ORIGINS

CANADA'S MULTICULTURAL HERITAGE

JULIA SAINT/JOAN REID

Origins

Canada's Multicultural Heritage

Printed in Canada by The Bryant Press Limited

ISBN 0-7747-1119-1

1 2 3 4 5 6 7 85 84 83 82 81 80 79

Acknowledgements

The authors and publisher wish to thank the following for permission to reproduce copyright material. Every effort has been made to acknowledge copyright. Any errors or omissions drawn to our attention will be corrected in future editions.
From *Defeathering the Indian* by Emma LaRoque, © 1975, reprinted with the permission of The Book Society of Canada Limited. From *Indians Without Tipis* edited by D. Bruce Sealey and Verna J. Kirkness, © 1974, reprinted with the permission of The Book Society of Canada Limited. From *My Heart Soars* by Chief Dan George and Helmut Hirnschall, published by Hancock House Publishers Ltd., 3215 Island View Rd., Saanichton, B.C. V0S 1M0. From *And What About Canada's Native Peoples?* reprinted by permission of the Canadian Association in Support of the Native Peoples. From the following CASNP bulletins, all reprinted by permission of the Canadian Association in Support of the Native Peoples: Vol. 17, NO. 3, December 1976; Vol. 17, No. 4, September 1977; Vol. 18, No. 2, October 1977. From *Northern Frontier, Northern Homeland* by Thomas R. Berger (The Report of the MacKenzie Valley Pipeline Inquiry), reproduced by permission of the Minister of Supply and Services Canada and James Lorimer and Company, Publishers. From *West Viking* by Farley Mowat, reprinted by permission of The Canadian Publishers, McClelland and Stewart Limited, Toronto. From *Seventeenth-Century Canada Source Studies* by Gary F. Coulson, reprinted by permission of The Macmillan Company of Canada Limited. From *Word from New France* by Joyce Marshall, by permission of Oxford University Press Canada. From statistics of Canada 1971 and New Brunswick 1971 census; *Everything You Always Wanted to Know About the Census;* and *Canada Year Book 1975* — all reproduced by permission of the Minister of Supply and Services Canada. From *The Ordeal of New France* by W.J. Eccles, published by Canadian Broadcasting Corporation. From *New France 1713-1760,* edited by Virginia R. Robeson, by permission of The Ontario Institute for Studies in Education. From *France in America* by W.J. Eccles, by permission of Fitzhenry & Whiteside Ltd. From *The Government of New France* by W.J. Eccles, Canadian Historical Association Booklet No. 18. From "To Be French in North America" by Robert Guy Scully, by permission of *Canadian Forum.* From "Youth Speaks Out on Essex French School" by Bruce Ward, reprinted with permission — *The Toronto Star.* From *America's French Heritage* by Jacques-Donat Casanova and Armour Landry, reproduced with the permission of the Editeur officiel du Québec. From *History of England* by G.M. Trevelyan, reproduced by permission of Longman Group Limited. From *England Under the Stuarts* by G.M. Trevelyan, published by Methuen & Co. Ltd. From *The Backwoods of Canada* by Catherine Parr Trail, reproduced by permission of The Canadian Publishers, McClelland and Stewart Limited, Toronto. From *To Their Heirs Forever* by Eula C. Lapp, reproduced by permission of Mika Publishing Co., Belleville, Ont. From *Canada and the American Revolution* by G.M. Wrong, published by Cooper Square Publications, Inc. From *The Highland Clearances* by John Prebble, published by Martin Secker & Warburg Limited. From *Emigration from Europe 1815-1914* by Charlotte Erickson, published by Adam and Charles Black. From *Sybil* by Benjamin Disraeli, by permission of Oxford University Press. From *The Great Hunger,* copyright © 1962 by Cecil Woodham-Smith, reprinted by permission of Harper & Row, Publishers, Inc. From *Cuthbert Grant and the Métis* by D. Bruce Sealey, copyright © 1978, reprinted with the permission of The Book Society of Canada Limited. From *Early Ukrainian Settlements in Canada, 1895-1900* by Vladimir J. Kaye, published by University of Toronto Press. From *Vilni Zemli: The Ukrainian Settlement of Alberta* by J.G. MacGregor, reprinted by permission of The Canadian Publishers, McClelland and Stewart Limited, Toronto. From *Strangers Within Our Gates* by J.S. Woodsworth, published by University of Toronto Press. From *A Chinaman's Opinion of Us and of His Own Country* by Hwuy-ung, translated by J.A. Makepeace, reprinted by permission of Chatto and Windus. From *Under the Ribs of Death* by John Marlin, reprinted by permission of The Canadian Publishers, McClelland and Stewart Limited, Toronto. Article "Japanese-Canadians: Did Canada Treat Them Fairly During World War II?" by Bruce Cushing, reprinted by permission of *Canada & the World.* From "Back Home in Italy Canadian Dollars Buy a Better Life" by Robert Reguly, reprinted with permission — *The Toronto Star.* From "A Super Agency Helps Solve Immigrants' Problems" by Bob Pennington, reprinted with permission — *The Toronto Star.* From "Hey! Black Banana," reprinted with permission — *The Toronto Star.* From "Toronto's Italians Say Mafia Legend Is Over-Exploited," reprinted with permission — *The Toronto Star.* From "The East Indian Presence in Canada" by R.T. Samuel in *Outreach for Understanding,* by permission of the Ontario Minister of Culture and Recreation.

Preface

One in every five Canadians today is a person who has immigrated to Canada. The rest of us are descendants of immigrants, who, at widely different times, came to North America from other continents.

The members of each immigrant group had their special reasons for leaving their original homes. Each had to overcome difficulties in adapting to a new country. Each group changed and was changed by the Canadian environment.

To begin to understand ourselves and other Canadians we need to share this common experience. It is the purpose of this book to provide that opportunity.

The authors wish to acknowledge the help of many people in the preparation of this book. Staff members and students at Applewood Heights and Central Peel Secondary Schools gave support and many helpful suggestions. Professor Gary Smith of the Department of History, Faculty of Education, University of Toronto, made perceptive comments on the early manuscript. Alan Hux of West Toronto Secondary School offered many constructive suggestions. Ruth Koretsky gave valuable early help. Norman Houghton, our editor, gave us the benefit of his long experience. Our special thanks go to Paul Paquette, Manager of the School Book Division Academic Press, for his unfailing patience and enthusiasm. Any weaknesses remain those of the authors alone.

Contents

To the Student

This book can be used by you in two quite different ways:

  (i) As a source book. We hope you will find valuable information here, organized in such a way that it is interesting and clear.

 (ii) As a series of challenges to you to investigate a topic more fully or to give more thought to a particular question or problem.

In using this book:

  (i) *Condense* what you have learned so that only the most important parts remain. These summaries can help you in remembering what you have learned, and in your review.

 (ii) Search for the connection between what happened "there and then" with what is happening "here and now." Ask yourself, "What has this information to do with me and my world at this moment?"

(iii) Ask, "How do the new pieces of information I am given relate to each other?" or "Where does all this new information fit into what I have already learned?"

(iv) Challenge your classmates to a debate, or try to win over the rest of your class by playing the part of some historic or imaginary person, and give a speech in his or her support.

    You may, on the other hand, want to listen to more evidence or hear different points of view before making up your mind where you stand on a particular issue. If so, as you listen to the student advocates, keep a record of their major points, and be ready to attack them when you feel their facts or arguments are weak.

 (v) Find out more about a topic by consulting as many *sources* as you can. These include (i) written records: printed materials including newspapers and magazines, or original letters or diaries; (ii) illustrations: pictures, drawings, or photographs; (iii) statistical information in tables, charts, and graphs; (iv) old buildings, bridges, or cemeteries in your area; (v) artifacts (any objects made by human skill); (vi) people: older members of your own family, a neighbour, or one of your classmates.

To the Teacher

Origins is an examination of the roots of Canada's multicultural heritage. Organized chronologically, it emphasizes three aspects of the history of our country:

(i) *Waves of immigration*

The major waves of immigrants to our country — from those of Canada's original peoples to the great influx of many different ethnic groups following World War II — are studied through the exploration of several themes. These include: why the immigrants left their homelands, what problems they faced, what they contributed to Canada's development, and how their cultures were changed by their new environment.

(ii) *Institutional roots*

Many aspects of our Canadian culture have been preserved in the basic legal and political institutions established during the French and British colonial periods. Our continuing political connection with Great Britain in particular largely determined the form of political organization we developed. The strength of British institutions also made it possible for many aspects of British culture to become dominant in Canada. For these reasons we have included a chapter on the development of our political and legal institutions in Great Britain and a section on the establishment of French legal institutions in Quebec.

(iii) *Origins of our modern technology*

A third vital element in our present urban, industrialized society had its roots in the agricultural and industrial revolutions of the eighteenth century in Europe, in particular in Great Britain. These revolutions led not only to mass emigration from Europe to our continent but also to the great technological changes that are still revolutionizing our whole way of life in Canada today.

Technological change is therefore a recurring theme throughout the text. In the final chapter it is reconsidered as the single most dominant component in our culture.

The organization creates a framework of study emphasizing historical continuity; this is true both of the Canadian sections of the book and of those studies describing the roots of our culture that come from outside Canada.

Possible Uses of *Origins*

The organization of *Origins* permits its use in a number of different ways:

(i) As a source book for material not generally available in other texts and studies.

(ii) As the central source for a unit or semester study at the Intermediate Level of one important aspect of Canadian history or of a very important contemporary issue.

(iii) As the framework for a year's course of study, into which additional related materials can be integrated.

The organization is also flexible enough to permit teachers to change the order of studying some of the chapters. Some teachers may prefer to begin their study of immigration with the wave after World War II or with a consideration of our present immigration policies in the Immigration Act and Regulations proclaimed in April 1978. Others may choose to begin by examining the two letters on pages 139 and 140. These were chosen to help students to understand the meaning of the word *culture* and to appreciate some of the difficulties in cross-cultural understanding.

Students for Whom Origins Was Written

While *Origins* was written for all students studying intermediate history, we have had two groups particularly in mind: (i) the many students who are enrolled in courses at general and basic levels, whose reading levels are relatively low and for whom the study of history may have lacked relevance; (ii) the new Canadians among our students who are attempting to adapt to a new society and, perhaps, to a new language. While some of the materials in the book are clearly beyond the scope of the first group of students, there are a number of sections designed specifically for their use. These include "Looking at Canadians," "Why They Left Home," "The Atlantic Crossing," and the many interviews and case studies that are used throughout the text. For the second group we hope that *Origins* will be of value in providing an opportunity to study the experiences of other groups who have immigrated to Canada and to investigate, if they choose, the roots of their own culture. We have included two guides in the appendix to help them in their research.

Materials and Methods of Presentation

Immigration has touched on every aspect of life in Canada. We have attempted to use a wide range of materials, including the following: original government documents, family documents including letters and diaries, photos, graphs and charts, personal interviews, newspaper accounts, hypothetical and actual case studies.

In presenting the materials we have attempted to find balance between narrative and investigation. The narrative sections are content-centred; the information presented has been collected, sifted, and organized. In the exploratory sections students are to locate and select materials and organize and present their findings in written or oral form.

Assignments and questions used throughout the text were created as aids in learning a number of basic skills:

> The skill of summarizing, which also tests the student's comprehension of the material studied.

> The skill of establishing relevance to the student's own experience or of drawing parallels either to modern situations or to other periods of history.

> The skill of analyzing new evidence and synthesizing or integrating it into knowledge already gained .

> The skills of research: gathering data from a variety of sources, formulating hypotheses, applying the skills described above to independent study.

> The skill of evaluating: judging from observation, communicating orally and formulating value judgments.

Many questions are "open-ended" to encourage further research and debate. Others are designed to enable teachers to use the resources available in their local communities and particular provinces.

Choice of Representative Groups

Origins recognizes the dominant influence of the British and French cultures in Canada. It also recognizes the unique place in our history of the Indian and Inuit peoples.

The many other groups — over fifty in all — who are today part of the Canadian mosaic could not all be included for individual study. There are several obvious omissions. For this reason we have included sections designed to encourage students to investigate their own heritage as well as those of other groups represented in their class and in their community.

Looking at Canadians

Let us begin our search for our origins with you and your own family. Imagine for a moment that you are able to return to the year 1860 and want to talk about your family with each of your great-great grandparents. How many people will you need to contact?

If you stopped to work out the answer, you will see that tracing your family tree quickly involves the study of many persons. Since each of us has two parents, the number of our ancestors *doubles* with each generation.

Perhaps the chart below will help you to trace your family. Make your own copy, filling in as many blanks as you can.

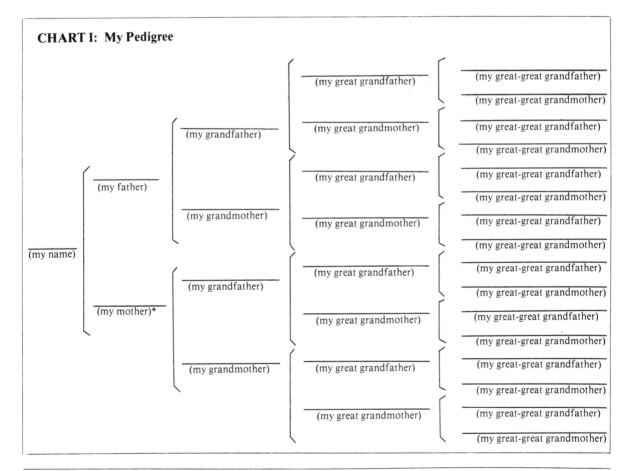

CHART I: My Pedigree

(my name)

(my father)

(my mother)*

(my grandfather)

(my grandmother)

(my grandfather)

(my grandmother)

(my great grandfather)

(my great grandmother)

(my great grandfather)

(my great grandmother)

(my great grandfather)

(my great grandmother)

(my great grandfather)

(my great grandmother)

(my great-great grandfather)

(my great-great grandmother)

(my great-great grandfather)

(my great-great grandmother)

(my great-great grandfather)

(my great-great grandmother)

(my great-great grandfather)

(my great-great grandmother)

(my great-great grandfather)

(my great-great grandmother)

(my great-great grandfather)

(my great-great grandmother)

(my great-great grandfather)

(my great-great grandmother)

(my great-great grandfather)

(my great-great grandmother)

*Remember to use the maiden names of all female ancestors.

While you are filling out the chart, try to find out when each branch of your family came to Canada and the country or countries your family emigrated from. Your parents will be able to help you and will probably suggest other older members of their families who may know more than they about your family history.

If you wish to continue the investigation of your family still further, make out a sheet similar to the one below for each separate family member you identified in Chart I. You should begin with your own immediate family, then with the family of each of your parents, then with each of your grandparents, and so on.

As you work, you may find many persons or things to help you. Have you a relative who has already made a study of your family? Have you a family photograph album? family Bible? a collection of old postcards, letters, or diaries? If your family has lived in the same area for some time, is there a family plot in the cemetery? Does your local church or synagogue have records of family births, marriages, or deaths?

There are also government officials who can help you, either in your local area or in Ottawa. Your teacher or librarian will tell you how to get in touch with them.

In many towns and cities there are *genealogical* societies. Their members are people who are skilled in tracing family trees. You might invite one of the members to talk with your class about this very interesting hobby or profession. Since you may want to trace your ancestry outside of Canada, be prepared to ask your visitor about government offices in other countries.

When you are well along in your investigation, prepare a report for your class. Bring photographs and other documents with you, and be sure to explain how you went about your detective work.

CHART II: My Family

My father's name: _____

Date and place of birth: _____

My mother's maiden name: _____

Date and place of birth: _____

Children's names: _____

CHART III: My Father's Family

My grandfather's name: _____

Date and place of birth: _____

My grandmother's maiden name: _____

Date and place of birth: _____

Date and place of death: _____

Children's names: _____

Make a Statistical Study of Your Class

The next step is to find out the origins of the other members of your class:

1. As a group, begin your study by finding out these things:
   (i) the country or countries of origin of each member's family. (It is usual to use the father's family to trace country of origin.)
   (ii) the approximate time of each member's family's arrival in Canada. (Not all Canadian families have records of the time of their arrival. Some students may not have this information.)
2. Tabulate (*i.e.,* show in tables) your statistical findings to show:
   (i) the number of students who originated from each of the countries on your lists.
   (ii) the number of students whose families arrived in Canada within certain time blocks (*e.g.,* within your own lifetime, between 1946 and 1960, between 1920 and 1939, etc.).
3. Have two or three volunteers convert the numbers of students in 2(i) and (ii) into percentages of the class.
4. Now find a way of making your statistical findings so *clear* that they can be rapidly understood by anyone reading them. The statistician regularly uses three kinds of diagrams:
   (i) the *bar* chart (or histogram): this is a useful method to compare quantities by columns or bars. If the widths of the columns are the same, then their heights are directly proportional to the quantity each represents. Use a bar graph to illustrate the percentage of the class who originated in each country.
   (ii) the *pie* chart: this chart shows at a glance comparisons between different quantities. Slices of a circular pie are cut in different sizes, each representing a different quantity. When taken together they must equal the total amount represented by the whole pie. (The pie represents 100 percent; each slice represents part of that percentage.) Two or three volunteers should make a pie chart to illustrate the per-

centage of the class who originated in each country. These can be drawn on a ditto for all students to keep.
   (iii) the *line* chart: this chart shows change over time and is often used to project change into the future, or to establish trends. If enough members of your class know when their families came to Canada, make a line chart to show this information.

Look at Canadians As a Whole

Ethnic Origin of Canadians 1971   *Study the charts shown below:*

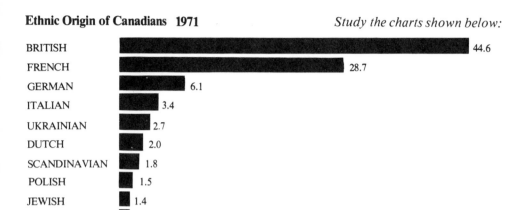

BRITISH	44.6
FRENCH	28.7
GERMAN	6.1
ITALIAN	3.4
UKRAINIAN	2.7
DUTCH	2.0
SCANDINAVIAN	1.8
POLISH	1.5
JEWISH	1.4
NATIVE INDIAN	1.4

Groups of Less Than 1 percent

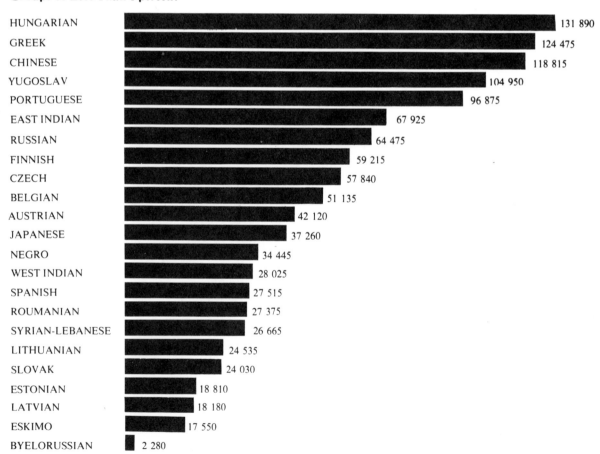

HUNGARIAN	131 890
GREEK	124 475
CHINESE	118 815
YUGOSLAV	104 950
PORTUGUESE	96 875
EAST INDIAN	67 925
RUSSIAN	64 475
FINNISH	59 215
CZECH	57 840
BELGIAN	51 135
AUSTRIAN	42 120
JAPANESE	37 260
NEGRO	34 445
WEST INDIAN	28 025
SPANISH	27 515
ROUMANIAN	27 375
SYRIAN-LEBANESE	26 665
LITHUANIAN	24 535
SLOVAK	24 030
ESTONIAN	18 810
LATVIAN	18 180
ESKIMO	17 550
BYELORUSSIAN	2 280

Ethnic Origin of Canadians
1971

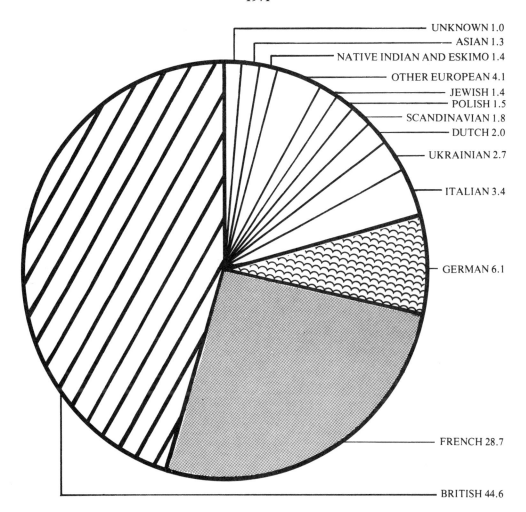

UNKNOWN 1.0
ASIAN 1.3
NATIVE INDIAN AND ESKIMO 1.4
OTHER EUROPEAN 4.1
JEWISH 1.4
POLISH 1.5
SCANDINAVIAN 1.8
DUTCH 2.0
UKRAINIAN 2.7
ITALIAN 3.4
GERMAN 6.1
FRENCH 28.7
BRITISH 44.6

- How do the findings shown in Figures 1 and 2 compare with the ones you made of your class? Is your class typical of Canadians as a whole?
- How do the findings in the following chart on the ethnic origins of your province compare with the ones you made in your class? Is your class typical of your province's population?
- Compare the ethnic composition of your own province with that of Canada as a whole.

- Does any one group of Canadians form a majority over all other groups? Taken together, what percent of Canadians are represented in the *two* largest groups? Can you think of any ways this fact has influenced the development of our country?
- The Canadians in the other minority groups are sometimes referred to as "the Third Force"? Why?
- Look back at your own family tree. How many of the separate groups did you find in your family?

5

ETHNIC ORIGIN OF CANADIANS
1971

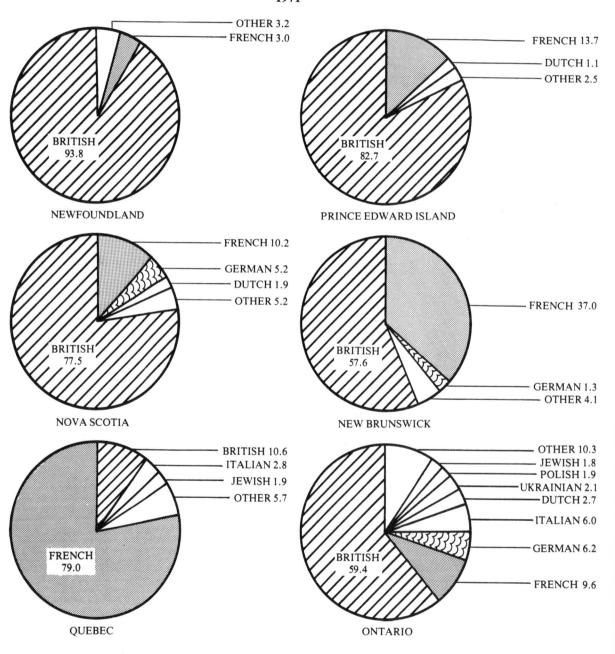

OTHER 3.2
FRENCH 3.0

BRITISH
93.8

NEWFOUNDLAND

FRENCH 13.7

DUTCH 1.1

OTHER 2.5

BRITISH
82.7

PRINCE EDWARD ISLAND

FRENCH 10.2

GERMAN 5.2

DUTCH 1.9

OTHER 5.2

BRITISH
77.5

NOVA SCOTIA

FRENCH 37.0

BRITISH
57.6

GERMAN 1.3

OTHER 4.1

NEW BRUNSWICK

BRITISH 10.6
ITALIAN 2.8
JEWISH 1.9
OTHER 5.7

FRENCH
79.0

QUEBEC

OTHER 10.3
JEWISH 1.8
POLISH 1.9
UKRAINIAN 2.1
DUTCH 2.7

ITALIAN 6.0

GERMAN 6.2

BRITISH
59.4

FRENCH 9.6

ONTARIO

ETHNIC ORIGIN OF CANADIANS
1971

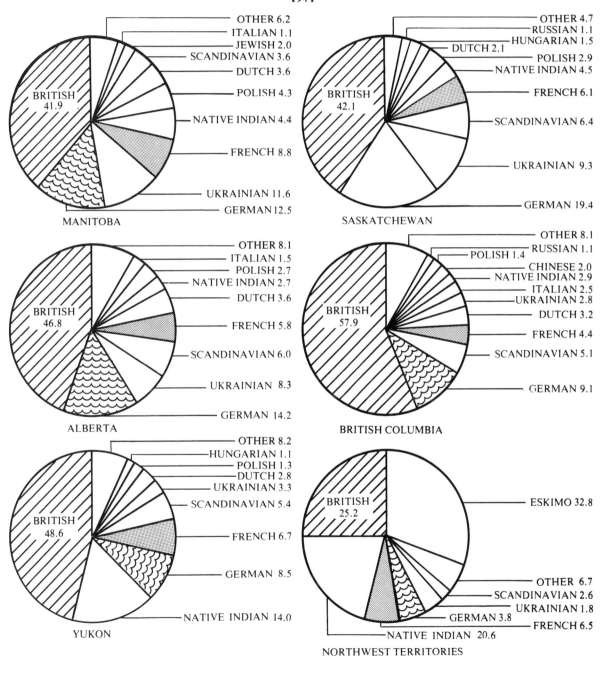

MANITOBA

OTHER 6.2
ITALIAN 1.1
JEWISH 2.0
SCANDINAVIAN 3.6
DUTCH 3.6
POLISH 4.3
NATIVE INDIAN 4.4
FRENCH 8.8
UKRAINIAN 11.6
GERMAN 12.5
BRITISH 41.9

SASKATCHEWAN

OTHER 4.7
RUSSIAN 1.1
HUNGARIAN 1.5
DUTCH 2.1
POLISH 2.9
NATIVE INDIAN 4.5
FRENCH 6.1
SCANDINAVIAN 6.4
UKRAINIAN 9.3
GERMAN 19.4
BRITISH 42.1

ALBERTA

OTHER 8.1
ITALIAN 1.5
POLISH 2.7
NATIVE INDIAN 2.7
DUTCH 3.6
FRENCH 5.8
SCANDINAVIAN 6.0
UKRAINIAN 8.3
GERMAN 14.2
BRITISH 46.8

BRITISH COLUMBIA

OTHER 8.1
RUSSIAN 1.1
POLISH 1.4
CHINESE 2.0
NATIVE INDIAN 2.9
ITALIAN 2.5
UKRAINIAN 2.8
DUTCH 3.2
FRENCH 4.4
SCANDINAVIAN 5.1
GERMAN 9.1
BRITISH 57.9

YUKON

OTHER 8.2
HUNGARIAN 1.1
POLISH 1.3
DUTCH 2.8
UKRAINIAN 3.3
SCANDINAVIAN 5.4
FRENCH 6.7
GERMAN 8.5
NATIVE INDIAN 14.0
BRITISH 48.6

NORTHWEST TERRITORIES

BRITISH 25.2
ESKIMO 32.8
OTHER 6.7
SCANDINAVIAN 2.6
UKRAINIAN 1.8
GERMAN 3.8
FRENCH 6.5
NATIVE INDIAN 20.6

7

II. Time of Immigration

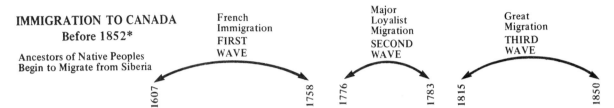

IMMIGRATION TO CANADA
Before 1852*

Ancestors of Native Peoples
Begin to Migrate from Siberia

French
Immigration
FIRST
WAVE

Major
Loyalist
Migration
SECOND
WAVE

Great
Migration
THIRD
WAVE

1607   1758   1776   1783   1815   1850

*There are no reliable immigration statistics before 1852

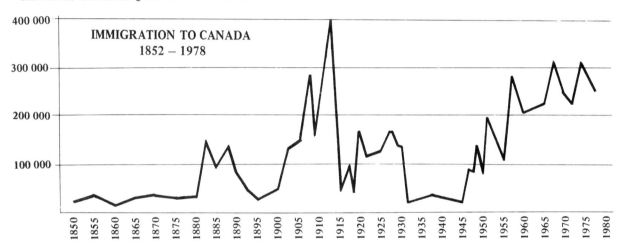

IMMIGRATION TO CANADA
1852 – 1978

- Canada's population for over eighteen *thousand* years was composed entirely of the Indian and Inuit peoples. Why is it impossible to draw a chart of their immigration?
- Later immigrants did not enter Canada in a steady stream but in a series of *waves*. When did each wave begin? How long did each last? What important events might have caused people to leave their homes and come to Canada in great numbers at these times?
- If you traced your family's immigration to Canada to any of these waves, were you able to discover why your family came? Compare your findings with those of other members of your class.
- In one clear paragraph, explain the caption, "Canada, a Land Of Immigrants."
- Why will we often refer to the charts on these pages throughout our study of immigration?

FOR FURTHER READING

Baker, Eunice R. *Searching for Your Ancestors in Canada.* Ottawa: Heritage House Publishers Ltd., 1977.

Baxter, Angus. *In Search of Your Roots: A Guide for Canadians Seeking Their Ancestors.* Toronto: Macmillan of Canada, 1978.

Doane, G. H. *Searching for Your Ancestors.* Minneapolis: University of Minnesota Press, 1973.

McLeod, Joan. ed. *We Are Their Children: Ethnic Portraits of British Columbia.* Vancouver: Comm Cept Publishing Ltd., 1977.

Sheffe, Norman, ed. *Many Cultures, Many Heritages.* Toronto: McGraw-Hill, 1975.

Starbird, Ethel. "The People Who Made Saskatchewan." *National Geographic,* Vol. 155, No. 5, May 1979.

The First People

You have probably heard people say that Columbus "discovered" America. This sounds strange to the Native peoples of America — the Indians and Inuit. How, they wonder, could a European "discover" a land where they already lived?

Did the Indians and Inuit Originate in America?

Were the Native peoples always here? In Europe, Africa, and Asia the bones and skulls of early man-like creatures have been found. In America scientists have not been able to find evidence of man's long occupancy. Only the bones and remains of modern man — *Homo sapiens* — have been found in America. This fact has led many scientists to believe that the Native peoples did not originate in America but were the first immigrants to reach her shores.

SOME SCIENTISTS WHO STUDY THE PAST

An *archaeologist* studies past human life and activities by excavating prehistoric sites which contain bones, man-made objects, buildings, and other evidence of man's occupancy.

Some *anthropologists* specialize in studying the physical characteristics of men by comparing their skeletal remains.

A *geologist* studies the history of the earth as it is recorded in rocks and land formations.

A *paleontologist* studies fossil animal remains to learn about the habitat and eating habits of early man.

Where Did the Native People Come From?

The Native legends and stories passed down from father to son do not contain any definite clues to an answer to the above question. With few exceptions, none of the Native peoples had developed a form of writing with which to record their past. Fitting together the story of their past is rather like trying to put together a jigsaw puzzle — without a picture to guide you.

Study a map of the world. What land masses lie closest to America? What are the most likely routes that the first immigrants might have followed?

You probably listed the following routes:
(i) across the Pacific using islands such as Hawaii as stepping stones to Central or South America;
(ii) across the Bering Sea to Alaska;
(iii) across the north Atlantic to Iceland to Greenland to America;
(iv) across the middle Atlantic to South America.

Similarities in physical appearance and blood type between Mongolians from Siberia and Indians from the Americas encouraged scientists to look for more definite evidence to support their idea that the *Indians and Inuit originated in Asia and migrated to the Americas.* Answers to two very important questions had to be found before they could be certain:

How did the Indians and Inuit come to the Americas?

When did they come?

They had arrived long before Europeans had boats capable of crossing the oceans. In their search for explanations, the scientists turned to geologists for help.

Geologists, who study the history of the land and rivers and climate of our continents, know that much of Canada was once covered by heavy, thick, slow-moving sheets of ice called glaciers. Where the cities of Toronto and Montreal now stand, the ice is estimated to have been a thousand feet thick.

Four times the glaciers moved southward. Four times the climate became warmer and the ice "retreated" north. It is believed that man moved into America before the final advance and retreat of the ice — at least twenty thousand years ago. How was man able to cross the ocean from Siberia to Alaska?

Soviets say Indians came from Siberia

MOSCOW (Reuter) — Soviet archeologists have found fresh evidence that the Indians of North America emigrated to the New World from homelands in Siberia, the news agency Tass reported yesterday.

Professor Nikolai Dikov, leader of an expedition working at ancient sites in northeast Siberia and the Kamchatka Peninsula, said the latest diggings also showed that the ornaments worn by American Indians had an Asian origin.

The migration of the tribes who later became known as Indians took place during the ice age when Siberia and Alaska were linked by a land bridge across what is now the Bering Strait, the archeologist added.[1]

The Bridge

When Did They Come?

Glaciers need a great deal of moisture to "feed" themselves. It is believed that they drew quantities of water out of the oceans. This moisture fell as snow and remained unmelted. The water level of the oceans was lowered, therefore, and the ocean floor was exposed where the water had been shallow.

In the Bering Sea a land bridge once connected Siberia and Alaska. Parts of the land in Alaska were not always covered with ice. Several open pathways of vegetation through the ice attracted wandering animals in search of food. The land bridge was probably covered with long, thick grass like that which grows now on the Alaskan peninsula.

Open paths in the ice allowed the immigrants to move from Alaska, down the eastern side of the Rockies, and into the ice-free plains of modern Colorado and New Mexico. The route followed would roughly match the route of the Alaska Highway today. The glaciers may have grown again and closed the pathway behind them.

Archaeologists have a test that they can use to establish the age of *once-living* materials such as bones. This test, called the Carbon 14 test, is like having a metre stick to measure time.

If bones are found which the Carbon 14 test shows are about ten thousand years old, then archaeologists know that the person or animal lived about ten thousand years ago. Sometimes *artifacts* (man-made objects) are found along with bones. The archaeologist can tell when the objects were made by testing the age of the bones found with them.

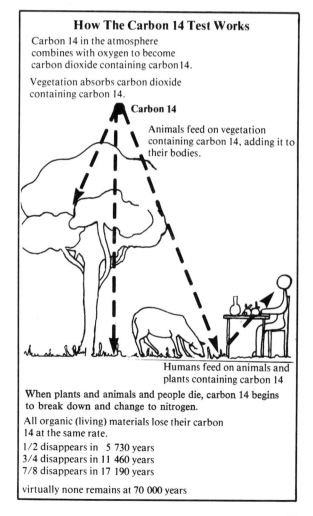

How The Carbon 14 Test Works

Carbon 14 in the atmosphere combines with oxygen to become carbon dioxide containing carbon 14.

Vegetation absorbs carbon dioxide containing carbon 14.

Carbon 14

Animals feed on vegetation containing carbon 14, adding it to their bodies.

Humans feed on animals and plants containing carbon 14

When plants and animals and people die, carbon 14 begins to break down and change to nitrogen.

All organic (living) materials lose their carbon 14 at the same rate.

1/2 disappears in 5 730 years
3/4 disappears in 11 460 years
7/8 disappears in 17 190 years

virtually none remains at 70 000 years

Why Did They Come?

Consider the following clues left behind by early man in the Americas:

(i) A ten-inch-long caribou bone scraper found in the Yukon was dated at 27 000 years by a Carbon 14 test in 1972.

(ii) A man-made flint spear point was found embedded in the ribs of an ice-age bison, now extinct, near Folsom, New Mexico. A Carbon 14 test showed that the bones were 10 000 years old.

(iii) At Debert in Nova Scotia evidence was found to suggest that man lived there 11 000 years ago on the very edge of the glacier.

Photograph of caribou bone scraper found in the Yukon. Carbon 14 establishes the bone as 27 000 years old.

This does not necessarily mean that man used it as a scraper 27 000 years ago. Can you explain why?

From pieces of evidence such as these, archaeologists have been able to put together the story of early man in America and find some of his routes of travel. As more clues in the form of man-made objects are found, more of the puzzle of ancient man will be solved.

Archaeologists believe that the first immigrants followed the animals that were their chief source of food. The tremendous changes in climate and vegetation caused by the advance and retreat of the glaciers drove animals and plants from one part of the continent to another. Early man followed. These *nomadic* (wandering) hunters left evidence of their presence at their "kill" sites. Their artifacts are found with the bones of the animals they killed for food.

- What evidence is there to support the idea that the Indian and Inuit reached America from Asia?
- How has the time of their arrival been estimated?
- What are the probable reasons for their coming?

What Happened After They Arrived?

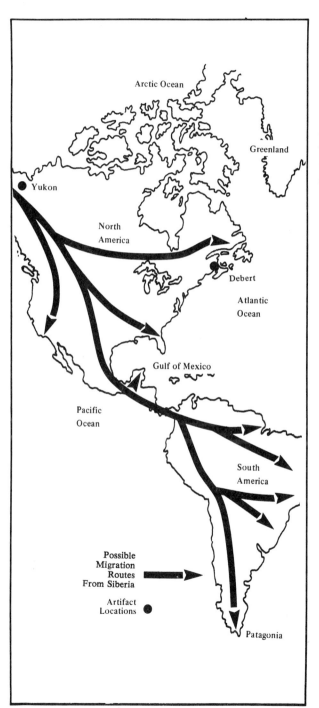

In slow-moving groups, over thousands of years, wandering families and tribes spread east and south as far as Patagonia at the southernmost tip of South America. Stone tools and spearheads which are about ten thousand years old have been found in Patagonia.

As the ice began its final retreat — about fifteen thousand years ago — the climate gradually became warmer. Many of the animals which had been hunted became *extinct* (no longer in existence). As the first immigrants moved to new regions, they had to adjust themselves to new food supplies.

For thousands of years they had the two continents of the Americas to themselves. No other immigrants arrived. During that long period of time separate groups built up their own ways of life. The hunting life-style of the first nomads who came from Asia across the Bering Sea changed as they adapted to new environments. By the time Europeans arrived a variety of cultures existed. These cultures changed as various Native peoples came in contact with European cultures. Changes are still occurring.

- Investigate the way of life of a Native society in your area before the coming of Europeans. Find out how the people dressed, what their homes were like, the equipment and utensils they used, and the food they ate. Pay particular attention to the way in which they adapted their way of life to the environment in which they lived. What were their religious beliefs? How did they feel about the land? What attitudes and behaviour did they admire? Find examples of their artistic skill and their legends. Build models which show their original way of life.

- Some Native peoples are concerned about museum displays of Native "culture" because observers often fail to distinguish between the past and the present. Others are alarmed by the digging up of their cemeteries and the lack of respect shown for their ancestors in the name of "science." Keeping these two points in mind plan one or more of the following activities:

Cultures Meet

(i) Invite a Native person to your classroom to discuss past and present life-styles.

(ii) If there is a museum in your area that has a display of Indian or Inuit artifacts, make a class visit.

(iii) Invite a speaker from your local archaeological society to your school or find out whether there is a "dig" nearby that you may visit.

- If your area was "shaped" by glaciers, find out how this was done and what features of the landscape show it.

European explorers and traders first came into contact with the Native peoples of Canada nearly five hundred years ago. Indians lived in every area of Canada, as the map below shows. They were divided into eleven major language families and over fifty tribes and tribal divisions. It must be kept in mind that there was no single Indian language or way of life. The Hurons of southern Ontario were farmers who lived in settled villages. The Micmacs of Nova Scotia were nomadic hunters. The Haida of British Columbia, famous for their carvings, depended heavily on salmon. The Blackfoot of the plains hunted the buffalo. The Inuit were spread across the Arctic regions from Newfoundland to Alaska.

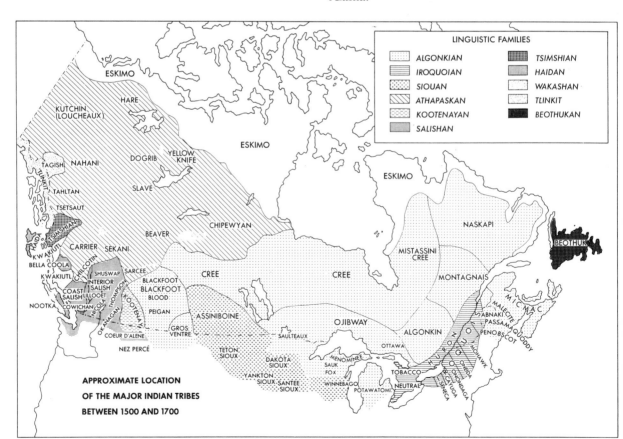

Map of Language and Tribal Divisions, c.1500 A.D.

The first Europeans brought with them their own way of life, their religious beliefs, and their technology. As native peoples and Europeans met, an exchange of cultures took place. The following model outlines the typical pattern of events when European and native cultures met. The period of first contact did not occur at the same time for every region of Canada. In eastern Canada the period of first contact generally occurred in the 1500's or 1600's. Europeans generally came into contact with the Plains Indians and the tribes of the west coast in the 1700's or early 1800's. Other contacts did not occur until the 1900's.

Use the model on the next page as a guide. Study the pattern of events which occurred when Europeans met the Native peoples of your area. Pay particular attention to the exchange of cultures that took place and to the effects on each culture. Determine how well the model fits each of the four periods outlined.

MAKING CANOES

Building a Birch Bark Canoe

Felling trees by burning and chopping with a stone axe.

Stripping Birch Bark

A Dug out Canoe was made by shaping a log, charring the inside, and then scraping it with sharp stones.

SKIN DRESSING AND MEAT DRYING

Leather

Method of using Scraper & holding it rigid

Rubbing fat into the skin

Scraping flesh from Moose Hide with Beaming Tool made from leg bone of Deer

Bone-handled Scraper with stone blade

Smoking & drying moose meat

Model

(i) *Period of First Contact:*
— The Indian was independent of the European. He followed his own religion and managed his own economic life.
— He voluntarily accepted some of the products of European technology, such as metal knives, copper kettles, guns, steel traps, and so forth. Often these products made his life easier.
— Europeans adopted certain Indian technology such as the birch bark canoe and snowshoes.

(ii) *Period of Deepening European Influence:*
— The Indian became more dependent on European trade goods.
— He became deeply involved in the European economic system through the fur trade and sometimes became involved in European wars.
— He began to lose control of his economic, social, and political life. He sometimes lost the old skills of his culture.
— Europeans made serious efforts to convert him to their religion and teach him the behaviour and attitudes of their culture.
— European diseases such as smallpox reduced his numbers.

(iii) *Period of European Dominance:*
— The Indian found himself greatly out-numbered by settlers who had different ideas from his about the land and how it should be used.
— Indians were moved onto lands reserved for them. In western Canada this was done from 1871 to 1921 through a series of eleven land treaties.
— The Indian came under the control of the federal government.
— He became dependent.
— Strong efforts were made to change his ideas, his behaviour, and his way of life.
— Native values and white ones conflicted causing serious disruptions in native life such as poverty, poor health, alcoholism, and apathy.

(iv) *Period of Reawakening:*
— Native people begin to speak out against their treatment.
— They seek recognition for their contributions to Canada and respect for their heritage.
— They begin to form nation-wide organizations to demand settlement of their land claims and treaty rights.
— An increasing number of native artists and writers win recognition for their work.
— Native people show an increasing desire to take control of their schools and economic life.
— Native people show an increasing desire to choose their own future path, whether that be to enter the highly industrialized and urbanized society of the majority, or to preserve a more traditional way of life, or some other option.[2]

What Do You Know About Indians Today?

- As individuals, Native people have made many contributions to Canada. Select one Native person and research his or her contributions. Here is a short list. You will be able to add many others to it: Pontiac, Joseph Brant, Tecumseh, Pauline Johnson, Poundmaker, Dan George, Harold Cardinal, Norval Morriseau, Buffy Sainte-Marie, Tom Longboat, Frank Calder, George Clutesi, Duke Redbird, Crowfoot, William Wuttunee, Ralph Steinhauer.

Ask yourself, "What do I know about Indians today?" Write down your information in a brief list and then read the quotation below.

> Recently, I had the task of speaking to a class of grade 3 students. . . . When the children entered the classroom they brought with them a painted cardboard model resembling a totem pole which they placed beside me. Out of curiosity I asked them to tell me all they knew about the Indians of today. Without much hesitation they gave me the following information: that the Indians live in teepees, other Canadians live in houses; Indians use bows and arrows for hunting, others have guns; Indians use horses for transportation, others have cars; Indians use buffalo for food and clothing, others do not; and that Indians wear feathers.[3]

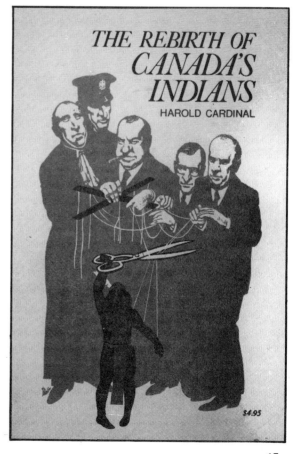

Two book covers by Harold Cardinal — "The Unjust Society," "The Rebirth of Canada's Indians" — illustrating the difference between periods 3 and 4 in the model.

Without realizing it the Grade 3 students gave Emma LaRoque a *stereotype*. They had a picture in their minds of perhaps the Plains Indians of over one hundred years ago. Like any other group of people, Indians have changed and adapted their way of life over the years. You and I do not follow a life-style exactly like that of our ancestors; neither do Native peoples.

Here is the way another writer explains how stereotypes develop:

The mass media have developed the stereotype that all Indians wore beaded buckskins and feathered head dresses when in fact only certain Plains Indians wore the huge feathered war bonnets. Yet, on ceremonial occasions, from the Pacific to the Atlantic, many Indian leaders feel constrained to

wear a brightly hued feather head dress. In short, it has become a modern ceremonial dress trait and can be equated with that of a person having one-seventh Scottish blood whose ancestors came to Canada five generations ago and who proudly parades in a kilt, misquotes the poetry of Robbie Burns and courageously eats a small portion of haggis one evening every year. To both the Scotsman and the Indian, these are ceremonial trappings and of little importance in daily living.[4]

- Define *stereotype*. How does the second quotation explain how stereotypes are spread? What are the mass media the author is referring to?
- The second author is not trying to make fun of people who are of Scottish or Indian ancestry. What point, then, is he trying to make about dress?
- How does dress affect our sense of identity?

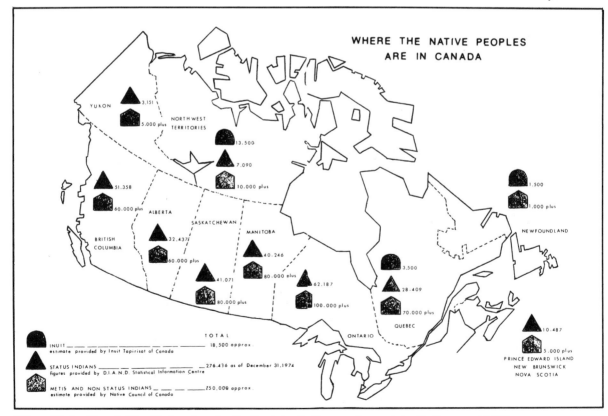

Where Native People Live Today showing Inuit, status Indians and non-status Indians and Métis.

Culture and Heritage

A few years ago, a friend and I were watching color television in a modern high-rise apartment. Like thousands of other Canadians, we were enjoying the Stanley Cup Playoffs. Suddenly my friend burst out, "I don't know anything about my culture! I am supposed to be an Indian working for a Native organization, but I don't know anything about my culture."

On many occasions the concern my friend raised had been my concern, too; a concern which causes an inner struggle shared by most contemporary Indians. But just then it struck me that perhaps the high-rise, the television and hockey were our culture, too. This was our present life-style; so then was it not our culture? Perhaps we needed to rephrase the question. Obviously, we were living our *culture*; it was our *heritage* we knew so little about.[5]

This quotation is from the book *Defeathering the Indian* written by Emma LaRoque, a Métis from northeastern Alberta. Miss LaRoque defines culture as life-style. This is how we will define it in this book. Your life-style, for example, consists of the things you do every day: the food you eat; the clothing you wear; the house you live in; the games and sports you play; the way you travel; the music you listen to; the school you go to; the television programs you watch; the institutions such as church, government, courts that you come in contact with; the language you speak.

But your culture also includes things that are harder to pinpoint and certainly more difficult to explain. These include attitudes, behaviour, hopes, and dreams. A working definition of culture might be "the sum total of the way in which people live."[6]

Neither Miss LaRoque, nor her friend, nor you live a life-style exactly like that of your parents or remote ancestors. New methods are adopted; old ways are abandoned or changed. Your life-style twenty years from now will probably be different in some ways from what it is now. You may be happy or unhappy about the changes.

All of us, however, do follow certain ways of living which we have inherited — our heritage — from the original culture or way of life of our ancestors. The interesting thing about Canadian culture is that the heritages of many people enrich it. Miss LaRoque's friend expresses a very human desire to learn about her Indian heritage. Sometimes people call this seeking their identity. Who am I? What have my people done in the past? What part of their achievements and contributions have added something to the way I live now? These are questions we will ask over and over again in this book, not only about people of Native ancestry but about those whose ancestors came from many cultures in Europe, in Asia, in Africa, and in other parts of the world. Canadians are a lucky people. They are the heirs of the best the world has to offer.

In the next section we shall take a brief look at what Native peoples of the Americas have contributed to our life-style and to the world.

The Indian Contribution

The greatest contribution Indians have made to the world is in the realm of food. The tremendous population of the present day would be unable to feed itself were it not for the food originally developed in the Americas by Indian people. The foremost food is corn . . . [which] provides basic sustenance for millions of people and is a basic fodder for countless millions of animals. The Indian habit of flaking kernels and roasting them has been adapted by industrial societies to provide a quick nutritious breakfast food. The delight of Indian children in popping a variety of corn kernels has spread throughout the world. . . .

Potatoes . . . revolutionized agricultural practices and food habits of Europeans. . . . [Native peoples also contributed] beans . . . squashes and pumpkins . . . cucumber and the tomato . . . syrups derived from maple trees . . . peanuts . . . chocolate, vanilla, pineapples, avocado, wild rice, tapioca, pecans, cranberries, chili and peppers . . . tobacco . . . turkeys . . . rubber . . . the gum of the chicle tree .

. . . Indians of America north of Mexico alone have contributed over a hundred medicines listed in standard Pharmacopeia used in Canada and the United States. . . .

. . . white people discarded their clumsy wooden row boats and quickly utilized the paddle driven birch bark canoe . . . to travel swiftly over long distances and explore the well-travelled water highways of the Indians.

In winter they used Indian snowshoes. Explorers simply hired Indian guides who took them along well-established Indian paths.

. . . Europeans soon adopted the clothing of the Indian . . . the parka of the Eskimo . . . mocassins and mukluks. . . . After centuries of complaining about the immorality of the breech clout worn by Indians during hot weather, modern North Americans have adopted it as suitable for beach wear [renaming it trunks or bikinis].

Indian designs influence modern jewellery. . . . Indian housing designs have also been adopted to modern use. The army's Sibley tent is an adaptation of the teepee. The Quonset hut is an Indian design . . . which allows a relatively flimsy structure to withstand strong winds and heavy rains. . . . The

cube style of Pueblo apartment blocks with a terrace set back on each level grace the horizon of modern skyscraper cities. . . .

Canadian Indian art, as exemplified by Mrs. "Odjig" Beavon, Jackson Beardy, N. Morriseau . . . to name just a few, has gained an honoured place in modern art circles. The subject of Indians also has inspired many white artists who have achieved world recognition.

The Globe and Mail — Toronto

Indian artist Novel Morriseau works on his painting "Child of the Year."

The designs of the cradleboard have been adapted to a light aluminum frame which many a white mother now finds perfect as a way of transporting her child in safety through urban crowds.

Only now are Indians beginning to put in printed form some of their legends and history which has been preserved through an oral tradition. Nevertheless the influence of the Indian in terms of supplying themes and heroes for white literature has been significant. . . .

To European ears, Indian singing in minor keys appears weird and spine tingling. . . . Modern white youth with its drum- and chord-dominated rock bands is showing more interest than any previous generation. . . .

English uses Indian words for the name of Canada, four provinces and two territories. Indian words are . . . scattered across our country . . . Miramichi, Nipigon . . . Okanagan . . . Winnipegosis . . . Temiskaming . . . Ottawa . . . We use Indian words for animals; caribou, chipmunk, moose, coyote,

"The People and the Land Are One"[8]

jaguar, racoon, skunk, and woodchuck. . . . We have muskegs and savannas and we love chinook winds. . . .

Words and phrases . . . have come directly as loan words or as English translations of Indian words. Hootch, punk, peewee, caucus, mugwump, podunk, tuxedo, war paint, fire-water, great white father, Indian summer, go on the warpath, bury the hatchet, have a pow-wow, run the gauntlet, a fast buck, and low man on the totem pole. . . .

Indian words exemplifying courage and endurance are used by athletic teams such as the Black Hawks, Redskins, Warriors, and Braves. We drive Pontiac and Jaguar cars. . . .

Original native place names were translated directly into English or French . . . Medicine Hat, Moose Jaw, White Horse Plains, Pembina Hills. . . .

In our schools we don't pow-wow but an equivalent called a pep-rally is felt to be a necessary ingredient to ensure victory for the basketball team. . . . Indeed, our obsession with lakeside cottages, fishing, hunting, and canoeing, add truth to the observation that Canadians work like dogs eleven and one-half months a year in order to live for two weeks like the Indian once did all year round.[7]

- Plan a series of posters illustrating the contributions of Native peoples. For example, one person might do a poster on food, another on transportation, a third on articles of clothing, a fourth on architecture and design, a fifth on animals and plants with Indian names.
- Collect pictures and slides of the art of Native peoples, both past and present.
- Draw a map of Canada or your province highlighting Indian place names and place names translated into English or French.
- Do a display of books written by Native peoples and novels and poems written about them.
- Research the game of lacrosse and the sport of throwing snow snakes.
- Invite Native people who are willing to demonstrate music and dancing to visit your class.

In recent years many Canadians have become concerned about pollution and the damage that is being done to our environment. They have shown a new interest in the values and attitudes of Native peoples towards the land and its uses. In the following excerpt Chief Dan George of the Coast Salish tribe of British Columbia describes his people's attitude to the land and also the family and social values they cherish.

I am a native of North America.

In the course of my lifetime I have lived in two distinct cultures. I was born into a culture that lived in communal houses. My grandfather's house was eighty feet long. It was called a smoke house, and it stood down by the beach along the inlet. All my grandfather's sons and their families lived in this large dwelling. Their sleeping apartments were separated by blankets made of bull rush reeds, but one open fire in the middle served the cooking needs of all. In houses like these, throughout the tribe, people learned to live with one another; learned to serve one another; learned to respect the rights of one another. And children shared the thoughts of the adult world and found themselves surrounded by aunts and uncles and cousins who loved them and did not threaten them. . . .

And beyond this acceptance of one another there was a deep respect for everything in nature that surrounded them. My father loved the earth and all it's [sic] creatures. The earth was his second mother. The earth and everything it contained was a gift from See-see-am . . . and the way to thank this great spirit was to use his gifts with respect. . . .

And I shall never forget his disappointment when once he caught me gaffing for fish "just for the fun of it". "My Son" he said, "The Great Spirit gave you those fish to be your brothers, to feed you when you are hungry. You must respect them. You must not kill them just for the fun of it.". . .

I see people living in smoke houses hundreds of times bigger than the one I knew. But the people in one apartment do not even know the people in the next and care less about them. . . .

It is hard for me to understand a culture that not only hates and fights his brother but even attacks nature and abuses her. I see my white brother going about blotting out nature from his cities. I see him strip the hills bare, leaving ugly wounds on the face of mountains. I see him tearing things from the bosom of mother earth as though she were a monster, who refused to share her treasures with him. I see him throw poison in the waters, indifferent to the life he kills there; and he chokes the air with deadly fumes. . . .

I am afraid my culture has little to offer yours. But my culture did prize friendship and companionship. It did not look on privacy as a thing to be clung to, for privacy builds up walls and walls promote distrust. . . .

My culture did not price [sic] the hoarding of private possessions, in fact, to hoard was a shameful thing to do among my people. The Indian looked on all things in nature as belonging to him and he expected to share them with others and to take only what he needed. . . .

We have taken much from your culture . . . I wish you had taken something from our culture . . . for there were some beautiful and good things in it.

Soon it will be too late to know my culture, for integration is upon us and soon we will have no values but yours. Already many of our young people have forgotten the old ways. And many have been shamed of their Indian ways by scorn and ridicule. My culture is like a wounded deer that has crawled away into the forest to bleed and die alone.[9]

• Compare the information below with the description given by Dan George.
— 64% of status Indian homes have no running water; 25% of these rely on water from sources known to be contaminated.
— The average earned Indian income on reserves is under $2000 a year.
— 53% of status Indians are unemployed.
— 41% of Indian families live on welfare, compared to the national rate of 3.7%.
— The average age at death of Indian males is 41.5 years; of females, 43.3 years.

— The death rate for preschool-aged children is almost three times the national average, and for Inuit children four times.
— 28.5% of Native deaths are suicide, as compared with the national average of 9.7%.
— 80.9% of status Indian children drop out before completing high school. 1% of all Indian students in Canada are attending university.
— In 1971 Indian unemployment in urban areas was estimated at 68%.
— Native people make up as much as 44% of total inmate populations in provincial jails and federal prisons. In 1970-71, 87.2% of the inmates in one western provincial women's institution were of Native extraction.[10]

• What attitudes towards nature did Chief Dan George's people have?
• In what ways does he feel his culture is different from the culture of the majority?
• Are your personal values similar to or different from his?

Cultural Conflicts

Here is how another writer shows some of the main differences.

Indian Culture

1. *Time is unimportant.*
   Seasonal jobs do not require "clock" watching. At peak seasons you might work from 4 a.m. to 12 p.m. When not on the job, it is not necessary to get up early.

2. *Today concept.*
   Today is more important than the future. Enjoy your resources while you can.

3. *Patience.*
   The way of livelihood such as hunting, fishing and trapping instills a patient approach. Weather often hampers keeping a tight schedule in the north.

4. *Extended family.*
   The family extends from mother, father, and children to aunts, uncles, grandparents, cousins, etc. The household often consists of more than the immediate family.

5. *Age.*
   Respect is for the elders. Their experience is recognized as being important. Little effort is made to conceal signs of old age. Aged are usually cared for by the family.

6. *Giving.*
   The respected member is one who gives.

7. *Lives in balance with nature.*
   Uses the lakes and streams, animals and birds but does not attempt to control them.

Non-Indian Culture

1. *Time is important.*
   Rigid schedules such as an 8:00 to 5:00 job, use of buses, planes and so forth lead to the watching of time. It is a time-orientated culture.

2. *Tomorrow concept.*
   This is a future-orientated society. This is shown through the interest in saving money and buying insurance.

3. *Action.*
   The man who is admired gets things done quickly. People are caught up in the race of time. Result — a tension-orientated society.

4. *Nuclear family.*
   The emphasis is on father, mother and children. Each unit operates independently.

5. *Youth.*
   People admire youthfulness. Thousands of dollars are spent on hair dyes and make-up to cover wrinkles. The aged are put in "old folks' homes."

6. *Saving.*
   An individual with the quality of "thrift" is felt to have a valuable trait.

7. *Controls nature.*
   Searches for ways to control nature. Artificial lakes are made, rivers are dammed, electricity is generated.[11]

- Discuss the differences in cultures described above. Why would a Native person who comes to live in a large Canadian city for the first time find it difficult to adjust?
- What Native values are shared by other cultures that you have studied?
- What Native values might improve Canadian society?

Who Are Canada's Native Peoples Today?

In Canada "Native peoples" is a comprehensive term which includes all those persons descended from the aboriginal inhabitants who are conscious of being Canada's "first citizens". . . . The term "Native" when used by Canada's Native peoples, implies a sense of pride in heritage. However, its use is not universally accepted: Indians in the Maritimes, for example, prefer to be called Indians or "Native Indians".[12]

Today there are approximately 1 000 000 Native persons. There are three categories: status Indians, Métis and non-status Indians, and the Inuit ("the people").

Approximately 276 000 Native persons are status Indians. They are members of 565 bands. They live on or have rights to 2274 reserves of varying size across Canada. They hold certain rights under the Indian Act. They are considered treaty or registered Indians.

Some Indians became treaty Indians when they signed treaties surrendering their claims to the land in exchange for sections of it called reserves. Europeans occupied and settled the lands surrendered. (See map page 127.) The provinces of Ontario, Manitoba, Saskatchewan, Alberta, and parts of the Yukon and Northwest Territories are covered by treaties.

Approximately 50 percent of Canada's registered Indian bands made no treaties and therefore have never formally surrendered their claims to the land. Europeans occupied and settled these areas without formal agreements with the Native peoples. However, reservations were established in these areas and Native peoples became registered or status Indians. This is the situation in most of British Columbia, all of Quebec (until 1975), all of the Maritime provinces, and large sections of the Yukon and Northwest Territories.

Métis and non-status Indians are Native persons who identify as Indians but are not legally recognized as such. Their numbers are estimated at 750 000. For a variety of reasons they either never had or they lost or gave up the right to "status."

The Inuit number approximately 18 500. They occupy the land north of the tree line in the Yukon, the Northwest Territories, Quebec, and Labrador. They have never signed any formal treaties. No reserves have been set aside for them although they now live in government promoted communities. The federal government has generally treated them as registered.[13]

- Study the terms of the Indian Act, first passed in 1876 and now revised.

Aboriginal Rights

As the first occupiers and users of the land Native peoples feel they have certain aboriginal rights. The British and later the Canadian government seemed to recognize this idea. Government officials understood that the treaties *extinguished*, or ended, Native claims to the land in return for reserves and certain payments and services. On November 11, 1975, the Cree and Inuit in Northern Quebec extinguished their aboriginal rights to 410 000 square miles of territory in return for certain payments and benefits. (See map below.) The James Bay Agreement is considered to be very important because it recognized the aboriginal rights of Native peoples who had never received such recognition before.

Some Indians who signed treaties in the past, however, insist that these treaties did not extinguish their aboriginal rights. They also are now asserting claims to the land. The Dene* are one example. They claim that under the terms of Treaties 8 and 11 they did not surrender their aboriginal rights to the land. They understood that they were signing treaties of peace and friendship. They would be free to hunt and trap over the treaty lands, and their way of life would not be interfered with. They are now concerned about the damage that large-scale developments in the North could have. They want their aboriginal rights recognized, not extinguished. They do not want a James Bay style treaty.

> We cannot understand how anyone could seriously suggest that we would consider negotiating the extinguishment of our rights. What we insist upon is a departure from the tradition in Canada that rights must be extinguished. We want our property rights to our land recognized and preserved, not extinguished.[14]

Other Native peoples who originally signed treaties are also concerned about their aboriginal rights, especially when treaty terms are not honoured and pipelines and mining and forest projects encroach on their hunting grounds and pollute the waters of their

reserves. The following excerpts suggest the concerns of the Cree and Ojibway of northern Ontario:

> Unlike you, we have no memory of an existence in other lands across the sea. We have prior rights to the custody of this land, which precede and supersede all your claims. . . .

Category I lands
Category II lands
Category III lands

JAMES BAY AGREEMENT

The James Bay agreement includes a land settlement covering 410,000 square miles, 60 per cent of Quebec. Some 2,095 square miles (the black areas) will be set aside for the Crees, 3,250 for the Inuit, as Category 1 land over which the native people will have almost full control. In the further 60,130 square miles of Category II land (diagonally striped) they will have exclusive hunting, fishing and trapping rights; In the rest of the territory, Category III land, certain animal species will be reserved for the native peoples, and forest products will be free for their use.

---

* Indians and Métis of the Northwest Territories.

This custody must remain with us. It is our sacred duty to pass it on to our unborn children. . . .

In your rush for materialistic gain, you are threatening nature's very limits. Now it is our sacred duty to slow you down before she is destroyed. . . .

We can no longer permit the progressive rape of our mother earth, and its life-giving forces. We have our children to save. The continuance of our race is a sacred mandate passed on to us by our ancestors.[15]

Louise Frost of Old Crow in the Yukon expressed deep concern for the land to the group investigating the building of an oil pipeline through the Mackenzie River valley:

I see our country being destroyed and my people pushed on reservations, and the white men taking over as they please. . . . The pipeline is only the beginning of all this. If it ever does come through, there will be a time when other companies will want to join in on this. . . . Their only purpose in coming here is to extract the non-renewable resources, not to the benefit of northerners, but of southern Canadians and Americans. . . . you can describe it as the rape of the northland to satisfy the greed and needs of southern consumers, and when development of this nature happens, it only destroys; it does not leave very much for us to be proud of, and along with their equipment and technology, they also impose on the northern people their white culture and its value systems, which leaves nothing to the people who have been living off the land for thousands of years. . . . the white man is destroying the Indian way of life.[16]

- Investigate the terms of Treaties 8 and 11. Which terms have never been carried out?
- Do further research on the developments which affect Native people in the Treaty 9 area. Examine the problems caused by mercury pollution for the Natives of northern Ontario and other parts of Canada. Why do the Ojibway-Cree refer to their "custody" of the land?
- Select one of the treaties made with the Plains Indians such as Treaty 3. Study the "medicine chest" clause in it. How is this clause interpreted today?

In parts of Canada where no treaties exist, such as in the Maritimes, British Columbia, and the eastern Arctic, Natives are also stating their aboriginal rights to the land. Some may be willing to extinguish their rights, others are not. The Nishga Indians of British Columbia are not. They have stated simply that "Nishga land is not for sale."[17] For over one hundred years they have sought recognition for their land claims. Métis and non-status Indians have also begun to state their claims, although not all may want the same type of settlement or recognition.

The Inuit speak of Nunavut — Our Land:

It has been said that the land belongs to the white people, but we say it is our land. We, the Inuit, were born on this land and we have grown up here. That is why we say it is our land. Now it amazes us to learn that it belongs to the government. Government people keep telling us this, even though there is proof that this is our land. . . . I often tell my white companion that if the Qadlunaat (whiteman) had lived here before us, we would have discovered pieces of glass and metal from long ago buried deep in the ground. But we can tell from the digging that while we have found pieces of flint that were used as harpoon points by the Inuit, we have not found any traces of metal. . . . We have found not a single item mingled with these ancient Inuit tools that belonged to the whiteman.[18]

- Do further research on the land claims of the Nishga Indians of British Columbia.
- Find out what other claims are being advanced by Native peoples of your province or territory.
- The Inuit are thought to be the last to arrive from Asia. Their time of arrival is uncertain. Investigate the culture of the Inuit according to the model on page 16.

FOR FURTHER READING

Barnett, Donald C. *Poundmaker.* The Canadians.
  Fitzhenry & Whiteside, 1976.
Coatsworth, David. *Farmers of the East: Huron
  Indians.* Ginn Studies in Canadian History. Ginn,
  1975.
Coatsworth, Emerson S. *Nomads of the Shield:
  Ojibwa Indians.* Ginn Studies in Canadian
  History. Ginn, 1970.
Coatsworth, Emerson S. *Treaties and Promises:
  Saulteaux Indians.*
  Ginn Studies in Canadian History. Ginn, 1971.
Embree, Jesse. *Let Us Live. The Native Peoples
  of Canada.* Dent, 1977.
George, Chief Dan & Hirnschall, Helmut. *My
  Heart Soars.* Hancock House & Clarke Irwin,
  1974.
Gooderham, Kent. *The Days of the Treaties.*
  Griffin House, 1972.
Gooderham, Kent, ed. *I am an Indian.* Dent, 1969.
Hacker, Carlotta. *Crowfoot.* The Canadians.
  Fitzhenry & Whiteside, 1977.
Patterson, P. & Patterson, N.L. *The Changing
  People: A History of the Canadian Indians.*
  Collier-Macmillan Canadian History Program.
  Collier-Macmillan, 1971.
Sheffe, Norman, gen. ed. *Many Cultures, Many
  Heritages.* McGraw-Hill Ryerson, 1975.
Symington, D.F. *Hunters of the Plains: Assiniboine
  Indians.* Ginn Studies in Canadian History. Ginn,
  1972.
Symington, D.F. *Seafaring Warriors of the West:
  Nootka Indians.* Ginn Studies in Canadian
  History. Ginn, 1970.

Did the Vikings Settle in North America?

Today Denmark is a rich agricultural country. In the days when the Vikings lived there, however, the soil was so poor that few crops could be grown. Other Vikings lived in the rugged lands of Norway and Sweden, often in small farming settlements scattered at the ends of deep inlets or fiords.

The Vikings were, apparently, a violent people, often at war among themselves and with their neighbours. For over two centuries they were the terror of Europe, attacking and destroying villages along the Atlantic coast. During the ninth century they conquered and ruled parts of France and the British Isles.

Later, when Europeans became strong enough to resist their attacks, the Vikings became traders, venturing southward along the coast of Europe and eastward far up the great rivers of Russia into the interior.

To the west, they formed colonies in Iceland (about 870) and Greenland (about 985). But Greenland, in particular, was almost valueless: a great island of packed ice, entirely without trees, and, except in a few small areas, almost useless for agriculture.

Did the Vikings living on Greenland, then, look farther west? Did they plan voyages of discovery, driven by the need to find new lands for settlement by their growing population? Or did they, perhaps, stumble on our continent through an error in navigation or while lost in a storm?

Those historians who claim that the ancient Vikings attempted to form settlements in North America usually emphasize the evidence given below. With two or three of your classmates, study each of the sections of the chart. Make a list of the information you find in each section.

Evidence of Settlement

Legends or Sagas

. . . They hurried to the land where a river flowed from a lake into the sea. . . . There was no shortage of salmon in the river or the lake, and these were larger salmon than they had ever seen before.[1]

In the morning Leif said to his crew: "Hereafter we shall either gather grapes and cut vines, or fell timber to make a cargo for my ship."[2]

Excavation at l'Anse aux Meadows

The excavation revealed:
- ruins of nine buildings, with earthen floors and turf walls;
- some iron nails and a stone anvil;
- charcoal in ember pits, revealing the pits were used about 1000 A.D.

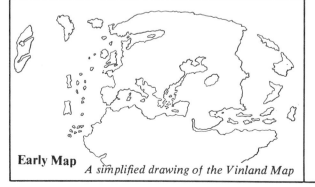

Early Map *A simplified drawing of the Vinland Map*

Ocean Currents

Viking Ships

In this vessel, Viking raiders travelled southward from the Baltic Sea to the Mediterranean Sea and westward to Iceland and Greenland.

In investigating the past, the historian often follows an educated guess or *hypothesis* about what may have happened. We followed a hypothesis — that the Vikings *did* attempt to settle in Canada — to gather the information shown in the charts.

- Using a scale of 1 to 5, grade the information you listed for reliability. (1 is for lowest reliability, 5 for highest.)
- Does the evidence *prove* that the Vikings reached North America? Why or why not?
- If the Vikings did found settlements in North America, suggest reasons for their final failure.
- How might our life in Canada be different if the Vikings had been successful in establishing settlements? (No one can really answer this question, but if you have read further about the Vikings, it might be fun to write a description of Vinland, 1978.)

FOR FURTHER READING

Donovan, F. *The Vikings.* New York: American Heritage Co., 1973

Kirby, Michael. *The Vikings.* Oxford: Phaidon Press, 1977.

La Fay, Howard. *The Vikings.* Washington: National Geographic, 1972.

Madsen, O. *The Vikings.* Barcelona: Minerva Press, 1976.

After Columbus: Competition for Empire

The settlements in North America believed to have been formed by the Vikings were probably abandoned in the eleventh century. For four more centuries our continent remained isolated from Europe. Then, at the end of the fifteenth century, everything changed. Within ten years after Columbus' famous voyage of discovery, the rulers of France, England, and Portugal sent out expeditions to explore new routes to the East. Gradually the eastern coastline of North America was explored and mapped.

After the explorers and adventurers came fishermen, merchants, and settlers. The monarchs of competing countries granted government contracts — or royal charters — to trading companies or groups of settlers. By 1700 eastern North America and the West Indies were divided among the European powers.

- What products were Europeans in competition for?
- As far as Canada is concerned, what two countries were in major conflict?
- What territories did each of these countries claim and why?

Over the one hundred and fifty years after the first successful settlement at Quebec in 1608, the French came to control a large part of present-day Canada. In the next section of our study we will examine the roots of our culture established during that very important time in our history.

The French in Canada

People of French ancestry have lived in Canada for nearly four hundred years. The two oldest European settlements in Canada were founded by French traders and explorers. They were Port Royal, founded in 1605, and Quebec, founded in 1608.

Did you ever wonder why both French and English appear on Canadian money, food container labels, and post offices? Can you think of any other places where both languages appear?

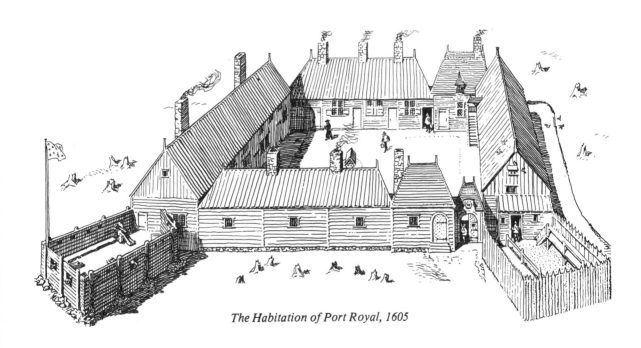

The Habitation of Port Royal, 1605

The Founding of Port Royal

At the beginning of the seventeenth century, European traders were eager to develop the wealth of the New World. In return for a promise to bring out settlers, the kings of France granted these traders a *monopoly* (sole right) to the fur trade.

The Sieur de Monts held a fur-trading monopoly for the area called Acadia. In 1605 he established a small group of French settlers at Port Royal on the Bay of Fundy. This colony became France's first permanent colony in the New World.

In 1606 de Monts asked Jean de Biencourt, Seigneur de Poutrincourt, to take charge of the tiny settlement of Port Royal. Marc Lescarbot, a Paris lawyer, accompanied de Poutrincourt to the New World. Lescarbot wrote a lively account of his voyage across the Atlantic:

On Saturday, . . . the 13th of May, we weighed anchor and put out to sea. . . . The great towers of the town of La Rochelle faded from our view. . . .

Storms were often presaged by the porpoises, which surrounded our ship in thousands. . . . we had a watch set below the bowsprit, harpoon in hand, who ran them through . . . and brought them on board with the aid of the rest of the crew, who hoisted them on deck with gaffs. . . . The meat tastes exactly like pork. The most delicate portion is the ridge along the back, and the tail. . . . These porpoises are the only fish which we caught before reaching the Grand Bank of codfish. But we saw other large fish at a distance, which showed more than half an acre of their back above water, and threw in the air to a height of more than two lances great streams of water from the blow-holes and openings in their heads.

. . . we encountered several storms which made us lower sail and sit with folded arms, borne at the will of the waves, and buffeted in strange fashion. . . . Sometimes the soup-kettle was upset, and at dinner or supper our dishes flew from one end of the table to the other. . . . To drink, one had to sway one's mouth and glass according to the motion of the ship. . . . However, most of us took it as a joke, for danger there was none, at least so far as we could see, since we were in a stout ship strong enough to resist the waves. Sometimes too we had very tiresome calms, during which we bathed in the ocean, danced

on the upper deck, climbed to the cross-trees, sang in harmony. . . .

. . . about . . . June 18th, we found for the space of three days the water of the sea quite warm . . . though the air was no warmer than before. And the 21st . . ., on the contrary, we were for two or three days so surrounded with fog and cold, that we thought we were in the month of January, and the

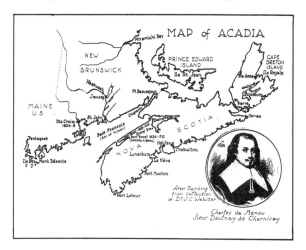

MAP of ACADIA

Charles de Menou Sieur Daulnay de Charnisay

After Painting from Collection of Dr. J.C. Webster

SHIPS & BOATS OF CHAMPLAIN'S TIME

sea-water was extremely cold. . . . When I seek for the cause of this alteration, I attribute it to the icebergs of the north, which came down upon the coast and into the sea which washes the shores of Newfoundland and Labrador. . . .

On Tuesday, the 25th [of July] we were off Cape Sable. . . . The next day we cast anchor at the entrance of Port Royal.[1]

- How long did Lescarbot's voyage take? Why did it take so long?
- What are the large "fish" described in lines 13 to 17?
- What evidence can you find which suggests that Lescarbot found the trip a great adventure?
- What is the explanation for the "warm" sea they encountered on June 18th?
- Is his explanation for the fog mentioned in lines 38 to 42 correct?

Establishing a Colony

Marc Lescarbot made his ocean voyage sound like a happy adventure, but he was very serious when it came to the business of setting up a settlement. "Many who are ignorant," he wrote, "think that the establishment of a settlement in an unexplored country is an easy matter but they will see that it is much easier said than done." He goes on to explain some of the difficulties:

I have been told by a pilot . . . who was with the English in Virginia twenty-four years ago, that after their arrival there, thirty-six died in three months. And yet Virginia is supposed to lie . . . where the climate is good. . . . Considering this I repeat my conviction . . . that such a high death-rate comes from bad food; and there is special need in such a country to have from the first . . . domestic animals of all sorts, and to transplant many fruit-trees and slips, in order speedily to have the change of diet necessary to the health of those who wish to people the land.[2]

- What advice does Lescarbot have for those who are planning settlements?

- What evidence can you find that he is eager to see a prosperous colony, not just a fur-trading post?

The Order of Good Cheer

Lescarbot spent the winter of 1606-1607 at Port Royal. The members of the tiny settlement, which included Samuel de Champlain, developed a way to make the long winter pass quickly and to maintain their health:

. . . in order to keep our table joyous and well-provided an Order was established. . . which was called the Order of Good Cheer. . . . each . . . man was appointed Chief Steward in his turn, which came around once a fortnight. . . . there was no one who, two days before his turn came, failed to go hunting or fishing, and to bring back some delicacy in addition to our ordinary fare. So well was this carried out that never at breakfast did we lack some savoury meat of flesh or fish, and still less at our midday or evening meals.[3]

Lescarbot explained that the evening meal was the "chief banquet" of the day. The ruler of the day's feast marched in "napkin on shoulder, wand of office in hand, and around his neck the collar of the Order which was worth more than four crowns." Each member followed him carrying one of the dishes which the cook had prepared. Geese, ducks, bear, and rabbit were plentiful. Lescarbot was particularly fond of tender moosemeat but felt that nothing could rival beaver's tail. Wine, of course, was served with every meal.

The Settlement at Quebec

The Abandonment of Port Royal

In 1607 de Monts lost his monopoly of the fur trade in Acadia. He had depended on the money he earned from the fur trade to support the colony at Port Royal. Lescarbot was bitterly disappointed and full of grief "to abandon a soil which had produced for us such goodly wheat."[4] He believed that in one more year the colony could support itself because "the soil was ample to produce the necessities of life." He realized that "de Monts and his partners were losing money, and receiving no help from the King, could not support without much difficulty a colony overseas."[5]

De Poutrincourt and his son made a brave attempt to re-establish the colony in 1610, but an English expedition from Virginia destroyed it in 1613. Only a handful of French settlers stayed on to form the nucleus for future settlements.

During the next one hundred years Acadia passed back and forth between Britain and France. In 1713 Acadia and her 2500 French settlers came under British rule. The story of these "Acadians" will be told later.

- How did Lescarbot believe colonies should be financed?
- Why did he believe Port Royal was an excellent site for a colony?

Meanwhile Samuel de Champlain had established the second permanent French settlement at Quebec in 1608. The colony grew very slowly. Champlain blamed the fur-trading companies, who were given the responsibility of bringing in settlers in return for a monopoly of trade.

In a letter to the King of France and his council in 1618 Champlain tried to stir their interest in Canada and gain their financial support for permanent colonies. As you read the following statements from his letter, you will realize that there were several motives for establishing colonies.

> Should this said country [New France] be given up and the settlement abandoned, for want of bestowing upon it the needed attention, the English or Flemings, envious of our prosperity, would seize upon it, thereby enjoying the fruits of our labours, and preventing by this means more than a thousand vessels from going to the dry and green [wet, salted]fisheries, and for whale-oil, as they have already done . . . in the Sieur de Poutrincourt's settlements. . . .

> His said Majesty will establish the Christian faith among an infinite number of souls, who neither hold nor possess any form of religion whatsoever. . . .

> The King will make himself master and lord of a country nearly eighteen hundred leagues in length, watered by the fairest rivers in the world. . . . full also of the greatest meadows, fields, and forests. . . .

> The Sieur de Champlain undertakes to discover the South Sea passage to China and to the East Indies by way of the river St. Lawrence. . . . His said Majesty would derive a great and notable profit from the . . . customs' duties on the merchandise that would come from China and the Indies. . . .

> I had no other purpose than to see the country inhabited by industrious people, for the clearing of the land.[6]

- Why might the fur-trading companies neglect their responsibility to bring in permanent settlers?
- Why would French settlers be reluctant to come to the New World at this time?
- According to Champlain, how could the New

World be a valuable source of wealth to the King?
- How does Champlain try to appeal to the King's vanity and his concern for the prestige of France?
- Why might the King of France be interested in spreading the Christian religion? Was Champlain correct when he said that the Indians "neither hold nor possess any form of religion whatsoever"?
- What exploration was Champlain interested in? Why?

The Habitation of Quebec, 1608.
In 1627 the population was only 65. The tiny colony survived English occupation from 1629-1633. Under the Jesuits missionary work, especially among the Hurons, was undertaken. Montreal was founded in 1642. The very existence of the colony was threatened in the 1640's and 1650's by Iroquois attacks.

Advice to Those Wishing to Settle in New France

Pierre Boucher came to New France from Normandy in 1635. He "made good," and in his *True and Genuine Description of New France Commonly Called Canada* in 1664 he explained what kind of settlers Canada needed:

> You ask me in the first place whether you are fit for this country. The answer I make you is that this country is not yet fit for people of rank who are extremely rich, because such people would not find in it all the luxuries they enjoy in France. . . .
>
> The people best fitted for this country are those who can work with their own hands in making clearings, putting up buildings. . . .
>
> It would be well for a man coming to settle, to bring provisions with him for at least a year or two years if possible, especially flour. . . .
>
> It would be well also to bring a supply of clothes, for they cost twice as much here as they do in France.
>
> Most of our settlers are persons who came over in the capacity of servants, and who, after serving their masters for three years, set up for themselves. They had not worked for more than a year before they had cleared land on which they got in more than enough grain for their food.
>
> Poor people would be much better off here than they are in France, provided they are not lazy; they could not fail to get employment and could not say, as they do in France, that they are obliged to beg for their living because they cannot find any one to give them work; in one word, no people are wanted, either men or women, who cannot turn their hands to some work, unless they are very rich.[7]

- Would you give the same advice as Pierre Boucher did to someone who wanted to settle in Canada today? Why or why not?

Canada's First Census, 1666

Today, the Canadian government takes a *census,* or count of the population, every ten years. The 1971 census showed that Canada had a total population of over 21 000 000 people. A census tells us more than just the total number of people in a country. It also explains where people live and how they make their living.

During the winter of 1666 a general census of the colony of New France was taken by the *Intendant,* or king's manager. This was the first Canadian census of which we have any record. According to this census, the total European population of New France was 3418. Most of these people lived in or near the three main towns of Quebec, Trois Rivières, and Montreal.

Louis XIV King of France 1643-1715

The First Wave of Immigrants

During the ten years from 1663 to 1673 Canada received her first wave of immigrants. Contrast the slow growth of population before 1663 with the rapid growth in the ten years which followed:

Year	Population
1653	2000 (estimate)
1663	3000 (estimate)
1666	3418
1668	5870
1672	7000 +
1674	7800

What had caused such remarkable growth in such a short time? In 1663 New France came under the direct control of the young king of France, Louis XIV. For nearly ten years he took a keen interest in the colony and its growth. He saw that colonies could bring wealth, power, and prestige to France. He appointed Jean Talon as his Intendant in New France. Talon was eager to promote settlement and growth. During this ten-year period France gave help and encouragement to those who wished to settle in the colony.

The King's Daughters

When Talon took the first census in 1666, he noticed a very interesting fact: men outnumbered women by nearly two to one. Considering the motives for early settlement, why would this be so?

The shortage of women was remedied by sending groups of young single women to be the brides of the young bachelors of the colony. Some of these young women had been raised in orphanages. Because they were the responsibility of the king, they were called *les filles du roi,* or the king's daughters. Others were from poor peasant families. Priests recruited the young women, who were chaperoned by a responsible married woman during their long sea voyage to Canada.

Marie de l'Incarnation, who was Mother Superior of the Ursulines, an order of nuns in Quebec, wrote regularly to her son in France. In the following letter of 1667 she describes *les filles du roi:*

> Ninety-two girls have come from France this year, who are already married . . . to soldiers or labourers. . . . A great many men have also come this year at the expense of the King, who wishes the country to be peopled.[8]

In another letter she writes:

> The vessels have no sooner arrived than the young men come here to seek wives and, as there are so many of both men and girls, couples are married by thirties. The most prudent young men commence to build a habitation a year before they marry, because those that possess a habitation have a better choice; this is the first thing the girls inform themselves about and they are wise to do so, because those that are not already established suffer a great deal before they become well off.[9]

Talon gave fifty livres in goods to each young woman who found a husband. The king gave every young man who married at or before age twenty a gift of twenty livres, called the "King's gift." Fathers were fined if their sons had not married at twenty and their daughters at sixteen. It is not surprising, then, that Talon reported in 1670 that all the girls who came that year were married except fifteen.[10]

Many years later, in 1709, La Hontan described the meeting of brides and bridegrooms:

> . . . the bridegrooms chose their brides as a butcher chooses his sheep. . . . here were to be seen the tall and the short, the blonde and the brunette, the plump and the lean; everybody, in short, found a shoe to fit him. At the end of a fortnight not one was left. I am told that the plumpest were taken first, because it was thought being less active they were more likely to stay at home, and that they could resist the winter cold better. Those who wanted a wife . . . were obliged to make known their possessions and means of livelihood. . . . The marriage was concluded forthwith with the help of a priest. . . . the next day the governor-general caused the couple to be presented

Mother Marie de l'Incarnation teaching Indian children

with an ox, a cow, a pair of swine, a pair of fowls, two barrels of salted meat, and eleven crowns in money.[11]

- In what ways did King Louis XIV encourage immigration to New France?
- How did his interest help to promote rapid growth?
- In what ways does La Hontan's account differ from that of Marie de l'Incarnation?
- Why does our society discourage rather than encourage young marriages?

Landing of the girls sent out as brides

Population Growth by Natural Increase

It is estimated that over fifteen hundred government-assisted immigrants reached New France between 1665 and 1671. During the same period of time nearly one thousand young women arrived to be wives for the young men. After 1678 immigration from France slowed down. Further increases in population were mainly due to a very high birth rate. Between 1689 and 1760 the population increased sixfold as the following figures show:[12]

Year	Population
1689	12 000
1713	18 000 +
1734	37 000 +
1754	55 000 +
1760	76 000 (est.)

It was the high birth rate that enabled the population of New France to grow so rapidly in spite of a high death rate and low immigration after 1678.

In New France large families were encouraged and rewarded. All families with ten children were entitled to a pension of 300 livres a year. Families with twelve children received 400 livres. In 1671 Talon reported that between 600 and 700 babies had been born that year and more than this were expected the next.[13]

- A country's birth rate is worked out by counting the number of babies born for every 1000 people.

   Between 1751 and 1760 the birth rate in New France rose to 61.7 per thousand — one of the highest rates ever recorded.[14] In 1973 the birth rate in Canada was 15.5. In the province of Quebec it was 13.8.[15] Show this on a graph.

- A country's death rate is worked out by counting the number of people who die for every 1000 people.

Between 1700 and 1770 the death rate in New France ranged from 23.9 to 38.2 per thousand.[16] Even with this high death rate, the number of births was much greater than the number of deaths. The death rate in Canada in 1973 was 7.4 per thousand.[17] Show this on a graph.

- The infant mortality rate (death rate of children less than one year old) was 15.5 in Canada in 1973.[18] It is estimated that 246 of every 1000 babies born in New France died before their first birthdays.[19] The infant mortality rate in old France was even higher according to some estimates. Show this on a graph.
- In Jean Talon's census of 1666 only 152 of the 3418 people were older than fifty years. Why would this be so? What is the life expectancy of Canadians today?
- Why did so many babies die before they reached their first birthdays?
- In his census Talon made a careful list of the occupations and trades of New France. This is the first Canadian manpower and employment survey. Members of the nobility, clergy, and government service are not included. He also left out farmers. Here is his list:[20]

Armourers	4
Bailiffs	4
Bakers	11
Braziers	11
Brewers	3
Brick Makers	1
Butchers	7
Button Makers	1
Carpenters	36
Carpet Weavers	3
Chandlers	3
Charcoal Burners	1
Confectioners	5
Coopers	8
Curriers	1
Cutlers	1
Drapers	4
Edge Tool Makers	14
Furriers	1
Foundrymen	1

Gardeners	3
Gentlemen	3
Gunsmiths	7
Hatters	7
Jewellers	1
Joiners	27
Locksmiths	3
Masons	32
Merchants	18
Millers	9
Nailers	4
Notaries	2
Printers	1
Rope Makers	6
Saddlers	3
Servants	401
Sailors	22
Ship Captains	1
Slaters	1
Shoemakers	20
Stone Cutters	1
Surgeons	5
Sword Grinders	1
Tailors	30
Teachers	3
Tinsmiths	1
Turners	1
Weavers	16
Wheelwrights	2
Wooden Shoemakers	1

- With the aid of a dictionary or encyclopedia find out about the occupations that are unfamiliar to you. Which of these occupations, very necessary in the 1600's, are no longer practised today? Why?
- Historians consider *primary* information (from first-hand sources) valuable in learning about life in New France. How many different kinds of primary information have been drawn upon so far in this unit? What kinds of primary information are available today?

  What do historians mean by secondary sources of information? Find some examples in this unit.

  What kind of information — primary or secondary — do you think would be the most trustworthy? Why?

The Society and Institutions of New France

- Find out what the following sailing terms mean: bowsprit, harpoon, watch, gaffs, cross-trees.
- Play the role of a *fille du Roi*. Interview a prospective bridegroom about his life and income or write a letter to a friend in France describing your voyage across the Atlantic and your observations of New France.
- It has been estimated that approximately 10 000 immigrants reached New France between 1608 and 1760. The origins of about 5000 of them have been identified.[21]

  Study the accompanying map of eighteenth-century France, which shows the provinces that supplied the greatest numbers of immigrants.
- A second important wave of immigration occurred between 1740 and 1759, the year Quebec fell to the British. Why would this wave make less impact than the earlier one under Jean Talon?
- The following classification of immigrants has been made: 3900 tradesmen; 3500 military recruits; 1100 marriageable girls; 1000 deported people. The population also included a sprinkling of non-French immigrants and the descendants of mixed French and Indian marriages. Account for the large number of military immigrants. Explain why the French government received angry requests to stop sending deported people.[22]

The basic political, social, and legal institutions of France, the mother country, were established in New France. The familiar land-holding system, the courts and laws, the Roman Catholic Church, and a social structure based on clear class differences were all brought to New France. The French language, French habits, styles and customs, French values and attitudes crossed the Atlantic to find root in New France. In short, the first French immigrants brought with them their seventeenth century French culture, or way of life.

None of the institutions or attitudes remained identical to those of old France. New conditions such as the climate and geography of the St. Lawrence Valley, new economic activity such as the fur trade, and new ways of doing things adapted from the customs of the Native peoples all helped to bring about certain "Canadian" variations of this seventeenth century way of life.

By 1713 New France, although clearly a French colony, had developed an identity of its own. "Its French people, with two or three generations of North American ancestors behind them, now called themselves not Frenchmen, but 'Canadiens' — Canadians."[23] By 1763 when New France became a colony of a foreign power — Great Britain — the great majority of Canadians who were farmers, craftsmen, labourers, and small shop-keepers had few direct ties with old France. Their livelihood and their culture were firmly planted in Canada where most of them had been born.

- Identify the Native peoples with whom the early French explorers, traders, and settlers came into contact and investigate the features of Native culture such as food, transportation, and dress which the French adapted.
- Using the model on page 16 investigate the effects of French culture on the life-style of the Huron Indians.

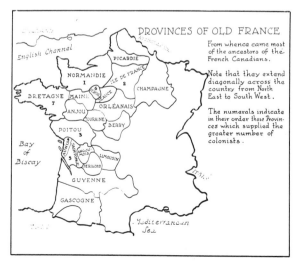

PROVINCES OF OLD FRANCE

From whence came most of the ancestors of the French Canadians.

Note that they extend diagonally across the country from North East to South West.

The numerals indicate in their order those Provinces which supplied the greater number of colonists.

The Seigneurial System

The land-holding system of New France was called the seigneurial system. It was modeled on the feudal land-holding system of northern France. It preserved the class structure of France and used some feudal ceremonies and words. However, special conditions in New France and deliberate French government policies caused it to become very different after it crossed the Atlantic.

The purpose of the seigneurial system was to settle the land. At first the fur-trading company and later the king's government granted a *seigneur*, or lord, a large block of land called a *seigneury*. The land was not simply a gift to reward an individual or to make him a wealthy man. Anyone who became a seigneur had to accept a whole series of duties, the first of which was to bring in colonists who would clear and settle the land.

When the seigneur received his land, he had to go through an old feudal ceremony called *foi et hommage*. To do this he went to the governor's home in Quebec City where he took off his hat, laid down his weapons, knelt, and declared himself to be the king's man. He promised to be a faithful subject and swore to carry out his duties as a seigneur.

The seigneur kept a portion of the land on his seigneury for his own use. This was called his domain. Parcels of land were allotted to *censitaires*, who were later called habitants. The seigneur might lose his land, and thus the livelihood he could make from it, if he did not try to find habitants to clear and settle it. The king's agent, the intendant, could and sometimes did insist on a detailed report to prove that this was done.

It was the seigneur's duty to build a manor house on his seigneury. He did not have to live in it all the time, but he or his agent had to be there once a year on St. Martin's Day, November 11, to collect the annual rent. He had to help pay for the cost of a church and presbytery for which some land on the seigneury might be set aside. If the intendant called for compulsory work on the roads, the seigneur had to do his share of the work. He had to build and operate a flour mill for the habitants. He had to reserve all the oak growing on the seigneury for the king. Oak was the most important wood for ship-building. The seigneur could not cut or sell it unless an agent of the king gave him permission. All mines and minerals that might be developed on a seigneury belonged to the king. Some seigneurs also had to establish courts on their seigneuries.

As you can see, the seigneur did not actually own the land. He did not buy it. The government could take it back. He and his descendants received the right to use it and enjoy certain profits from it only if they carried out their duties. A seigneur could sell his right to use the land, but if he did, the king collected a large tax.

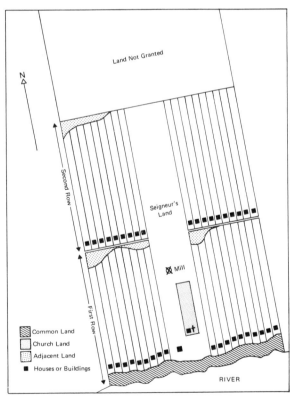

The first seigneury was granted to Robert Giffard in 1634 at Beauport near Quebec City.

Historians agree that the seigneur got very small profits in return for the duties he performed and the services he provided. He received certain payments from his habitants, in money or produce or work. These payments were fixed in a contract, and the seigneur could not charge more or add new ones. Habitants had to make him a yearly payment called *cens et rentes*. They might have to perform one or two day's labour a year for him. The seigneur could collect a fee of one-fourteenth of the amount of grain ground at the mill. Some habitants had to pay a fee to use the common pasture land on the seigneury. Others might have to pay for the privilege of fishing. The occasional seigneur had the right to collect wood on the land of his habitants or to require them to set up a Maypole in front of his manor house every May 1. If a habitant wished to sell his right to his parcel of land to another, he had to pay a transfer tax to the seigneur.

- List the duties a typical habitant might have to his seigneur.
- What security and services did the habitant receive as long as he carried out his duties?

Although the seigneur might receive little financial reward, his social position as a noble entitled him to certain honours and privileges. In the local church he had a free pew which was twice as wide as those of the habitants. It was located in an important place, the first row to the right. The *curé* (parish priest) would name the seigneur and his family in prayers. The seigneur had the right to be buried inside the church beneath his pew. In public ceremonies he came first behind the curé. He could expect to be appointed to certain government positions, and his sons might become officers in the army.

In old France the feudal system tended to favour the seigneur. In New France the seigneurial system tended to favour the habitant. This was partly because of conditions in the new world and partly because of government policies. Consider the following:

(i) It was difficult to persuade settlers to come to New France. Therefore seigneurs had to offer them attractive terms. Rents and duties tended to be lower in New France than in old France.

(ii) There was an abundance of land in the early days. A seigneur who put too much pressure on his habitants might lose them to another or they might prefer the free life of the *coureurs de bois* (independent traders).

(iii) As long as the habitant performed his contract duties, his right to the land was secure and he could pass it on to his heirs. The seigneur could not throw him off the land, rent it to others, or increase his contract payments.

(iv) A seigneur could not hold his land for speculation because he might lose it if he did not bring it into cultivation.

(v) Certain rights of French seigneurs were not permitted in Canada. They could not collect a hearth tax from the habitants or hunt across their crop lands. They were usually denied the right to force their habitants to use the seigneury bake oven for a fee.

(vi) Canadian seigneurs came from a wide variety of backgrounds. Seigneurs were legally nobles; but those who had come from either the ranks of the habitants or the middle class would never be treated with quite the same respect as the centuries-old noble families of France.

(vii) The government of New France required all inhabitants to do militia duty and road work. The militia captain for each parish was a habitant, not a seigneur. When the militia captain was carrying out the intendant's orders, the seigneur had to take orders from him. The seigneur had to do his share of road work.

(viii) In old France it was estimated that a peasant family paid between one-third and one-half of its produce in government taxes. There were no direct taxes of this kind in New France. The only taxes ever collected were import duties on wine, spirits, and tobacco and an export tax which merchants paid on beaver.

(ix) In old France nobles who engaged in trade or commerce would lose social standing. In New France seigneurs did engage in trade and commerce.

A number of observers commented on the higher standard of living enjoyed by the habitants of New France compared to their peasant counterparts in France. Some observers liked the difference; others felt that the habitants had become "too independent."

The habitants who really labour on their land are well off, or at least live very comfortably, having their fields, a goodly number of cattle, and good fishing close to their homes.[24]

Truly, if the many poor people who drag on a wretched existence in France only knew the advantages that are here for those who wish to work, and who have strong arms, I think that many of them would come over here. . . . We know nothing of taxes.[25]

They warm themselves as they please by using the firewood at their disposal in unlimited quantities. They differ in this respect from the French living in a great number of the French provinces which are short of wood.[26]

The ordinary *habitants* would be scandalized to be called peasants. In fact, they are of better stuff, have more wit, more education, than those of France. This comes from paying no taxes, that they have the right to hunt and fish, and that they live in a sort of independence.[27]

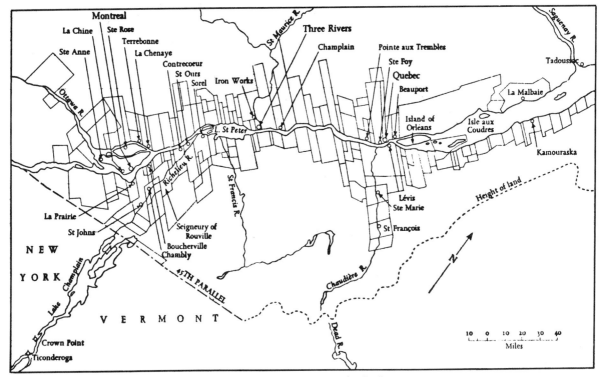

There were about 250 seigneuries in 1760, spread along the St. Lawrence, Richelieu and Chaudiere rivers.

The average Canadian is unruly, obstinate and will do nothing but what he wants or fancies. . . .

The habitants generally live in great comfort. They never travel on foot. In summer, they have carriages and in winter they have sleighs. In general, all of the habitants own horses. It is quite common to have as many horses in a household as there are boys. The latter use the horses only when they wish to go out in style and to go courting.[28]

- In what ways was the Canadian habitant better off than the French peasant according to these observers?
- What evidence is there in these quotations that seigneurs placed very light obligations on their habitants?
- Some observers commented that the health of Canadians was better than that of the population of France in spite of a more severe winter climate. What might account for this?

In old France peasant villages with houses clustered together were the normal situation. This type of village was almost unknown in New France. Habitants wanted farms that fronted on the St. Lawrence or its tributaries. Narrow strip farms, each with a habitant's house and river frontage, running back from the river were typical. By 1760 the St. Lawrence River from Quebec to Montreal might almost be described as a long straggling village on both sides of the river. Under French law all children were entitled to a share of the family property. Some farms became so narrow through subdivision that the government set a minimum width of one and one-half arpents (slightly over sixty metres) in 1745. The narrow strip farms along the river were "Canadian." There was nothing similar in old France.

Typical early Quebec home:

Montreal type, with double chimneys & parapet at gable ends.

- Construct a model of an early French-Canadian farmhouse or seigneury.
- Investigate more fully the relationship between seigneur and habitants. Draw up an imaginary contract between a seigneur and habitant.
- Do an investigation of the economy of New France. What food crops were grown? Were they exported? Where? How important was the fur trade? What industries were there? Did they export their products? What businesses and trades developed in the towns? What percentage of the population lived in towns?

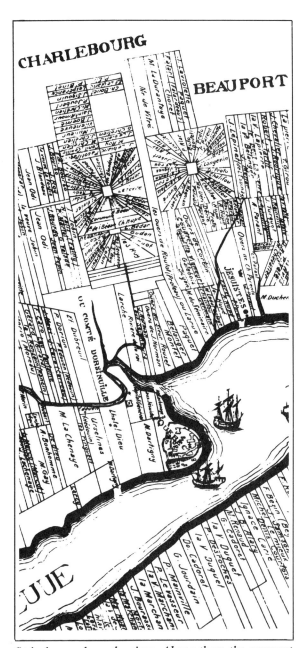

Strip farms along the river. Above them the compact radial villages, modelled on those of old France, with which the intendant Talon experimented. This type of village was unpopular. Why?

The Church

The familiar religious practices and religious orders of the Roman Catholic Church in France were brought to New France. In 1615 four monks of the Récollet Order arrived to do missionary work among the Indians. In 1625 five members of the Jesuit Order began their missionary work. Protestants were discouraged from settling in New France after 1625; therefore the Roman Catholic Church played a central role in the society of New France. The yearly reports, called *The Jesuit Relations,* sent by the Jesuits to their superiors in France are a main source of information about New France.

As the population of New France increased, women's religious orders such as the Ursulines, who devoted themselves to teaching, arrived. Other religious orders did educational, hospital, and

charitable work, including caring for the aged and orphans. The number of parish priests also increased.

The normal practice of all European countries was to have a state or established church (a church recognized and given financial support by the government). This practice was followed in New France. The Roman Catholic Church was entitled to collect a *tithe* (tax) from the inhabitants. In old France the customary tithe was one-thirteenth of the produce. In New France when the tithe was introduced, the Church had to accept one-half this amount to be paid on grain alone. In order to finance their educational, missionary, hospital, and charitable work religious orders normally became *seigneurs.*

In 1760 the clergy in Canada consisted of approximately 160 persons, including some seventy parish priests. About one-half the number were Canadian, the others French. In personnel the Church was becoming "Canadianized."

The Government of New France

The government described below was established in New France in 1663. It remained in operation until New France came under British rule.

All power came from the king of France who gave specific powers and responsibilities to such officials as the minister of marine, the governor general, and the intendant.

The governor general was responsible for military matters and for relations with the Indian nations and the European colonies to the south. He was answerable to the minister of marine and thereby to the king of France.

The intendant had very important duties. He had to keep law and order, to see that justice was done in the courts, and to manage and direct the economy of New France. He had to feed, arm, and clothe all military forces. He was responsible for building and keeping military fortifications repaired.

The superior council registered laws and acted as a court. The intendant became the main official in the council. French laws were enforced, and if laws for local conditions were needed, it was the intendant who made them.

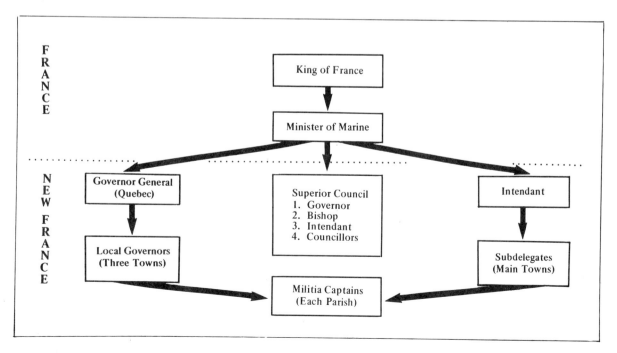

A militia captain from among the habitants was chosen for each parish. The militia captains were the local agents for the intendant. They gave his orders and called for compulsory work on roads and bridges. They also had to muster the militia for military service.

There was no popularly elected assembly as there was in the British colonies along the Atlantic coast. Many critics have noted that this made the government of New France very dictatorial. (It might also be noted that the British colonies cherished the right of their assemblies to consent to taxes. New France did not have taxes except for the import and export duties named on page 44. The king of France did want, however, to be sure that the governor and intendant found out the views of the population before any local laws were passed. ". . . it was customary to call an assembly of the people at large, or at least of those directly affected, and be guided by the majority opinion. Between 1672 and 1700 seventeen such assemblies were held and on at least one occasion the intendant subsequently enacted legislation in accord with the expressed wishes of the assembly, and contrary to what he himself had recommended."[29]

Each year in the fall, before the annual freeze-up of the St. Lawrence, royal officials in New France would send long reports and requests to the minister of marine in France. In the spring or early summer, dispatches from France would be sent to Quebec. Ten months or more might pass between the time that a report was sent and a reply was received from France.

- After doing further research on the government of New France, debate the following question: Was the government despotic, that is, did it strictly control and direct the lives of all the inhabitants?

The Legal System and Courts

Law is divided into two main types. A crime is an action that is considered harmful to the community as a whole. Crimes include such actions as murder, robbery, and arson. The government acts for the community through courts and judges. It takes responsibility for bringing the accused to trial and punishes him if he is found guilty. Civil cases deal with matters that involve two parties in a dispute, such as the terms of a mortgage or contract. Civil cases also deal with matters that affect family life, such as property and inheritance, marriage and divorce, adoption and care of children. In civil cases the government will step in to help individuals settle their differences.

The courts and the legal system of New France were the responsibility of the intendant. From 1640 on the code of law used was the *Coutume de Paris* (Custom of Paris). In 1663 a revised version of the *Coutume de Paris* was declared to be the law of New France. This was the common law or customary law as built up through the centuries and followed in most of the central and northern provinces of France at the time. To this basic code of law was added the king's *Ordonnance Civile* of 1667 and *La Grande Ordonnance Criminelle* of 1670.

In New France the intendant could judge minor civil cases worth small amounts of money. His decision could be appealed to the superior council. In more serious civil cases, if both parties requested it, he could decide the matter. There was no appeal. There was no charge for the intendant's service. A poor habitant could have the intendant judge a dispute with his seigneur free of charge. Under certain circumstances, the intendant could take a case out of court if he felt that justice was not being done. His judgment could be appealed.

There were three types of courts in New France. Seigneurial courts usually heard minor civil and criminal cases. Royal courts at Montreal, Trois Rivières and Quebec handled more serious ones. The superior council heard both civil and criminal cases and acted as a court of appeal.

Historians have both praised and criticized the legal system of New France. They have looked with favour on the following practices: there was no imprisonment for debt as there was in England and the British colonies; a habitant's livestock and tools could not be seized for debt; cases were decided swiftly

The Effects of British Rule

because courts sat weekly; the fees that court officials could charge were strictly limited so that justice was available to all; the superior council heard appeals free of charge and reviewed sentences imposed before they were carried out.

Historians have also noted the following less favourable aspects of the legal system of New France: there were no juries; lawyers were not allowed to practise, so an accused person would either have to present his own case or have someone else do it for him; witnesses could not be cross-examined although their testimony could be questioned; the accused was considered guilty unless he could prove his innocence; torture might be used; a judge could choose any punishment he thought suitable; there was no right of habeas corpus (freedom from arbitrary imprisonment).

It should be noted that lawyers were not allowed to practise because they had gained such a bad reputation in France. There were, however, notaries to record wills, search land titles, and draw up contracts. When King Louis XIV received complaints that the governor of Montreal had imprisoned people arbitrarily, he ordered his legal officials not to imprison anyone who had not been properly charged by a court.

When New France became British at the conclusion of the Seven Years' War (1756-1763), the people of New France became subjects of the British king. Their ties with France were broken, and they lost their links with the Mississippi Valley, Prince Edward Island, and Cape Breton.

At the time of their surrender the people of New France had been promised the peaceful enjoyment of their homes, property, and religion. French officials and a few seigneurs and clergy returned to France. The great mass of the population could not afford to do this, nor did they have their roots in old France.

British officials assumed that the approximately 76 000 *Canadiens* would be assimilated, that is, they would begin to speak English and adopt British customs and values. This did not happen, for several reasons. The *Canadiens* had a deep and enduring will to maintain their unique identity. English-speaking newcomers remained a tiny minority. Governor Carleton remarked: "Barring catastrophe shocking to think of, this Country must, to the end of time, be peopled by the Canadian race, who already have taken such firm root."[30]

The thirteen American colonies were on the point of revolting against their mother country, Britain, in 1774. The British government, urged on by Carleton, passed the Quebec Act. This law has been criticized by many because it favoured the clergy and the seigneurs at the expense of the habitants. Looking back, it now seems to some to be the "Magna Carta" of Quebec because it provided the legal means by which the French could preserve important parts of their cultural heritage. The seigneurial system of land-holding was kept. French civil law remained, although English criminal law was introduced. Roman Catholics were allowed to practise their religion freely, and the Church could continue to collect the tithe for its religious, educational, hospital, and charitable work. The boundary of Quebec was extended to the Ohio and Mississippi Rivers, although this was not permanent.

During the American Revolution (1775-1783), the majority of *Canadiens,* having given up their hopes for liberation and a restoration of French rule, decided that British rule was preferable to American. As thousands of Loyalists moved north into the Maritimes and Quebec, the British government was forced to reorganize its possessions in British North America. Quebec was split in two along the line of the Ottawa River. The eastern half — the heart of New France — became Lower Canada. Here the guarantees of the Quebec Act continued. The Constitutional Act of 1791 granted Lower Canada the right to an elected assembly. Land that had not yet been granted to seigneurs could be granted according to the British system of land-holding called freehold tenure. Under freehold tenure an individual could buy or sell his land as he wished. The population in Lower Canada at this time was approximately 145,000 French and 10,000 English. Sheer weight of numbers, as well as the legal guarantees of the Quebec and Constitutional Acts, enabled the French heritage to survive. Since the French had a majority, they could dominate the new assembly. Although the assembly's powers were weak compared to those of the British governor, it did give the French an institution which could provide them with experienced political leaders.

The Church became the key institution in preserving the French heritage. Only a handful of priests returned to France. Most of them, including the leaders, remained in Canada. The British, although officially opposed to religious orders such as the Ursulines, allowed them to continue their vital work. When the bishop of Quebec died in 1760, many feared that the British would not permit the con-secration of a new bishop. Their fears were un-necessary. Bishop Briand was consecrated, and he in turn was able to consecrate Canadian priests. The Church continued its educational work. The French language continued as a result, although there were strong pressures to adopt English. The seigneurial system may also have helped to preserve the heritage:

> The French Canadians, concentrated in their seigneuries, bound together by their language, their old culture, and their religion . . . successfully resisted the continual fumbling efforts of the Anglo-

Canadians and British officials to assimilate them, to make them over into English-speaking Protestants.[31]

The seigneurial system continued until 1854, when it was abolished. It no longer met the needs of a society that was increasingly urban and industrialized. It did, however, leave a mark on the physical appearance of the land which is still visible along the St. Lawrence and in the boundaries of certain counties. As a group, the seigneurs lost whatever special status they had enjoyed.

- The French seigneurial system and the English freehold system of land-holding show the different economic interests and social values of the two societies; the former emphasizes community welfare, the latter individual enterprise. What are the advantages of each system? What economic interests do each promote?

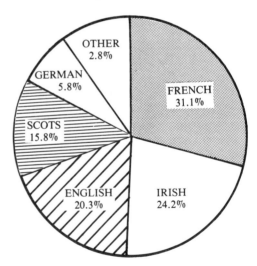

Canada's Population 1871 Census

Canadians of French Origin at the Time of Confederation

At the time of *Confederation* (union of the provinces to form Canada in 1867) people of French origin formed nearly one-third of the total population. At

The French Heritage

this time they were the largest single group in the country. The Irish, English, and Scots together formed a large English-speaking group. This is one reason why both French and English are *official* (recognized) languages in Canada. This is why our country is often described as *bilingual* (having two recognized languages).

Canadians of French Origin Today

The 1971 census of Canada showed that Canadians of French origin numbered over six million people. Turn back to the pie graph of the ethnic origin of Canada's population in 1971 (page 5). You will see that Canadians of French origin from nearly 30 percent of Canada's total population. The great majority of them are the descendants of settlers who came to Canada over three hundred years ago. As the pie graphs on page 6 and 7 show, people of French origin live in every province and territory in Canada.

If you had lived nearly three hundred years ago and had studied a map of North America, you might have predicted a predominantly French-speaking North America with a small English-speaking area along the Atlantic coast — the opposite of what actually happened.

With the above prediction in mind, here is how one writer explains how it feels to be French in North America today:

We had it made, so to speak, and we blew it. Demography, and war, changed everything. But because our ancestors came here as conquerors, their

Map of North America just before 1713.

descendants have never really, deep down, accepted defeat. They cannot be considered in the same light as other North American "ethnic" minorities, who came as immigrants, and who understood, therefore, that they would have to "assimilate". The integration of these people was a painful process, but at least it was voluntary. . . . Whereas the Cajuns of Louisiana, the Canucks of New England, the Francos of Ontario and Manitoba, have something in common with the Indians and the Blacks: they were all *forced* into the Anglo-Saxon Mainstream. . . .

When the French empire in America broke up, it left behind remnants of its original colonies: Louisiana, Acadia, Canada. . . . These old colonies refused to disappear, as they normally should have. . . . the French tried to remain French as long as they could.

They lost their struggle, everywhere but in Quebec, where they were luckier, stronger, fared better under foreign rule, and today hold a majority.

- Why does the speaker feel that the French must be treated differently from later immigrant groups?
- Why does he compare the French to the Native peoples and the Blacks?
- Demography is the statistical study of populations. Study the pie graphs on pages 5, 6, and 7. How has demography defeated French hopes except in Quebec?
- What war is the author referring to?
- Define: assimilation, integration.

Language

Many people consider language to be the most important means by which a person may keep his or her cultural heritage. The French language did not receive any legal protection until the British North America Act, Canada's written constitution, came into effect in 1867. Section 133 of the British North America Act states:

Either the English or the French language may be used by any Person in the Debates of the Houses of the Parliament of Canada and of the Houses of the Legislature of Quebec; and both those Languages shall be used in the respective Records and Journals of those Houses; and either of those Languages may be used by any Person or in any Pleading or Process in or issuing from any Court of Canada established under this Act, and in or from all or any of the Courts of Quebec.

The Acts of the Parliament of Canada and of the Legislature of Quebec shall be printed and published in both those languages.[33]

The Official Languages Act was passed in 1969 by the federal government in Ottawa. The federal government collects taxes from and represents people from all over Canada whether they speak French or English. It provides a variety of services, such as the Post Office and unemployment insurance, for all Canadians whether they speak English or French. The government employees who provide these services are civil servants. The Official Languages Act was passed to ensure that government services were available in English for those who spoke English and in French for those who spoke French. Some civil servants would speak English; some would speak French; and some would be bilingual so that contacts could be kept between the two language groups. The law has been widely criticized by those who fear that all civil servants will have to become bilingual.

Since 1960 many Quebeckers have been alarmed by certain trends which they fear threaten their ability to maintain their identity: non-French and non-English-speaking immigrants to the province of Quebec have tended to identify with the English-speaking minority; the birth rate in Quebec has fallen rapidly (17.6 in 1969 and 13.8 in 1973);[34] many Quebeckers themselves have become "Anglicized." As a result Bill 101, which became law in 1977, was passed.

The purpose of Bill 101 is to make French, "the distinctive language of a people that is in the majority French-speaking," the official language of the province of Quebec.[35] French is called "the instrument" by which people have given expression to their identity. French will be the language of government and of the courts, schools, and businesses of the province. People will be able to work, study, play, eat, and entertain themselves in French. In short, their life-style will be French. An English-language school system will be maintained for children who have at least one parent who attended an English-language school in Quebec, or one older brother or sister in such a system. Newcomers to Quebec, both from within Canada and from abroad as immigrants, are expected to enter the French-language school system. Native peoples on reserves may use their own language, but they are expected to use French as their second language.

- What groups have protested against Bill 101? What are their reasons in each case?

The graph below shows how difficult it has been for people of French ancestry to maintain their language outside Quebec.

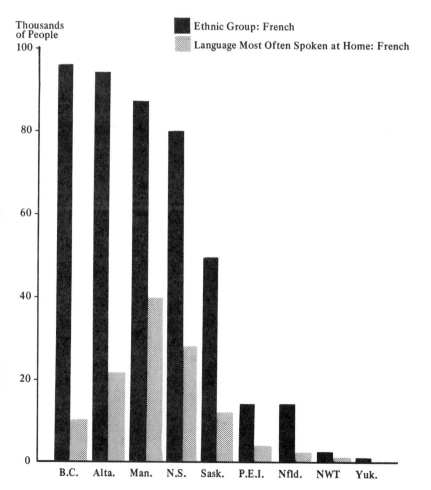

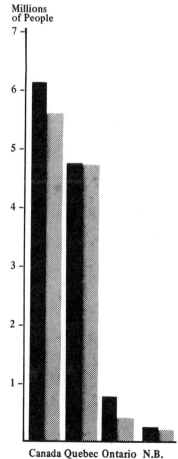

People of French ancestry outside of Quebec have been bitterly disappointed in their struggle to win official recognition for their language from provincial and territorial governments. The right to have their children educated in French has caused bitter controversy for over one hundred years. There are some signs that French-language education is winning support. In Ontario in 1978 the Minister of Education stated:

> I support the effort and intent of the francophone minority in this Province to preserve their language without feeling awkward or out-of-place, and to achieve conditions in which they can feel more comfortable living and working in their own language to the extent that it is practical. . . .
>
> It is not my feeling that the French-speaking citizens of this province are asking for the world. By the very foundations upon which this nation was established, they have a right to feel at home here, to feel self-respect, to be treated equally and to lead fulfilling lives free of political squabbles.[36]

However, not all English-speaking people share this view:

> Jean-Paul Beneteau, 12, offers a simple yet strong argument in favor of the controversial bill that will force construction of a secondary school for French-language students in Essex County. . . .
>
> "That school will help me to be me," he says.
>
> "I don't want to forget my French because my parents and grandparents are French-Canadian and I am too. . ."
>
> "I'm very happy now because I know when the new high school is built I'll be going there."

But there are boys in Jean-Paul's neighborhood who wish he'd shut up about his roots.

> Stevie Wilson, 14, feels that Francophones are trying to "take over" in Stoney Point, a village of 500 about 30 miles from Windsor.
>
> "They're trying to push that crap down our throats," he says. "They think everybody should cater to the French." . . .

There are about 50 000 Francophones in the county, some 70 per cent of whom are bilingual. Population of the county is about 300 000.

> Most French-speaking communities in Essex are clustered on the outskirts of Windsor. The "north shore" area — Stoney Point, Belle River, Tecumseh, and Tilbury — is heavily Francophone.
>
> The government's action isn't likely to lessen the racial friction in Essex.
>
> Board trustee Ted Boutette . . . says . . . the French-language students have "every right to their own school. . . ."
>
> "They are here in sufficient numbers to warrant building the school and there is no reason — besides pettiness and bigotry — why it shouldn't have been built years ago."

Francophones are always the losers in split French-English schools, he says.

> "They get bombarded with English and a lot of them wind up being assimilated."

Boutette, whose French ancestry goes back to the 18th century, cites himself as an example.

> "My French is just good enough to get by," he says. "My children didn't learn French when they were young but they managed to pick it up in college.
>
> "If you lose the language, you lose everything."

Gloria LeBlanc, 15, is convinced that English-speaking Canadians dislike Francophones.

> "How would you feel?" she asked. "The government almost had to put a gun to their heads to get the school. And they still won't give in.[37]

- Is it possible to maintain one's cultural heritage if one loses the ability to speak the original language?
- Investigate the way in which your province or local area has dealt with the question of French-language schools.
- Does your province provide provincial services in French?
- Does your area have French-language radio or television programs?
- Does your province or local area provide instruction in languages other than French or English

for those whose mother tongue is neither French nor English?

- Investigate the Manitoba Schools controversy in the 1890's.
- How did Ontario deal with French-language schools in the early years of the twentieth century?

Are You French?

Most French names have derivatives in the United States. They were "rebaptized." Some were translated outright:

Barrière became Gates and Berry
Beauchamp became Fairfield and Prettyfield. . . .

And that is only the beginning of the alphabet. Others underwent euphonic changes:

Auclair became O'Clair
Bouchard became Bouchor
Belair became Blair
Cartier becomes Carter . . .

Some underwent unexpected, amusing transformations:

Archambault became Scambo
Bilodeau became Bilow
Boucher became Bush. . .

Others have a number of derivatives:
Bellemare, Bealmear, Bealmer, Bellmar, Bellmard
Desrochers, Derusha, Desrouchie, Rock, Stone. . .

Nor is the picturesque absent from the changes:
Therien, Lander, Taylor, Farmer
Bélanger, Baker, Belonga
D'arsenault, Snow
Viens, Cummings, Come
Léviellée, Wideawake . . .

The descendant of a Frenchman may often be found behind an English name.[38]

- Although the above names have been recorded in the United States, a similar process of Anglicizing names has gone on in Canada. Research the origin of your own family name. Why do people change their surnames?

Civil Law

The civil law of Quebec, based on the *Coutume de Paris* along with some peculiarly Canadian additions, was left almost untouched by the British after 1763. Both the Quebec Act of 1774 and the Constitutional Act of 1791 guaranteed that such law would continue in Lower Canada, now the Province of Quebec.

In 1841 Upper and Lower Canada were reunited to form the Province of Canada. By this time the civil law code needed to be modernized. The original on which it had been based had already been drastically changed in 1804 by the Emperor Napoleon of France.

The Civil Code of France, or the Code Napoleon, established in 1804, was divided into three books. The first book dealt with the individual and the family, the regulation of marriage and divorce, the authority of the father, and the adoption and care of minors. The second book dealt with property. The third book dealt with contracts, mortgages, gifts, and obligations.

The Code Napoleon was much admired because its language was clear and simple. It could be understood by ordinary citizens, not just lawyers trained in the law. It has also been praised because it is based on principles of tolerance and *equity* (fairness).

The Code Napoleon had a wide appeal in Europe. It deeply influenced law in Spain and in turn spread to Spanish-speaking areas in the Americas. It is still the law of France, although like laws everywhere it has been modernized to suit twentieth-century conditions. It is found in the civil law of Puerto Rico and Louisiana.

In 1857 Prime Minister Macdonald of the Province of Canada set a committee to work to codify the civil laws of Lower Canada based on the updated civil code, commercial code, and civil procedure of France. Thus the 1804 civil code of France, the Code Napoleon, was adopted for Canada and officially proclaimed in 1866. Some sections were brought up to date between 1870 and 1879. The code is still being revised to reflect the needs of the people of Quebec in the last decades of the twentieth century.

- Make a montage of pictures that reflect the lively present-day culture of Quebec. Some topics to consider are: music, architecture, government, schools, theatre, television, newspapers, ballet, industrial development, films, sports, and festivals such as the Winter Carnival and St. Jean Baptiste Day.

Exploration

Guided and aided by Natives, French explorers penetrated and named vast areas of the interior of North America.

The map on page 51 indicates the extent of the continent claimed by the French empire at its height. Although France had to give up this vast area, the French heritage remains in place names that dot the map from the Gulf of St. Lawrence to the Gulf of Mexico and northwards and westwards into the Great Plains.

After 1666 the appearance of the *coureurs de bois* helped to advance France's claim to the interior of the continent. The government of New France had tried to discourage these men by severe penalties, but the attraction of the fur trade could not be stamped out. By the end of the seventeenth century, Montreal traders had established a base at Michilimackinac and were already conducting trade with the Indians of the plains. The voyageurs, who learned the art of making white birch bark canoes from the Indians, carried the trade of the interior waterways until early in the nineteenth century when the Hudson Bay Company assumed complete control of the fur trade.

- The following are the most important explorers of the seventeenth and eighteenth century. Try to find out what parts of North America they explored.
  Champlain 1609
  Brûlé 1615
  Nicolet 1634
  Radisson and Des Groseilliers 1659-60
  Jolliet and Marquette 1673, 1679
  Du Lhut 1678
  Iberville 1694-96
  La Vérendrye 1731, 1743
- Using a map of North America find as many places as you can that are of French origin. Some may be French versions of the original Indian place names.
- The following geographical terms used frequently in North America are of French origin: prairie, bayou, coulee, butte, cache, levee, portage. Using a dictionary, define each one.

- It has been said that the presence of French Canadians who have shown a determined effort to preserve their distinctive heritage has enabled Canada to develop into a multicultural society. Discuss this idea.
- Examine the role of French Canadians in Canadian political development. You might consider the following: Papineau, LaFontaine, Cartier, Laurier, St. Laurent, Trudeau.
- Investigate the contributions that French Canadians have made to the shaping of Canadian foreign policy.
- Why would a booklet prepared for people who are thinking of settling in Canada contain the following information?

Canada's historic and linguistic roots lie with two communities: one French-speaking, the other English-speaking. . . . Immigrants of other ethnic origins, in joining one of the two linguistic groups and accepting the spirit of their institutions, have contributed the wealth of their own backgrounds while preserving the best of their homelands.[39]

The Acadians

Acadia was the name given by France to her colonies along the Atlantic coast of Canada. Today the French-speaking ,nhabitants of Prince Edward Island, New Brunswick, and Nova Scotia call themselves Acadians. They are the descendants of the colonists who began to settle in this area in the 1600's. In the preceding chapter you read about the first colonists at Port Royal.

During the hundred years after the founding of Port Royal, Nova Scotia changed rulers many times. Both England and France claimed this territory. Although their rulers changed, the Acadians continued to develop their own society and customs. They had little or no contact with the settlements in New France, or even with France itself. Acadian farmers traded with the English colonies to the south and west of them. Hunting and fishing added to their food supply.

After Nova Scotia became British in 1713, the Acadians found themselves caught up in the wars between the French and English in North America. They occupied the land between the English settlements in New England and the French colonies along the St. Lawrence.

After over forty years under British rule, six thousand to seven thousand Acadians were expelled from their homes shortly before the outbreak of the Seven Years' War (1756-1763) between Britain and France. They were scattered far and wide among the English colonies from Massachusetts to Georgia. Some of their descendants now live in Louisiana and are proud of their "Cajun" ancestry.

As a people the Acadians survived their forced exile. In 1764 they were allowed to return to Acadia, provided that they took an oath of allegiance to Britain. Today the Acadians feel themselves to be a distinct group within Canadian society. They are bound together by a common language, French, a common religion, Roman Catholicism, and the memory of a common experience, the expulsion from their homeland in 1755. The Acadians of New Brunswick make up over one-third of the population of that province. Smaller numbers live in Nova Scotia, Prince Edward Island, and Quebec.

The Acadians: For and Against

The following dialogue is imaginary, but it is based on the arguments used by the Acadians and the British authorities in 1755.

British Governor: The Treaty of Utrecht signed by Britain and France in 1713 offered you a choice. You could leave Nova Scotia within a year, or you could take an oath of allegiance to Britain and become British subjects. If you chose to leave, you were given one year to remove yourselves to wherever you saw fit and take all your moveable goods with you. If you decided to stay, you were promised the right to practise the Roman Catholic religion and to keep your property.

Acadian Spokesman: How could we leave? Our ancestors worked to make our farms productive. Their bones lie buried in our churchyards. We could not leave the only homes we have ever known. We chose to stay and become British subjects.

Governor: Some of your people did move to nearby French settlements on Prince Edward Island and Cape Breton.

Acadian: A few did — but most of us wanted to stay. The British authorities did not seem to want us to leave.

Governor: We did not wish to see the land stripped of its people. But, as British subjects, you were obliged to do military service.

Acadian: The oath of allegiance said nothing about military service. We were willing to be loyal subjects as long as we did not have to do military service. We have been faithful subjects for over forty years.

Governor: Faithful? Even by 1720 your French priests were turning you against us. You traded freely with French settlements but were slow to sell your farm produce to us.

Acadian: We were willing to be neutral. We would not take up arms against Britain, but we would not take up arms against France either. How could we take up arms against our French and Catholic brothers in Quebec and Louisbourg?

Governor: French soldiers and priests were continually trying to persuade you to leave British territory and go to French settlements. They wanted to strengthen French power against us.

Acadian: In 1730 my people swore to be faithful and obedient to His Majesty King George II and to recognize him as King of Nova Scotia.

Governor: Faithful subjects must be prepared to do military service.

Acadian: The British governor promised us that we would be exempt from military service when we swore to be faithful to His Majesty. We swore the oath on the understanding that we would be exempt. Your authorities seemed to think so too. They called us "The Neutral French."

Governor: You did not act like "neutrals" when war broke out between Britain and France in 1744. When the priest Le Loutre urged the Indians to attack Annapolis Royal, none of you warned us. Some of you even helped the French to attack us at Minas in 1746. You gave information to the French who attacked New England soldiers at Grand Pré in 1747.

Acadian: Most of us stayed loyal in spite of the threats against us. We kept our oath. Your own governor, Mascarene, said that "the colony owes its safety to the refusal of the inhabitants to take up arms against us." My own priest insisted that we remain loyal to Britain. He threatened to drive us from the Church if we took up arms against the British.

New Englander: The British government has been far too easy with you rebels. It should have expelled your French priests. Anglican ministers should have been sent in to teach your children English. It was a great mistake to return the fortress of Louisbourg to the French in 1748. It became a base for French ships and a threat to our trade. The French became stronger on our borders. The

French governors of Quebec and Louisbourg openly encouraged raids on our settlements.

Governor: We founded the naval base at Halifax to prevent that from happening. We also built Fort Lawrence to guard against the French bases at Beauséjour and Gaspereau, and we settled new groups of immigrants such as the Germans at Lunenburg. Then the governor called on the Acadians to take a new oath of loyalty in 1749.

Acadian: You broke your previous promise to exempt us from military service. We offered to take another oath swearing our faithfulness.

Governor: You had been British subjects for nearly forty years. It was time for you to show your gratitude by taking the oath without hesitation. No one had the authority to promise you freedom from military service.

Acadian: Many of us were willing to go to the French settlements in the spring of 1750, as we were shortly after the Treaty of Utrecht. You wouldn't give us permission to leave.

Governor: The French were trying to trick you. Those of you who did move to French territory had to do military service for France. The French didn't treat you people as neutrals. Yet you find us unreasonable when we ask you to do military service.

Acadian: You know that we feared the Indians. If we fought for the British, the Indians would attack us. Some of us live on isolated farms. They would cut our throats and destroy our cattle. We don't want to fight the French or the Indians. We want to be neutral — the way we've always been.

Governor: The Indians are few in number. You could drive them away any time you wished. Your priests acted like agents of the French government.

Acadians: We had to have French priests. There were no others. Do our priests have to have your permission to do their religious duties? You promised that we could practise our religion freely.

Governor: You continue to sell supplies to the French, our enemies. We can never trust you. If the French invade this area, you will support them against us. If you do not take the full oath now, you will be driven from this land.

Acadian: You can not mean that! We've taken an oath to King George II. We simply cannot fight the Catholic king of France.

Governor: Your stubborn refusal leaves us no choice. You can no longer be treated as British subjects. You are enemies living in this colony. You no longer have any property rights.

Acadian: France and Britain aren't even at war right now. We turned in all our weapons to you. We will take another oath to be faithful. Why do you doubt our sincerity?

Governor: You have refused to take an oath which includes military service. We are not going to give you any more chances. You may take your household furniture with you, but we don't want our ships burdened with a lot of rubbish. You will be sent to various British colonies under the protection of the British governors.

Acadian: You have deceived us. You let us think we'd be sent to French settlements. You can't send us to live among the Protestants of New England.

Governor: There will be war soon. We must defend Nova Scotia against the French. We cannot let you live where you will add to the strength of our enemies.

Acadian: Why must you separate our families? You must let us sail together.

Governor: We don't want to break up your families, but it's getting late in the season. Winter is coming. Some of you must fill up the vacancies in these ships.

Acadian: You separate us from our loved ones. You deny us the right to go to French territory. You burn our homes and seize our crops and animals. You drive us from our native land and force us to accept the charity of strangers.

Governor: When you people have gone, we shall be able to settle this area with loyal people who won't demand such special privileges as exemptions from military service, people who won't stir up the Indians against us and help our enemies. This will become a peaceful and prosperous land.

Acadian: What have we done to deserve such a cruel punishment?

- The Acadians were once described as a people caught "between two fires. France claimed them on one side, and England on the other, and each demanded their adhesion, without regard for their own feelings or their welfare."[40] In what ways were the Acadians trapped between the two countries?
- Did the Acadians deserve the punishment — exile — that was given them after forty years under British rule?
- Should they have been permitted to go to French territory?
- Should a loyalty oath which exempted them from military service have been permitted?
- Do you think that people who refuse to do military service can be good citizens?
- The Acadians described themselves as "neutrals." Is it possible to be neutral in times of great emergency?
- The Acadians are not the only people in Canada whose loyalty in wartime has been questioned. You might compare their situation in 1755 with that of the Japanese in 1942 in British Columbia. (See page 154.) In each case consider the reasons given for their treatment.
- Investigate the aims and policies of the Parti Acadien in New Brunswick.
- Using reference books, find out about the daily life of the Acadians before 1755 and examine their relations with the Indians of Nova Scotia and New Brunswick.

FOR FURTHER READING

Robeson, Virginia R., gen. ed. *New France: 1713-1760. Documents in Canadian History.* Curriculum Series/23. Toronto: The Ontario Institute for Studies in Education, n.d.

Smith, D.C. *Colonists at Port Royal.* Ginn Studies in Canadian History. Toronto: Ginn and Company, 1970.

Smith, D.C. *The Seigneury of Longeuil.* Ginn Studies in Canadian History. Toronto: Ginn and Company, 1971.

Trudel, Marcel. *Introduction to New France.* Toronto: Holt, Rinehart & Winston, 1968.

The expulsion of the Acadians

Canada and Great Britain: A Unique Association

You already know that in 1759 the French army at Quebec surrendered to the British. Four years later the king of France signed a treaty giving up most of his possessions in North America to Great Britain. This meant that Acadia, New France, and the vast territory opened up by the voyageurs now became part of the British Empire.

The purpose of this section of our study is to search out those parts of our Canadian culture that are British in origin.

- Form a group with two or three other students, preferably from different ethnic backgrounds. Discuss how each of your lives has been directly influenced — or changed — by the fact that Canada has had a long and close relationship with Great Britain. Make a list of the most important influences.
- Study the diagram on the next page: *The Roots of Canada's British Heritage.*
- Compare your own lists with the information given in the diagram. Note particularly any blocks of information you did not include. Suggest additions to the diagram.
- Try to imagine a day in your life if government — as we know it — did not exist. There are no laws to be obeyed; no public services such as hospitals, fire departments, or schools; no courts. Make a list of the things you would need to do in order to survive.
- Which of the items in your list could you accomplish: (i) alone? (ii) with the help of close friends or your family? and (iii) only with the support of many people in your community? Which of the three categories is largest? Why?
- Discuss the statement: "Government is the organization of a group of people for their common survival."
- Re-study the diagram. Why did we give a central place to the block "Foundations of Government and Law"?

The Foundations of Government and Law

By the time of the Seven Years' War most of the leading countries in Europe were ruled over by monarchs — for example, Louis XV of France — whose power over their subjects was absolute. The British government, however, was already very similar *in its structure* to that of Canada today.

As you know, a particular form of government doesn't simply appear overnight. Throughout much of their early history, the people of Great Britain endured periods of chaos or disorder during which men fought against each other for control. The only rules were those imposed by brute force: by the club, the sword, and later, the gun. Periods of warfare alternated with periods of relative peace, during which strong leaders took control and imposed order on their followers. To prevent new outbreaks of war, bargains were agreed upon, often strengthened by contracts or oaths. These were the rough beginnings of what we today call the *rule of law.*

The Beginnings

In our study of the origins of our government we shall go far back in time to the year 1066. If your family originated in the British Isles, hundreds of your ancestors were living as members of a society almost totally different from our own today. All but very few of the people were farmers, living out their lives in the small villages scattered throughout the country. Most of the land was owned by former tribal leaders to whom their tenants paid rent in the form of produce and labour. Other farmers, called *freemen,* were owners of their own small plots of land.

In England the most powerful of the tribal leaders or lords had been united under the leadership of a king. Although the king's word was law, he was expected to uphold the traditions or customs of the people. The most powerful of the lords also acted as an advisory council, or *Witan,* which on the king's death chose his successor.

The Roots of Canada's British Heritage

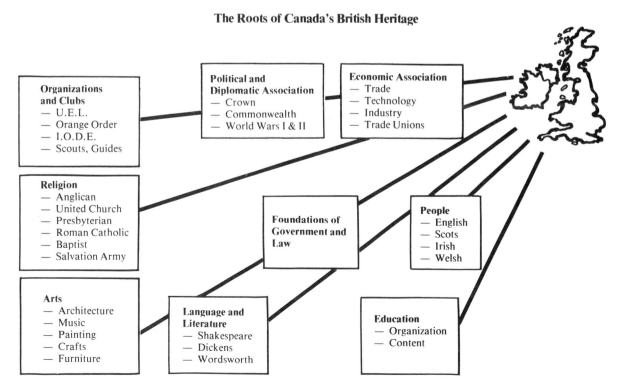

Organizations and Clubs
— U.E.L.
— Orange Order
— I.O.D.E.
— Scouts, Guides

Political and Diplomatic Association
— Crown
— Commonwealth
— World Wars I & II

Economic Association
— Trade
— Technology
— Industry
— Trade Unions

Religion
— Anglican
— United Church
— Presbyterian
— Roman Catholic
— Baptist
— Salvation Army

Foundations of Government and Law

People
— English
— Scots
— Irish
— Welsh

Arts
— Architecture
— Music
— Painting
— Crafts
— Furniture

Language and Literature
— Shakespeare
— Dickens
— Wordsworth

Education
— Organization
— Content

The king extended his power throughout England by appointing representatives to each of the counties or shires. These men, called *shire-reeves* or *sheriffs*, administered county government, assisted by local assemblies, called *moots*, which also acted as local courts. This arrangement provided a balance between central and local authority and gave the ordinary freeman a chance to participate in government.

Methods of trial were very rough and appear to us cruel or absurd. Under trial by ordeal, for example, the accused person might be bound by a rope and thrown into water. If the accused sank to a certain depth — usually about two metres — he or she was presumed innocent; if he or she floated, guilty.

- Using the information you have been given, draw a chart to show the structure of government in England by 1066. On the chart show the relationship between the central and local branches of government.
- Draw a similar chart to show the relationship between your provincial government and that of your own region and/or municipality.

The illustration is from the Bayeux Tapestry. The Tapestry is just under seventy metres long, and about fifty centimetres wide. It was apparently embroidered by Norman women for the Bishop of Bayeux, who was a half-brother of William the Conqueror. In a series of remarkable pictures it gives the full story of William's victory.

The Norman Conquest (1066)

In our own country in 1759 the French were defeated by British forces and placed under British rule. In England the opposite occurred seven centuries earlier when William, Duke of Normandy, successfully invaded England and made himself the first of a long line of Norman kings.

With a force of about two thousand knights and three thousand foot soldiers, William defeated the English forces under their king, Harold, at the Battle of Hastings. The details of the battle were recorded in the famous Bayeux Tapestry.

After being crowned in Westminster Abbey, the new king ruthlessly established his power. The lands of the English nobles were confiscated. Those nobles who were lucky enough to escape with their lives fled to Wales or Scotland. Three-quarters of the land of

England was redistributed by the king as booty to the Norman overlords and knights who had fought with him.

The mass of the people, including many former freemen, became serfs, bound to the land and forced to pay heavy rents in the form of labour and produce to the Norman overlords or barons. There were scattered unsuccessful rebellions, after which the people were forced to contribute their labour to build military towers and castles for their masters. From these the countryside could be supervised and kept under tight military control.

Once his conquest of England was complete, William developed an extremely efficient political organization. Building on the earlier system of local government, he appointed commissioners, or sheriffs, to enforce his will throughout the shires.

An example of the king's thoroughness is the famous Domesday Survey of 1086. His representatives visited every part of England and made a record of the property owned by all of his subjects. From the *Anglo-Saxon Chronicles* we have the following account:

> . . . Then at midwinter the king was at Gloucester with his witan [council] and there held his court five days; . . . After this the king had a great council, and very deep speech with his witan about this land and how it was peopled, or by what men; then sent his men over all England, into every shire, and caused to be ascertained how many hundred hides* were in the shire, and what land the king himself had, the cattle within the land, or what dues [taxes] he ought to have, in twelve months from the shire.
>
> . . . So very narrowly he caused it to be traced out, that there was not one single hide, nor one yard of land nor even . . . an ox, nor a cow, nor a swine was left that was not set down in his writ.[1]

- What uses, other than taxation, might William make of the information contained in the survey?
- What kinds of information can historians gain about Norman England from the Domesday book?

The Middle Ages

For four hundred years William's successors ruled England. During this long period of time, usually referred to as the Middle Ages, great changes took place. During periods of peace more land was cultivated. Some landowners turned to sheep raising, and England became the largest wool exporting country in Western Europe. As trade with other countries expanded and towns appeared, people began to earn their living in a greater variety of ways: as craftsmen, shopkeepers, and prosperous merchants.

Throughout the Middle Ages, however, one class remained by far the most powerful. This was the small number of Norman barons among whom

_____
* The amount of land that could be cultivated by one ploughman

William had divided much of the land of England. To William's successors they were to prove difficult to control. This class of warriors, each with his own army of knights, ruled large districts from heavily fortified castles. At times they turned against each other in support of rival claimants to the throne. At other times they joined forces against an unpopular king.

It was during this unruly time that the structure of our present government was established.

Henry II, the Courts, and the Common Law

The greatest of the kings who ruled England in the Middle Ages was Henry II. He was the direct descendant of William the Conqueror, and his father was the Count of Anjou, one of the most powerful nobles in France. From his father and from William, Henry inherited almost all of western France.

Henry became King of England in 1154 at the end of a period of civil war over a disputed claim to the throne between his mother and his cousin Stephen. He re-established order by forcing all nobles to contribute to the royal army and by ordering all castles and strongholds built without royal permission to be destroyed.

To strengthen his position, Henry issued new laws in the form of *writs* (direct royal orders) and of *assizes* (decrees issued by an assize or session of the king's notables or judges). By sending his judges to every part of England to hold assize courts, he undermined the local courts, often controlled by the nobles, and established a network of royal courts throughout England.

Since there could not be laws or traditions to cover every dispute or crime that the judges had to settle, they used their power in the assize courts to make decisions on their own in the name of the king. Records were kept of all decisions, and these were studied by the other judges. Gradually, therefore, a whole new body of law was created through *precedent* (the use of a legal decision made in one case at court to decide later penalties in similar cases). This body of law developed through the courts was known as *common law* because it was common or the same for all of England. This body of common law, added to and greatly changed throughout the centuries, is still practised in most parts of the English-speaking world today.

Henry also ordered groups of men, called jurors, to be appointed in each local area to investigate local crimes and make lists of persons who should be brought to trial in the assize courts. The importance of this action cannot be overemphasized; it recognizes that crimes are committed not just against individuals, but against the whole of the society. It is therefore the duty of all citizens to see that criminals are brought to justice.

Trial by jury, as we know it, was introduced soon after Henry's death, when groups of men were appointed to judge the guilt or innocence of a person on trial.

The law practised in Henry's courts was still very rough. The practice of trial by ordeal, for example, was not outlawed in England until after Henry's death. Also, individual judges might discard the law of precedent in favour of the traditional local punishment in a particular area. Nevertheless, the three major reforms Henry brought about — the beginning of the common law, the assize courts, the beginning of the jury — were not only important in themselves, but were the foundation on which many improvements could later be made. For these reasons Henry II is often referred to as the father of common law.

SUGGESTIONS FOR FURTHER INVESTIGATION

- If you were accused of a serious crime, would you prefer trial by jury to trial by judge alone? Give reasons for your choice.
- Try to interview a lawyer to find out more about the importance of the common law in our courts today. Alternatively, visit a court in your area to see our judicial system in practice.
- Although we no longer practise trial by combat or ordeal, there are still inequalities within our court

system. One of these is the matter of the expense of taking legal action. How is this problem being solved in your own community?

King John and Magna Carta

Henry's son John, who became king when his brother Richard the Lion-Heart was killed in France, was one of England's most unpopular kings. Unable to keep the loyalty of either his barons or his other subjects, he quarrelled with the Pope, lost his possessions in France, and tried to build up the royal treasury by forcing the wealthy to pay uncustomary taxes and forced payments or "loans." Finally, in 1215, John was forced by a group of his most powerful nobles to sign a contract, or charter, binding him to abide by a number of conditions. The king signed unwillingly, knowing that the alternative would be civil war.

Both John and his barons were attempting to protect their own interests. If you study the charter, you will notice that most of its terms are concerned with the direct relationship between the king and his most powerful subjects. Almost hidden by the other clauses, however, there are several statements that, in later times, were interpreted as guarantees of the freedom of all subjects and the superiority of the law over the king himself:

1. In the first place we [John] have granted to God, and by this our present charter confirmed, for us and our heirs forever, that the English church shall be free and shall hold its rights entire and its liberties uninjured; and we will that it thus be observed. . . .

12. No scutage or aid shall be imposed in our kingdom except by the common council of our kingdom, except for the ransoming of our body, for the making of our eldest son a knight, and for once marrying our oldest daughter, and for those purposes it shall be only a reasonable aid; . . .

20. A free man shall not be fined for a small offence except in proportion to the measure of the offence; . . . none of the above fines shall be imposed except by the oaths of honest men of the neighbourhood.

21. Earls and barons shall only be fined by their peers, and only in proportion to their offence.

39. No free man shall be taken or imprisoned, dispossessed, outlawed, banished, or in any way destroyed nor will we go upon him, nor send upon him except by the legal judgment of his peers and by the laws of the land.

40. To no one will we sell, to no one will we deny, or delay right or justice.[2]

- What does each statement tell you about the actions that John or his judges must have been taking?
- Restate each of the clauses in modern terms, substituting "government" for "we" and "citizen" for "freeman."
- In Canada today our basic freedoms are protected by the *Canadian Bill of Rights* which became law in August 1960. There is a copy in your school library.
- Read section 2 of the bill. What terms are similar to those expressed in Magna Carta?

The Beginnings of Parliament

Up to the time of Magna Carta the king was the chief lawmaker. Limited only by tradition and by the power of the Witan or, later, by the Great Council, he could make laws directly through royal writs or through assizes.

Following Magna Carta the nobles met regularly with the king to uphold the terms of their contract. These meetings came to be called *parliaments,* or discussions. John's grandson, Edward I, often had his lawyers prepare writs for the parliament to endorse. He also enlarged the Great Council to include representatives from the counties and the towns, who were encouraged to bring with them petitions from the people in their areas. The motives of the king in involving so many of his subjects in decision-making are revealed in the following document:

Writ of Summons to Parliament (1295)

—Since we intend to have a consultation . . . with the earls, barons and other nobles of our kingdom with regard to providing remedies against the dangers which are in these days threatening* the same kingdom; and on that account have commanded them to be with us on the Sunday next after the feast of St. Martin, . . . at Westminster, to consider, ordain and do as may be necessary for the avoidance of these dangers; we strictly require you to cause two knights from the . . . shire, two citizens from each city . . . and two burgesses from each borough, . . to be elected without delay. . . .

Moreover, the said knights are to have full and sufficient power for themselves and for the community of the . . . shire, . . then and there for doing what shall then be ordained according to the common counsel in the premises; so that the aforesaid business shall not remain unfinished. . . .

Witness the king at Canterbury, on the third day of October.[3]

- Make a quick list of the persons summoned.
- How might the summoning of representatives of the "common" people strengthen the king's power?
- How might this practice be used by these representatives in later times to undermine the king's power?
- The Parliament of 1295 is called the Model Parliament because it was often used as a model for later ones. To what extent was the Model Parliament representative of the people of England? Was it more or less representative of the different classes in society than our present-day parliament in Ottawa?

The One Hundred Years' War (1337-1453)

The descendants of the Norman kings continued to attempt to keep and, at times, to expand their

* The dangers threatening England were war with France and a rebellion of the Scots.

territories in France. To raise the money they needed for their campaigns, they often summoned parliament. Since the townspeople and the freemen of the counties paid heavy taxes and shared a number of interests, their representatives met separately from the Lords in what came to be called the House of Commons. From time to time the Commons presented petitions to the monarch. If they received support from the House of Lords and royal consent, these petitions or *bills* became law.

At the end of the One Hundred Years' War returning soldiers swarmed through the country, willing to attach themselves to any noble who would pay them. Large private armies once more supported rival contenders to the throne. For thirty years civil war raged. Finally, in 1485, Henry Tudor defeated his opponents and was crowned king. For the next century he, his son, and his granddaughter would lead England to a world position of great influence and power.

Before we look closely at the Tudor monarchy, however, let us briefly summarize how government in England had changed over the four hundred years after William's conquest:

(i) *The monarch:* The king still had great power: he was the hereditary ruler; the royal courts were under his direct control; royal decrees or writs were still a major part of law; he still summoned parliament only when he wished. At the same time the king was no longer absolute: in Magna Carta, John had promised to rule in accordance with the terms of a contract with his barons. This promise was binding on his heirs.

(ii) *Parliament:* The Great Council had been greatly enlarged to include representatives from classes other than the nobles. It now met in two Houses: the Lords and the Commons. Members of the Commons could originate law through their petitions or bills, although these had to be approved by the Lords and by the monarch.

(iii) *The courts:* Because of the important changes brought about by Henry II, the king's justice was

becoming more equally available to all subjects. These changes included the creation of the assizes, the use of precedent, and the development of common law.

Social Changes

Throughout our study of government in the Middle Ages we have scarcely mentioned the great majority of the people who worked on the land. This is because they took no part whatsoever in government. You remember that when the Normans conquered England, they forced most farmers to become serfs, forbidden to leave the land of their overlord. A great change in their condition occurred after the Black Death, a terrible plague that swept through the country in 1348 and killed between one-third and one-half of the working population. There was much confusion in many rural areas as serfs attempted to run away from their villages to find work as day labourers. When the landowners had parliament pass a Statute of Labourers to prevent a rise in wages, there was a peasants' revolt, which was brutally crushed. In the long run, however, many serfs were able to bargain for their freedom and became either tenant farmers or farm workers.

You learned earlier that during the later Middle Ages trade expanded between England and Western Europe. A new class of prosperous merchants was developing. It was the representatives of this class who were beginning to play a leading part in the work of the House of Commons.

The Age of the Tudors (1485-1603)

Henry VII

- Imagine yourself in the position of Henry Tudor in 1485. You have won the final battle in the Wars of the Roses. You must now break the power of your enemies and make the throne secure for yourself and for your heirs.

- What immediate action will you take? What other steps will you take during your reign to strengthen your power?
- If you decide to use parliament as a means of increasing your power, to what groups will you look for support?

The steps taken by Henry reveal how a master politician can use power to control events to his own advantage. Very briefly, that is what he did:

(i) The estates of his enemies were confiscated and the income used to build up the royal treasury. If civil war again broke out, he could afford a strong army equipped with the latest military equipment, especially guns.

(ii) He ordered all private armies disbanded.

(iii) He increased the power of local justices of the peace. These officials, largely small land-owners, were the direct representatives of the king. Their increased authority undermined the local power of the nobles.

(iv) Men who were too powerful to be tried in the ordinary courts were brought before the Court of the Star Chamber, a high court at Westminster presided over by members of the King's Council.

(v) He changed the membership in his Council to include representatives of the new middle class of educated lawyers, merchants, and small landowners.

(vi) He married members of his family to potential enemies at home and abroad; he himself married Elizabeth of York, the daughter of Edward IV. He married his daughter Margaret to James IV of Scotland, and he betrothed (engaged) his eldest son and heir, Arthur, to Catherine, the daughter of the rulers of Spain.

(vii) Soon after Columbus's voyage to the Americas in 1492, Henry commissioned an Italian seaman from Venice whose English name was John Cabot to search out lands in the New World for England.

- How many of Henry's actions are similar to those you would have taken?
- Which groups in parliament were now much more influential than previously? Which group had its power badly undermined?
- How would the invention of gunpowder change the military power of the nobles?

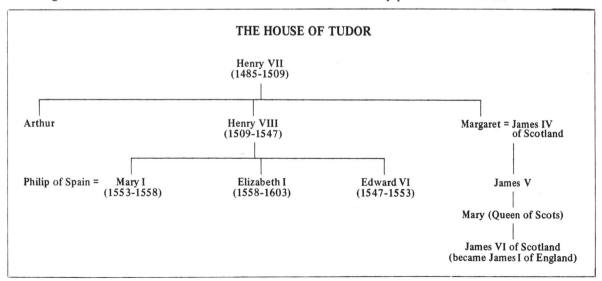

THE HOUSE OF TUDOR

Henry VII
(1485-1509)

Arthur

Henry VIII
(1509-1547)

Margaret = James IV
of Scotland

Philip of Spain = Mary I
(1553-1558)

Elizabeth I
(1558-1603)

Edward VI
(1547-1553)

James V

Mary (Queen of Scots)

James VI of Scotland
(became James I of England)

Henry VIII (1509-1547)

In 1509, all the king's subjects belonged to one united Christian Church which was under the leadership of the Pope in Rome. In 1534, as a result of a violent quarrel with the Pope, Henry VIII declared that the Christian Church in England would be separate and independent. He then called parliament and gained its support for his action. By the Act of Supremacy it was decreed that the king was the "Supreme Head" of the newly created Church of England.

Parliament had obviously let itself be used as a tool by Henry. Furthermore, the cause of his final break with the Pope was rather shabby: Henry wished to divorce his Spanish wife, Catherine, to whom he had been married after the death of his brother Arthur. The Pope had refused permission for such an action.

Why did parliament give the king its support? The answer is a complex one about which there is a good deal of disagreement. Some men must have acted through fear since Henry ruthlessly suppressed all who opposed him. Sir Thomas More, for example, formerly one of Henry's chief advisers, was put to death for treason when he refused to recognize the king as the head of the Church. More was not Henry's only victim. There were over four hundred monasteries with valuable lands and other property in England at that time. They were now closed and their property confiscated by the king on the grounds that they were centres of treason.

Aside from those who feared him, Henry was also supported by those who criticized the Church for its misuse of wealth and for the lack of education and dedication of many of its priests. Many people also resented the draining of church taxes from England to Rome. Those men to whom Henry had granted or sold the great estates of the monasteries now had a vested interest in supporting the new Church of England.

Added to these reasons, there was also the very practical problem of the succession. Catherine of Aragon had not had a son to inherit the throne. This meant that on Henry's death the country might return once more to a state of civil war.

Finally, Henry was popular with many of his people. He continued his father's practice of including members of the middle class among his advisers. His wars against France were generally supported, and his founding of the Royal Navy appealed to a growing nationalism in the country.

- What is an *established* church? Is there an established church in Canada?
- After further research, debate the resolution: "Henry VIII was justified in his suppression of the monasteries."
- Discuss the statement, "Henry VIII both strengthened and weakened parliament."
- What measures can be taken by our Canadian Prime Minister to persuade members of parliament to give him their support?

Elizabeth I (1558-1603)

Henry VIII's frantic attempts to have a royal son strong enough to rule England after his death were both sad and futile. It was his second daughter, Elizabeth, who during her forty-five-year reign brought the monarchy to the height of its prestige. Elizabethan England is perhaps the most vital period in English history: the time of the defeat of the Spanish Armada, of Sir Francis Drake's voyage around the world, of the plays and poems of the greatest writer in the English language.

When she first came to the throne, Elizabeth was faced with the problem of deciding the religious future of her people. Her older sister Mary had ruled for only five years, but during that time she had re-established the Roman Catholic religion in England and married Philip, the King of Spain. To make Elizabeth's position more difficult, a third religious group, the Puritans, were gaining in influence. The Puritans believed that the Bible was the only source of religious truth, and that all people were equal in the eyes of God. They therefore emphasized a simple form of church service and church government by elected members rather than by officials appointed by those above them.

Elizabeth immediately restored the Church of England. Although all her subjects were required to attend church on Sundays and holy days or pay a fine, they were free to follow any form of service they wished in private worship. Thus the Puritans could continue their own religious practices without real fear of punishment.

There were, however, other sources of conflict between Elizabeth and parliament. The queen insisted that she alone could make decisions on her marriage, succession to the throne, foreign policy, and religion. To control opposition, she had men whom she trusted always present in parliament to defend her interests. At one point a Puritan member of the Commons, Peter Wentworth, was imprisoned in the Tower for life for opposing the queen's command that two Commons bills on religion be dropped. There were other disputes, but open conflict was prevented. The special relationship that existed between the queen and her parliaments is described by one historian in the following paragraph:

On 30 November 1601 one hundred and forty Members crowded the Council Chamber at Whitehall to hear the Speaker return their thanks and the sovereign accept them. Elizabeth was in the sixty-ninth year of her age and the forty-fourth of her reign. Not many present could remember the time when she had not been Queen, and those who could did not cherish the memory. But all could imagine — as she herself must have done — that she was addressing them for the last time, and even those who were already looking forward to the exciting novelty of a King could not deny the majesty of this Queen's leave-taking. It was the majesty which stoops to conquer. "Though God hath raised me high," they heard her say, "yet this I count the glory of my crown, that I have reigned with your loves. . . . It is not my desire to live or reign longer than my life and reign shall be for your good. And though you have had, and may have, many mightier and wiser princes sitting in this seat, yet you never had, nor shall have, any that will love you better."[4]

- Working with two or three other students, draw up a list of the services that the Tudors performed for their subjects.
- Look back at the chart on page 63. What contributions to Canadian culture were made during the Tudor Period in each of the blocks shown in the chart?

The Stuarts (1603-1648, 1660-1688)

James I

The Scottish king who succeeded Elizabeth to the throne of England in 1603 was an outsider who had little understanding of the legal and political traditions we have traced.

James had quarrelled bitterly with the Presbyterians, the Puritans who had become a very strong religious group in Scotland. He was therefore outraged when Puritan bishops and members of parliament requested freedom to introduce simple forms of worship in the Church of England. More than anything else, though, he feared the democracy of the Puritan churches. Speaking of his experience in Scotland, he said:

A Scottish Presbytery* agreeth as well with a monarchy as God with the Devil. . . . Then Jack, Tom, Will and Dick shall meet and at their leisure censure me and my council.[5]

In his Speech from the Throne to his first parliament, James made his ideas about the nature of his own power very clear:

The state of the monarchy is the supremest thing upon earth: for Kings are not only God's lieutenants upon earth and sit upon God's throne, but even by God Himself they are called gods. . . .

As to dispute what God may do is blasphemy. . . I shall not be content that my power be disputed on.[6]

- What does James claim to be the source of his power? Why is this belief called the "Divine Right of Kings"?

---

* The elected governing body of the Presbyterian church

The leaders of James's last parliament made the following statement about their position in relationship to that of the monarch:

> We hold it an ancient, general and undoubted right of Parliament to debate freely all matters which properly concern the subject and his right or state.[7]

- What is the source of parliament's power? Could parliament's power coexist with that of the king?
- Why had the Tudor monarchs, who apparently also believed in the "Divine Right of Kings," been able to avoid direct conflict with parliament?

Charles I

Under James's son Charles, matters soon became worse. Despite his marriage to a French princess, Charles soon became involved in an expensive war with France. To pay for the war, he forced citizens to grant him special payments; those who refused were imprisoned. In addition, to save expense, recruits called up for service were temporarily billeted in private homes. Lawlessness resulted:

> The soldiers not only robbed and insulted the hosts on whom they were quartered, but broke loose in companies upon the countryside to pillage, rape, and murder; in some parts the highways and markets were deserted. . . . The attempt to restrain these rascals by Martial Law only incensed the jealous population. Men heard with alarm that the soldiers who had robbed them had been hanged by Court Martial, which might next be employed to punish all who resisted the Government; . . . The sound prejudice of the English against militarism, silently grown up during a hundred years of peace and civil life under the Tudors, now caused an outbreak of public feeling, which found voice at Westminster.[8]

In response to the public outcry, the House of Commons drew up a petition which, to keep the peace, the king signed. The *Petition of Right* is often compared to Magna Carta because it dealt with very basic rights. The king was prohibited:

(i) from forcing any of his subjects to make loans or pay taxes without the consent of parliament;

(ii) from detaining any citizen in prison without shown cause;

(iii) from billeting soldiers in private homes; and

(iv) from the trial of citizens by martial law.

- To many ordinary citizens during the reign of Charles I, who appeared to be their protector?

Charles kept an uneasy peace for several years after the Petition of Right by ruling without calling parliament. Then in 1639 there was rebellion in Scotland. When the king called parliament to raise money to suppress the rebellion, the money was refused. When Charles led a force of soldiers to parliament to arrest its leaders, he found that they had escaped and were gathering recruits to oppose him.

The Civil War lasted until 1648 when the king's forces met final defeat. "Charles Stuart" was put on trial by a parliament from which his supporters were excluded, found guilty of treason, and executed.

With the king dead, England became a republic. For eleven years the country was led by Oliver Cromwell, who united Ireland, Scotland, and England under one parliament. The experiment failed. Ireland had been forced by brutal war into joining the union. Like the Stuarts before him, Cromwell could not gain the support of parliament. Finally, like them, he ruled without it.

- What, if anything, had been achieved by the Civil War?
- What important link was lacking between the monarch (or Cromwell) and parliament?
- Cromwell's name was hated by many later generations of Roman Catholics in Ireland. Find out why.
- After further reading, prepare a defence of Charles I in which you attempt to prevent his execution.

When Cromwell died, the son of Charles I, Charles II, was asked to accept the throne. He managed to keep the country relatively peaceful until his death in 1685. His brother James, who succeeded him, was not so successful. Within three years he was forced to flee to France when the leaders of parliament became convinced that he was planning to rule as an absolute monarch and to restore the Roman Catholic religion in England.

- In 1679 parliament passed the Act of Habeas Corpus. Find out what this very important act stated.

William and Mary

Once more the leaders of parliament were forced to search for persons of royal blood who would be suitable monarchs. Their choice fell on the Protestant ruler of Holland and his wife Mary, the grand-daughter of Charles I. Before the new king and queen were permitted to take the throne, however, they were compelled to sign a *Bill of Rights* in which they recognized certain powers of parliament and of the courts, and certain freedoms for all citizens.

- You are a member of the British parliament in 1688. With a small group of your classmates draw up a Bill of Rights that you will have William and Mary sign before they are crowned. Be prepared to justify each of the terms of your bill.

- Study the extracts from the documents below. (In every case the language is simplified but the sense is retained.)

The Bill of Rights (1689)

No monarch may levy taxes, maintain an army, or suspend or dispense with laws without parliament's consent. Parliament is to meet frequently. Its members are to have full freedom of debate.

No Roman Catholic is to wear the crown.

The Coronation Oath

The monarch is bound to govern according to the laws and customs of parliament.

The Act of Settlement (1701)

Judges are to hold office for life and cannot be dismissed except on the request of parliament.

The order of succession to the throne is set down in law.

The Triennial Act of 1694

Parliamentary elections are to be held every three years.

- What clauses are included in the documents that you omitted from your bill?

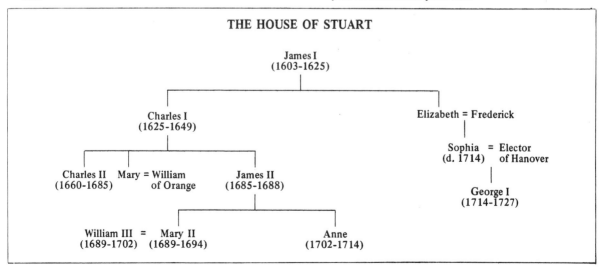

THE HOUSE OF STUART

James I
(1603-1625)

Charles I
(1625-1649)

Elizabeth = Frederick

Sophia = Elector
(d. 1714) of Hanover

George I
(1714-1727)

Charles II
(1660-1685)

Mary = William
of Orange

James II
(1685-1688)

William III = Mary II
(1689-1702) (1689-1694)

Anne
(1702-1714)

- What clauses did you include in your bill that are missing from the documents?
- Make a diagram showing the major parts of government in England by 1689. In your diagram include the major powers of each part.
- Compare your diagram with one of the Canadian federal government.
  What offices were not yet part of government in 1689? What powers have changed?
- How often must parliamentary elections be held today in Canada? What situation in parliament can lead to an *earlier* election?
- Do judges in Canada still hold office for life? Do you think this is wise? Why or why not?
- Investigate Canada's present relationship with the monarch. Find out what duties are performed by Queen Elizabeth or by her representative, the governor general. After further research, attack or defend the present official relationship between the government of Canada and the Crown.

The Prime Minister and the Cabinet

All the rulers of England from the time of William the Conqueror chose a small number of leading men from the Great Council or, later, from parliament as their chief advisers. The office of prime minister, or chief adviser, was not deliberately created. However, George I, a German prince who succeeded to the throne in 1714, spoke English badly and was not interested in attending all meetings of his ministers. His favourite adviser, Sir Robert Walpole, persuaded the king to appoint as ministers those members of parliament who agreed with Walpole on important matters of government. Walpole was also strong enough to insist that all ministers support him in a united front in parliament. In this way Walpole became Britain's first "prime minister."

As political parties grew stronger, it became the custom for the monarch to choose as his prime minister the leader of the party which was strongest in parliament. In Canada today, therefore, the prime minister is the leader of the party which has the largest number of followers in the House of Commons. He and the ministers he chooses form the *cabinet,* which is *responsible* to the Commons in two ways: (i) all cabinet ministers must be elected members of the Commons and available for questioning by other members, and (ii) if a bill introduced by the cabinet (a government bill) is defeated, the cabinet must resign.

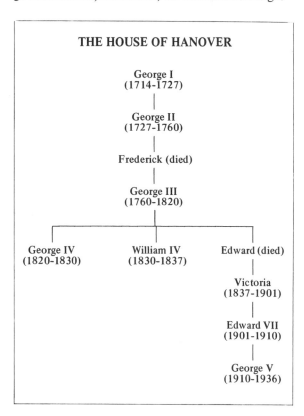

THE HOUSE OF HANOVER

George I
(1714-1727)

George II
(1727-1760)

Frederick (died)

George III
(1760-1820)

George IV (1820-1830)   William IV (1830-1837)   Edward (died)

Victoria
(1837-1901)

Edward VII
(1901-1910)

George V
(1910-1936)

Reconsider the position of our prime minister today:

- How did he gain the leadership of his political party?
- What other advisers may the prime minister have in addition to the members of his cabinet?
- How can the prime minister exert control over each of the following: (i) the members of his cabinet? (ii) the members of his party in the House of Commons?
- How can the ordinary citizen influence the prime minister and his cabinet to act in a particular matter?

With the beginning of cabinet government our brief study of the origins of our system of law and government in Great Britain comes to an end. By 1750 Great Britain was still an *oligarchy* (a government by a privileged few). Most of the population had "nothing to do with the laws but to obey them." Many of the punishments inflicted in the courts throughout the land were, by modern Canadian standards, harsh and cruel. But the *structure* of our modern parliamentary and judicial systems had been established in law and reinforced by tradition and custom.

By 1750 these systems were already taking root in the British colonies on this continent. Their adaptation to the needs of North American society was slow and, at times, painful. You have probably already studied about some of the conflicts between our colonial legislatures and the governors and their appointed councils. In a later chapter of this book you will learn how, in the greatest of these conflicts, Great Britain lost her original thirteen colonies.

In the unit on "The French in Canada" you have also learned that the people of Quebec decided not to join in the American Revolution against Great Britain. In later sections of our study you will learn about other successful experiments in adapting British forms of government to our Canadian environment.

FOR FURTHER READING

Brown, George W., ed. *Canada and the Commonwealth.* Toronto: J.M. Dent & Sons (Canada) Ltd., 1953.

Cowie, Leonard W. *The Black Death and Peasants' Revolt.* London: Wayland Publishers, 1972.

Derry, T.K. et al. *Great Britain: Its History to 1901.* Toronto: Oxford University Press, 1960.

Doughty, Howard. *British Roots.* Toronto: Wiley Publishers of Canada Ltd., 1978.

Furneux, Rupert. *Conquest 1066.* London: Secker & Warburg, 1966.

Labarge, Margaret. *A Baronial Household of the Thirteenth Century.* London: Eyre & Spottiswoode, 1965.

Reeves, Marjorie, ed. *Then and There Series.* London: Longmans, Green and Co. Ltd. The many booklets in this series include: *The Norman Conquest, Magna Carta, The Medieval Monastery, Elizabethan Citizen, Samuel Pepys in London, Richard Baxter, Toleration and Tyranny (1615-1691).*

Richer, J.C. et al. *The British Epic.* Toronto: Clarke, Irwin & Co. Ltd., 1956.

Tait, George E. *Proud Ages.* Toronto: Ryerson Press, 1958.

Trueman, John. *Britain: The Growth of Freedom.* Toronto: J.M. Dent & Sons (Canada) Ltd.

The Scots in Canada

On July 1, 1773, the sailing ship *Hector* left the Scottish port of Greenock with three families and five young men aboard. The small ship plodded north towards Lock Broom in Ross-shire. Thirty more families and twenty-five unmarried men boarded. The nearly two hundred immigrants crowded the ship.

As the ship was about to leave, a piper named John MacKay came aboard. The captain, John Spears, ordered him ashore, for the piper had not arranged his passage. The passengers, however, offered to share their rations with him in return for his music and he was allowed to remain. A schoolteacher, William McKenzie, was also one of those aboard.

At first the voyage went well. The ship sailed up the North Channel and around the northern coast of Ireland. Songs and music whiled away the hours. Dancing and wrestling provided amusement for the more active.

However, the voyage was to prove a long and dangerous one. The *Hector* was old and slow. Passengers found they could pick the rotting wood from her sides with their bare hands. A fierce storm off Newfoundland drove the ship back and added two more weeks to the voyage.

Smallpox and dysentery broke out. Eighteen people, mainly children, died and were buried at sea. One child was born. Food and water supplies ran low. The oatcake — the main food supplied to passengers — turned moldy. Salted meat increased the thirst of the passengers. Water was severely rationed.

- Dr. Samuel Johnson, the English writer, once described a ship as "worse than a prison." Do you think the passengers on the *Hector* would have agreed with him?
- Why were deaths at sea common at this time?
- At the time that the *Hector* sailed, there were no regulations covering passenger health and safety on emigrant ships leaving the British Isles. What kind of regulations would you have recommended?

"The Men in Petticoats"

On September 15, after eleven weeks at sea, the *Hector* dropped anchor at Pictou, Nova Scotia. A few British settlers were already established in the area. A story passed down from father to son tells us that the British settlers tried to frighten the Micmac Indians by warning them that "the men in petticoats" — Highland Scots — were coming. The Indians had seen such men before at the Battle of Quebec in 1759.

Although the wearing of Highland dress was forbidden by the British government at this time, the men of the *Hector* donned their kilts and plaids in honour of the occasion. Some even wore claymores. The piper led them ashore. According to the story passed down, the skirl of the bagpipes sent the Indians fleeing.

Perhaps the Highlanders had dressed up to give themselves courage. Several lay sick. The wife of Hugh McLeod died as the ship arrived. The child of Alexander McLeod died as the first group went ashore. Two graves were dug near the beach.

The Highlanders' first sight of shore was a shock. An unbroken forest barred their path. Already the leaves were tinged with autumn. No provisions or shelters had been provided for them. When they located their farm lots, they found that they were two or three miles inland. Shut off from the sea by dense forest, it would be difficult for them to fish.

They must have thought back to the advertisement in the *Edinburgh Advertiser* in September, 1772 which had promised them farms "on easy terms." At the time they had asked some searching questions. The doubters wondered how colonists could exist on uncleared lands. Who would buy their produce? Wouldn't they need large sums of money to clear the land?

However, John Ross, an agent of the Philadelphia Company which had placed the advertisement, had painted a glowing picture of a country where each man could *own* his own land. Each man was to have a free passage across the Atlantic, a farm lot in Pictou, and a year's provisions. To those whose farm was a rented patch of ground, the prospect was hard to resist.

Now, however, the Highlanders refused to settle the lands provided by the Company. The Company refused them supplies. Desperate, the men seized supplies. Word was sent to the British governor at Halifax that the "Highlanders were in rebellion."

The following winter was colder than the new immigrants expected. Some moved to Truro or Windsor or Halifax. Some became indentured servants or indentured their children. The seventy or so who remained at Pictou lived in simple huts covered with bark or branches. To obtain a bushel of potatoes or flour meant a long walk through snow-filled forests to Truro, the nearest settlement, which was eighty miles away.

Within a few years they learned to use the resources of forest and sea. Timber was cut and fields cleared. Wheat and potatoes were planted between stumps. Sea water, boiled down, gave salt. Moose provided meat, and maples gave syrup. Fish, clams, and lobster added to their food supply.

- What similarities and differences do you see between the voyage of Marc Lescarbot in 1606 and the passengers on the *Hector* in 1773?
- Why were the Scots dismayed when they saw the site of their new farms in Pictou? How did Nova Scotia differ from Scotland?
- Why were they perhaps too optimistic about the new land?

In the Highlands good land for crops was scarce. Oats and potatoes could be raised on the fairly flat areas along river valleys. The rivers and lochs (lakes) provided fish. Undrained bogs (swamps) provided peat for fuel. Although the general surface of the land was mountainous, it could support many cattle, sheep, and wild deer for hunting. Stone for building was plentiful. The rocky, indented coast line provided sheltered harbours.

Highlanders wore a plaid and kilt woven from hand-dyed wool. The kilt was a piece of tartan approximately four metres long and two metres wide. It was worn belted around the waist with a leather belt. The plaid was fastened around the left shoulder leaving the right arm — the sword arm — free. Unwound, the plaid formed a blanket. A sporan, a large purse of goat or badger, hung from the waist. A bonnet was worn on the head. Untanned leather tied with thongs completed the outfit. Stockings are a fairly recent invention. The clans did not have distinct tartans as they do today. A man wore the emblem of his clan on his bonnet.

Why Had They Come?

From the lone shieling of the misty island
Mountains divide us, and the waste of seas —
Yet still the blood is strong, the heart is Highland,
And we in dreams behold the Hebrides.

Canadian Boat-song[1]

The lines of this poem are carved in stone along the famous Cabot Trail, a highway that curves along the rugged and beautiful north shore of Cape Breton Island in Nova Scotia, where so many Highland Scots settled. Given such loyalty to their native land, why had the passengers aboard the *Hector* risked such a long and dangerous voyage across the Atlantic? What powerful forces had driven them from their beloved homeland?

- Why are most immigrants likely to feel homesick during their first years in a new land?
- Why is loneliness a particular problem for them?

"An Epidemical Fury of Emigration"[2]

Dr. Samuel Johnson, the famous English writer, visited the Highlands of Scotland in 1773 and noted the "epidemical fury of emigration" which was sweeping through the land. Before 1763 there were only a few hundred Highlanders in America. Between 1763 and 1773 nearly 25 000 Scots, many of them Highlanders, set off for America.

Dr. Johnson described the "America dance" performed by the inhabitants of Armadale. One couple started the dance. They started another couple going. The two couples started others:

> . . . and so it goes on till all are set a-going. . . . It shows how emigration catches till all are set afloat. Mrs. Mackinnon told me that last year when the ship sailed from Portree for America, the people on shore were almost distracted when they saw their relations go off; they lay down on the ground and tumbled, and tore the grass with their teeth. This year there was not a tear shed. The people on shore seemed to think they would soon follow.[3]

- Why did Dr. Johnson compare emigration to an epidemic?
- How does his description of the "America" dance help explain why so many decided to emigrate?

"There Were Too Many of Us"

What were the causes of this "epidemical fury of emigration" which drove the Scots to America?

"There were too many of us," said one immigrant. Strangely, it was the establishment of peace and order that contributed to the bitter problem of over-population in Scotland. Warfare among the clans ended. The introduction of the potato as a food crop and improvements in the control of smallpox also lowered the death rate. More people were living longer. As the population increased in size, the amount of land farmed by each man tended to become smaller and smaller. Many men on the land became a burden.

To understand why, we must look more closely at Scotland itself. Scotland is usually divided into two regions: (i) the Lowlands and (ii) the Highlands and Western Islands.

Over the centuries the Highlanders developed a special way of life. They spoke Gaelic, an ancient language of the Celtic peoples. After England and Scotland were united in 1707, people in the Lowlands followed a way of life that more and more resembled that of the English to the south of them. Behind a barrier of mountains the Highlanders continued to follow the old ways of clan life.

Clans were groups of interrelated families. Each clan was led by a chief. Every clansman claimed to be a blood relative and was the namesake of the chief. A Highlander's first loyalty was to his chief and his *glen* (valley). The clan chief acted as judge, military leader, and protector of his people. He was head of the clan family. The clan followed his standard in war. The clan chiefs were glad to have many men on the clan's land. Many men meant a strong clan and a strong clan army. In return for military service, each clansman had a share of the clan lands.

The close-knit economic, political, social, and military relationships between the chief and his clansmen was abruptly shattered in 1746. During that year some Highland chiefs supported the attempt of Prince Charles Edward Stuart, "Bonnie Prince Charlie," to seize the crown from King George II of England and Scotland. English and Scottish troops loyal to King George defeated Bonnie Prince Charlie and his Highland supporters at the Battle of Culloden in 1746.

The social, political, and economic system of England and the Lowlands was imposed by the central government in London on the Highlands. The chiefs became landlords with clear titles of ownership to the clan's land. Chiefs who had supported Bonnie Prince Charlie lost their lands, and new men became owners of their clan land.

Clansmen became tenants who had to pay rent to a landlord who often lived hundreds of miles away in Edinburgh or London. The old personal blood relationship between clansman and chief no longer existed for these men.

As the population increased, pressure on the land increased. Rents kept going up. In August, 1773, Dr. Johnson spoke to a man named Macqueen. Macqueen said that seventy men had already left his glen for America. He himself intended "to go next year." Twenty-five years before, the rent on his farm had been 5 pounds a year. His rent was now 20 pounds. He felt that he could not pay more than 10 pounds and still feed and clothe his family. After 1763, rents in the Highlands increased from 33-1/3 percent to 300 percent.[4]

Some Highlanders complained of losing their cattle in the severe winter of 1771. Crop failures were also mentioned. The most common complaint, however, was rising rents.

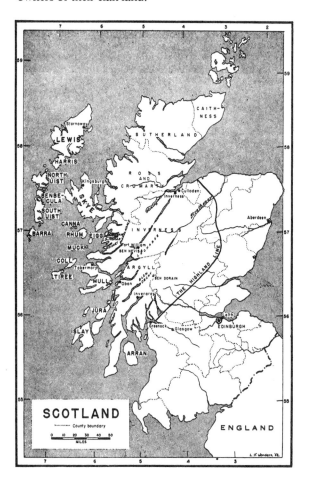

80

The Veterans

Two of the immigrants on the *Hector* had served in the British army during the Seven Years' War (1756-1763). Many Highlanders, estimated at twelve thousand, joined the British army. Service in the army was popular among those who found it difficult to find employment in the Highlands. Some Highlanders had participated in the capture of Louisbourg (1758) and Quebec (1759). After the war, many settled down on lands offered to veterans in Prince Edward Island, Quebec, and New York.

By 1770 many Scots had come to look upon America as a kind of paradise. Their friends and relatives who had already emigrated wrote them about cheap, abundant land, low taxes, high wages, and a healthy climate. The two veterans of the Seven Years' War on the *Hector* felt that Nova Scotia offered them better prospects than they could look forward to in Scotland.

- What were the economic, social and political forces that "pushed" the Highlanders from their homeland?
- What economic changes were under way before Culloden? How did the Battle of Culloden make these changes worse?
- What were the forces that "pulled" the Highlanders to America?
- Why would the British government forbid the wearing of Highland dress and the playing of bagpipes after the Battle of Culloden?

Later Scottish Immigration

The great Scottish immigration to Nova Scotia began in 1773 with the sailing of the *Hector*. Emigration worried the British government. Landlords and government officials feared the loss of agricultural and industrial workers. Military leaders wondered where they would find a large supply of recruits for the British army.

When the American Revolution broke out in 1776, the British government placed a temporary ban on emigration.

During and after the American Revolution, which ended in 1783, many Scots who had settled in the Thirteen Colonies, for example, in New York, came to Canada as Loyalists. They settled in Nova Scotia and Upper Canada (Ontario) where their most important settlement was at Glengarry. They were joined by thousands of their fellow countrymen. Heavy Scottish immigration continued throughout the first half of the nineteenth century.

The Selkirk Settlement

The first agricultural settlement in the Canadian West was established on land obtained from the Hudson Bay Company by Lord Selkirk, a Scottish nobleman, in 1811.

Lord Selkirk was deeply moved by the growing misery and poverty of the Highlands during the early years of the nineteenth century. Read the following quotations carefully. Work out an explanation for the poverty of the Highlands.

> The Highlands of Scotland may sell, at present, [1795] perhaps from £200 000 to £300 000 worth of lean cattle per annum. The same ground will produce twice as much mutton, and there is wool into the bargain. . . . the same ground under the Cheviot or True Mountain breed will produce at least £900 000 of fine wool.[5]

> The adoption of the new system, by which the mountainous districts are converted into sheep pastures, even if it should occasion the emigration of some individuals, is, upon the whole, advantageous to the nation at large.[6]

> One man will occupy the land that once starved fifty or more families; he gives a double or treble rent and is punctual to the day of payment.[7]

> The whole inhabitants of Kildonan parish, with the exception of three families, nearly 2000 souls, were utterly rooted and burned out. Many, especially the young and robust, left the country, but the aged, the females and children, were obliged to stay and accept the wretched allotments allowed them on the seashore and endeavour to learn fishing.[8]

> Our family was very reluctant to leave and stayed for some time, but the burning party came round and set fire to our house at both ends, reducing to ashes whatever remained within the walls. The people had to escape for their lives, some of them losing all their clothes except what they had on their backs. The people were told they could go where they liked, provided they did not encumber the land.[9]

> What crops they had, potatoes or grain, were left on or in the ground when Lord Stafford's agents came to their doors with writs of eviction. They were offered smaller lots of land, ten, fifteen or twenty miles away on the coast.[10]

> Our chief is losing his kin! He prefers sheep in his glens.[11]

> Upon the top of the hill, . . . you can set a compass, with 25 miles of a radius upon it . . . within this broad circumference you will not find a single human habitation, or one acre of land under cultivation save that occupied by shepherds belonging to some sheep-farmers [1856] . . . I recollect when 2 000 able-bodied young men could be raised within the same circuit in 48 hours![12]

You will be able to test the explanation you have worked out when you read the section entitled "The Great Migration."

- Find out more about Lord Selkirk's settlement at Red River and about the hardships and difficulties faced during the early years.
- Scots have played an important part in Canadian politics. Find out about the work of one of the following and report your findings to the class: William Lyon Mackenzie, Sir James Douglas, George Brown, Agnes Macphail, T.C. Douglas, Leonard Tilley, Alexander Galt, Sir John A. Macdonald, Alexander Mackenzie, Mackenzie King.
- Later in our study of the opening of the West, you will read about the work of Scottish explorers such as Simon Fraser and Alexander Mackenzie and traders such as George Simpson.
- Scottish traders were foremost in developing the North-West Company which was a rival of the Hudson's Bay Company in seeking to develop the fur trade of the west. Read about the development of this company.
- Find out what contributions Scots have made to music and sports.
- When and how do Scots celebrate Robbie Burns Day?
- In 1832 a visitor to Pictou, Nova Scotia wrote: "In the streets, within the houses, in the shops, on board vessels, and along the roads, we hear little but Gaelic and broad Scotch."[13] According to the 1971 Census of Canada, 1175 people listed Gaelic as the language they most often spoke at home.[14]

Sir John A. Macdonald

Simon Fraser

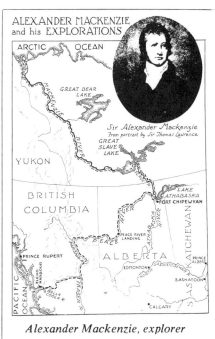

Alexander Mackenzie, explorer

*Prime Minister
Alexander Mackenzie*

Sir George Simpson

Sandford Fleming

William Lyon Mackenzie

Why does this language seem to be dying out? Why is it hard for a group to preserve its native language after the original immigrants have passed away? Should schools promote the learning of a language that is neither English nor French?

- In 1832 Thomas Traill and his wife Catharine left Greenock as emigrants. Mrs. Traill described their voyage in a letter to her mother:

After many delays and disappointments, we suc-ceeded at last in obtaining a passage in a fast-sailing brig, the *Laurel,* of Greenock. . . . The *Laurel* is not a regular passenger-ship. . . . The cabin is neatly fitted up, and I enjoy the luxury . . . of a handsome sofa, with crimson draperies. . . . We paid fifteen pounds each for our passage to Montreal. This was high, but it includes every expense; and, in fact, we had no choice. The only vessel in the river bound for Canada, was a passenger-ship, literally swarming with emigrants, chiefly of the lower class of Highlanders. . . . We came within sight of the shores of Newfoundland on the 5th of August, just one month from the day we took our last look at the British Isles. . . . At ten last night, August 15, the lights of the city of Quebec were seen gleaming through the distance.[15]

- In what ways did the Traills' voyage differ from that of the passengers on the *Hector*?
- Do you think that the Highlanders on the vessel described by Mrs. Traill would have a comfortable voyage?
- Why did Mrs. Traill say that they "had no choice" but to take the *Laurel?*

FOR FURTHER READING

McKiehan, Finlay. *The Highland Clearances.* Then and There Series. London: Longman, 1977.

The United Empire Loyalists

It is the year 1776. In many communities in Britain's Thirteen Colonies, neighbours and friends have turned in anger and hatred against one another:

Luke Carscallen (i.e. Edward) was an Irishman by birth, had served in the British army and . . . emigrated to the American colonies prior to the rebellion. He desired to remain neutral and take no part in the contest. The rebels, however, said . . . that inasmuch as he was acquainted with military tactics he must come and assist them, or be regarded as a King's man. His reply was that he had fought for the King and he would do it again; consequently an order was issued to arrest him; but when they came to take him he had secreted himself. His escape was a hurried one, and all his possessions . . . were at the mercy of the rebels. . . . They, disappointed in not catching him, took his young and tender son, and threatened to hang him if he would not reveal his father's place of concealment. The brave little fellow replied, "hang away!" and the cruel men, under the name of liberty, carried out their threat; and three times was he suspended until almost dead, yet he would not tell, and then, when taken down, one of the monsters actually kicked him.

The hero of the hanging story was George Carscallen, youngest son of Edward and Elizabeth. In 1776 he was thirteen.[1]

Along with this particular family, over 100 000 other people made the decision not to support the "rebels" but to leave their homes, their businesses, and all they had worked for in the American Colonies. Among the refugees there were not only families of Irish descent, but also blacks, Scots, English, Germans, and Indians. Some returned to the British Isles. Many others attempted to start a new life in the West Indies or in what are today Ontario, Quebec and the Maritime Provinces.

Why Had the Tragedy Occurred?

In 1776 the political leaders of Britain's American colonies declared their independence from their mother country. There were many reasons for the revolution that followed, and historians still cannot agree completely on which ones were the most important.

The following interview reveals why the British government took the actions it did between 1763 and 1776 and why the American revolutionary leaders were determined to create a new country independent of British authority. (The interview is, of course, imaginary, but the information given and opinions expressed are based on historical evidence.)

Interviewer: I realize that two men cannot be held accountable for the decisions of many. But you, Lord North, were King George III's Prime Minister from 1770 to 1782 while you, Mr. Jefferson, were the author of the Declaration of Independence, and later, President of the United States. Do you agree, then, to be spokesmen for your governments?

Lord North: Gladly! But may I first correct the most foolish charge made by Mr. Jefferson in the Declaration that His Majesty George III was guilty of tyranny. The measures I introduced and the king endorsed were similar to those put into effect by other prime ministers between 1763 and 1770. Further, all bills affecting the colonies were supported by a majority of members of parliament before becoming law.

Mr. Jefferson: I wrote the Declaration as spokesman for the representatives from all thirteen colonies who met at Philadelphia in 1775 to take common action against the king's government.
Do I need to remind Lord North that the measures to which he refers reached us over the signature and seal of the king? And the question surely is whether the king acted with the consent, not of your parliament, but of our assemblies!

Interviewer: Today, historians seem to agree that it was the Seven Years' War between Great Britain and France that was the direct cause of the American Revolution. Would you please describe the political relationship between the British government and her North American colonies before that time?

Lord North: We should not forget that the colonies were first established under *charters* [contracts] granted by the monarch to trading companies, individuals such as Lord Baltimore, or groups such as the early Puritan settlers. By the terms of those charters the colonists became the freest of those in any empire on earth. By this century each colony had its own assembly and remained largely free of any interference from the Crown.

Mr. Jefferson: What Lord North doesn't mention is that several charters — that of Massachusetts Bay, for example — gave to the founders of the colonies full authority of government. It was the settlers themselves who forced the founders to grant them elected assemblies. Lord North also ignores the fact that eight of our governors were still appointed by the Crown. These men, who possessed great power, stood for British interests, often opposed to our own.

Interviewer: Yet it seems that it was the commercial arrangements between Great Britain and her colonies that caused most resentment. What had happened?

Lord North: To preserve our reserves of gold and silver, we have always attempted to buy as little as possible from foreign powers. Our colonies have been valued by us as dependable sources of raw materials. Virginian tobacco planters, for example, were for many years granted a monopoly in the British market. In return we have provided our colonies with the manufactured products they require. From this arrangement we have all benefited: colonies, the mother country, and the ship owners — many of them colonials — who have had a monopoly of carrying goods throughout the Empire.
I recognize that we were far too lax in our enforcement of the Navigation Laws that regulated

our imperial trade. We encouraged lawlessness by overlooking widespread smuggling and the dishonesty of some of our customs officials.

Mr. Jefferson: The Navigation Acts may have regulated *your* trade, but they limited manufacturing in the colonies and cut off our trade with outside powers. For the New England merchant, who had established a profitable trade with the Spanish and French West Indies, and for the New York manufacturer, they were a source of deep annoyance and great expense. This is why smuggling was not generally considered a crime. The so-called "King of Smugglers" was none other than John Hancock, the President of the Philadelphia Conference and one of the wealthiest men in Massachusetts.

As for the Virginia tobacco planters, they were being gouged by the British merchants to whom they were forced to sell their tobacco. By 1763 many had mortgaged future crops. To paraphrase my colleague Patrick Henry's famous line: "Give me liberty, or give me debt!"

Interviewer: But, surely, the conflicting interests you have revealed could easily have been resolved. Why did it have to come to revolution?

Lord North: For one reason alone: the unreasonable reaction of the colonists when we attempted to find solutions to the very difficult financial problems our government faced after the Seven Years' War. It was a world war, fought in Europe and India as well as in North America. At its end, our government's debt was the heaviest in our history. Also, the war was no sooner over than there was a dangerous uprising of Indians under Chief Pontiac in the Ohio River area. Although the rebellion was crushed, we attempted to avoid further disasters by maintaining 10 000 troops in the area and by temporarily forbidding colonists from settling beyond the Allegheny Mountains.

We were also faced with the heavy responsibility of administering our new colony of Canada. Here there were over 60 000 people, who spoke the French language and followed the Roman Catholic religion, who had to be governed, and, if possible, made into loyal subjects.

Since the colonists had for many years enjoyed the free protection of the mightiest navy in the world, and since they were now freed from the threat of French invasion from the north and west, it seemed to members of parliament that they should now contribute to the costs of our garrisons in America.

The measures we took were restrained and just. The colonists were given a year to raise taxation money themselves, or to suggest suitable taxes to parliament. Only then, we imposed a Stamp Act, very similar to ones previously enforced in Britain, requiring all legal documents and newspapers to bear revenue stamps. We were met with lawless opposition: riots, attacks against officials selling the stamps, attempts to boycott all British imports, and cries of "Liberty, Property and No Stamps!" The following year we repealed the Act and took steps to revise our system of customs duties. Duties were lowered, but steps were taken to enforce their collection. Once more, there were organized boycotts. By 1770 we were faced with widespread resistance organized by a few radicals. Sons of Liberty they called themselves! Finally, in December 1773, a gang of rowdies boarded ships owned by the East India Company anchored in Boston Harbour and threw their cargo of over 300 chests of tea overboard.

This was the turning point. By order of the king, Boston Harbour was closed to all shipping. The Massachusetts Assembly was dissolved, and town meetings forbidden without the governor's consent.

Then, in April 1775, General Gage learned that the colonists had stores of arms and ammunition at Concord. He immediately sent troops to destroy the supplies.

Mr. Jefferson: It came to revolution because, as I wrote in the Declaration, George III and his ministers were guilty of a long train of abuses designed to establish an absolute tyranny over us. How were we to interpret the Proclamation of 1763, by which you prohibited settlement in the West, as other than a refusal to grant to our sons and daughters land we had helped to win during the war? The fact that the Proclamation was ignored by so many settlers who moved west despite the order ought to have warned you against making other arbitrary decisions!

And what can I say about the British government's policies toward her new subjects in Quebec? To enlarge the boundaries of that province to include the rich lands north of the Ohio! Lands rightfully ours, divided now between the Indians and our defeated enemies!

Lord North makes much of the problems faced by his government and mentions the protection we received from the Royal Navy. You should realize that Britain was protecting us not from our enemies but from her own. France and Spain were not our enemies, except as subjects of Great Britain.

Until after the war with France, it was generally recognized in the colonies that the British parliament had the authority to regulate imperial trade. Our objection to the Stamp Tax was that it was an internal tax, collected from citizens within the colonies. This was a clear infringement on the rights of our own legislatures. As for the Navigation Acts, what I said in the Declaration is clear: To enforce these laws, the British government sent swarms of officers [customs officials] across the Atlantic to harass our people: all to impose taxes on us without our consent!

Lord North makes much of the Boston Tea Party but ignores what preceded it: the seizing of John Hancock's sloop, *Liberty,* in 1768 because he did not pay duty on her cargo of wines. Lord North actually boasts of what followed the Tea Party: the cutting off of our trade from all parts of the world, taking away our charters, and abolishing our most valuable laws!

It was not enough for General Gage, the Governor of Massachusetts, to keep a standing army in our colony, but troops were actually quartered in private buildings in Boston. Shades of Charles I and the Petition of Rights!

At Lexington, General Gage's troops were met by a small group of armed patriots. The skirmish that followed ended all hope for peaceful settlement. Our great war for independence had begun.

- Two students who have done further reading on the events leading to the American Revolution should play the roles of a rebel and a "King's man" or a member of his family. Each should try to win over the rest of the class to his/her side. Take a poll. How many become Loyalists? How many become revolutionaries?

- Between London and any of the Thirteen Colonies was an ocean voyage of from four to twelve weeks. During the winter months the voyage took longer and was more dangerous. What significance might that fact have in explaining why no peaceful solution could be worked out to the conflicts that developed?

- Why do you think that some members of the British Parliament, for example, Edmund Burke, supported the Americans in their opposition to the actions of the British government after 1763?

- How might you expect the attitude of the British government to change toward her other colonies in North America after 1783?

Refugees

First Years in the Colony of Nova Scotia

Caught between the two sides in the revolution were those persons, like Luke Carscallen and his family, who opposed independence from Britain. During the revolution some United Empire Loyalists, as they called themselves, were able to escape to Canada. Thousands of others migrated to the colony of New York, where British forces were strongest. When the war ended, the British commander in New York organized their evacuation by the Royal Navy. Many of the Loyalists returned to Britain. Others went to the West Indies. Still others — probably over forty thousand — came to the British colonies of Nova Scotia and Quebec.

The Loyalists who came to Nova Scotia were refugees who flooded into a land that already had a mixed population of over sixteen thousand people. You have read about many of them in earlier chapters: the original Indian tribes, the Acadians (perhaps two thousand who had escaped exile or had returned), the Scottish settlers in Cape Breton, the Irish who had built their farms along the St. John River. There were also people who had immigrated to the colony after the Seven Years' War to take advantage of the government's offer of free land. These included a few German, Swiss, and French Protestant settlers from Europe and many New Englanders, who by 1780 outnumbered all other groups in the colony.

The governor of Nova Scotia was given the responsibility for settling the Loyalists. His descriptions of them were not always flattering. They came, he said, from all classes: some of those from New York were obviously very rich, while others were from the "dregs" of the working classes in the seaports. There were also Quakers from Pennsylvania. There were over three thousand black Loyalists who had been granted freedom because they had fought for the British in the revolution. There were many disbanded soldiers, some single, others with families. Finally, there were some of the leading professional people and government officials from several of the colonies. This last group he found particularly difficult: "an angel would not satisfy them."

The Loyalists were settled in two major areas: along the south shore of Nova Scotia near Shelbourne, and along the St. John River. In the beginning the first settlement thrived. By 1786 Shelbourne had more people than either Quebec or Montreal. Only three American cities — New York, Philadelphia, and Boston — were larger. Fishing was excellent. Game provided a cheap source of food. Thriving lumber and shipbuilding industries were created.

As new groups poured in, merchants built up their stocks to supply everyone's needs. Among the merchandise sold in one store were super-fine cloaks, beaver gloves, silk stockings, riding habits, Scottish carpets, and four-poster beds. Hardly what you would expect in a town surrounded by ocean and wilderness!

Unfortunately, the boom was soon over. The soil proved to be too rocky for successful farming. Quickly the timber reserves, covering a smaller area than supposed, were used up. Shipbuilding also died. With the end of prosperity, the community became very divided.

> There were disputes as to titles to land and charges of breach of faith against the government. . . . There were many grog-shops and much drunkenness. Soldiers . . . committed crimes that were punished brutally. The penalty of death was inflicted for trifling theft; there were whippings at whipping-posts, and also hangings.[2]

Many families left to form settlements in the Digby and Annapolis areas, where land had been cultivated earlier by the Acadian French (see page 58). Still others crossed the Bay of Fundy to settle with other Loyalists along the St. John River. A few went as far afield as Prince Edward Island and Cape Breton. By 1792 Shelbourne was almost a ghost town.

The second major settlement along the St. John River fared much better. Many later Loyalists came directly there from New York. By 1785 there were hundreds of new farms, and St. John itself had become Canada's first incorporated city.

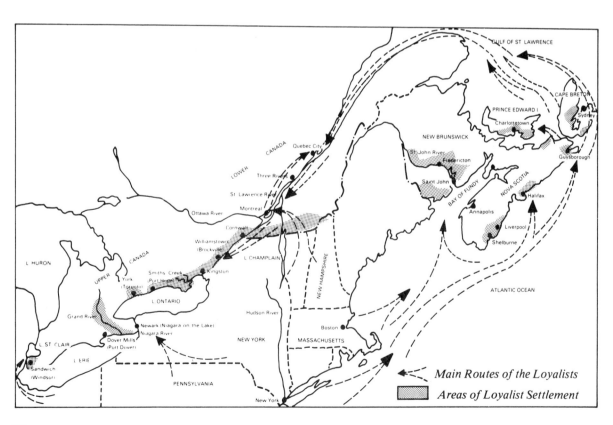

Main Routes of the Loyalists

Areas of Loyalist Settlement

First Years in the Colony of Canada

A second stream of Loyalists made their way to the British colonies from the interior of New York and Pennsylvania. They used one of the two trails shown below:

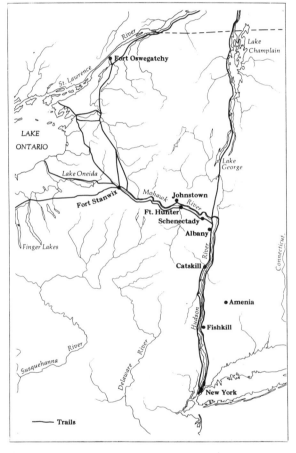

— Trails

Families often travelled by colonial flagships to a neutral point on Lake Champlain. There they transferred to Canadian vessels. Refugees carried their own provisions for two weeks. Some managed to bring other treasured possessions or necessities:

> As a rule, the women were allowed to bring with them only what belongings they could carry — along with provisions and small children. A few families who had servants were able to save one or two treasured belongings. Somehow Barbara Heck

managed to carry a large pewter tray and to bring the grandfather clock which had been a wedding gift, transported from Ireland in 1760! (This suggests that she came in 1777 under Burgoyne's protection, when some carts would be available for loyalists' possessions.)

> Mrs. Isaac Brisco of Arlington, whose daughter Nabby was to marry Luke Carscallen, had permission from Thomas Chittendon, the first Governor of Vermont, to take the following articles with her:

> 2 feather beds and bedding for same
> 6 pewter plates
> 2 pewter platters
> 2 basins
> 1 teapot or teakettle
> 1 small skillet
> 1 wardrobe chest

> Although this does not seem a great deal for the wife of the wealthiest man in Arlington to be allowed, we may be certain that it was much more than [many] women were able to salvage from their homes![3]

In 1783 a refugee camp was established at Sorel. The Loyalists were divided into groups according to their religion or area of origin in the Thirteen Colonies. They were then placed in one of thirteen townships, staked out by government surveyors, between present-day Cornwall and the Bay of Quinte area. North of Cornwall, in Glengarry County, for instance, a group of Scottish settlers originally from the Mohawk Valley were settled. Further west, between Cornwall and Belleville, Protestant English and Germans were settled.

One interesting Loyalist group comprised Iroquois bands who had fought under Sir William Johnson, the Loyalist governor of New York. One band, under Chief Deseronto, settled near the Bay of Quinte. A second, under the Mohawk chief Joseph Brant, was given a large tract of land on either side of the Grand River, just west of present-day Toronto.

Still another Loyalist group, composed of families of men who had belonged to Butler's Rangers, crossed over to Canada from Niagara and remained to settle in that area.

Government Help

The British government gave each family at least one hundred acres of land. To be fair to all, these were chosen by lot. Some were also given rations of food to tide them over and, since many had lost all their possessions, some tools and supplies. Despite this help, the first years were often harsh:

> For the women life was especially hard. The Valley wives had been used to strenuous work, but they were older now; and several years spent in refugee camps had told on their health. Life in Upper Canada was more of a change for Nabby Brisco who married Luke Carscallen, for she had grown up in a comfortable home with servants. Yet Nabby Carscallen, in a log cabin in the clearing by the river, bore twelve children — and without the benefit of a physician. As late in 1817, there was no resident doctor in the Midland District of Upper Canada.[4]

Loyalist Influences

The Loyalists changed the face of the Maritime provinces. For one thing, they outnumbered earlier settlers by about two to one. For another, they were quick to register complaints and assert their own interests in government. The large number who had settled along the St. John River, for instance, soon demanded their own legislative assembly, claiming that they were under-represented in the Assembly in Halifax. In 1784, therefore, New Brunswick was created as a separate colony from Nova Scotia.

In Canada as well, the Loyalists petitioned the British government to grant them their own assembly and a code of laws based on the British rather than the French system. Once more the British government agreed, and in 1791 the former colony of Canada became the two separate colonies of Upper and Lower Canada. These, of course, have become the present provinces of Ontario and Quebec.

Loyalists camping

U.E.L. Societies Today

In 1789 the governor general of British North America declared that all those who had joined the Royal Standard in America before 1783 should be permitted to use the letters U.E. after their names. A list of those who qualified was drawn up. Since then, those persons who can claim an ancestor on this list are considered to be of U.E.L. descent. Proud of their origins, they have formed a United Empire Loyalists' Association in Canada, which publishes a newssheet called *The Loyalist Gazette.* They also attempt to keep the Loyalist tradition alive in Canada by preserving letters, diaries, and other sources of information about the early settlement.

- "Mistakes made by government leaders are paid for by the sufferings of ordinary people." Discuss this statement using examples from current events or other periods of history you have studied.
- Do you agree with the decision of the governor of Upper Canada to settle different nationalities into different townships in Upper Canada? What disadvantages can you see in this plan?

It is quite possible that Canada would not exist today in its present form if it were not for the Loyalist immigration. Speculate about each of the following.

- Would what is now New Brunswick have fallen before the expansion of American settlement during the 1830's?
- Would Ontario not have been settled by the Post-Loyalists of the 1790's and, as a result, become part of the United States?
- Could Britain have defended Canada successfully against the Americans during the War of 1812 if there had not been Loyalist settlements close to the border?
- What special advantages would the Loyalists of British descent have over other cultural groups in preserving their culture?

FOR FURTHER READING

Doughty, Howard, et al. *Canadian Studies: Culture and Country.* Toronto: Wiley Publishers of Canada Ltd., 1976.

Fryer, Mary. *Caleb Seaman: A Loyalist.* Toronto: Ginn and Co., 1970.

Lapp, Eula C. *To Their Heirs Forever.* Belleville, Ontario: Mika Publishing Co., 1977.

Miller, Orlo. *Raiders of the Mohawk: The Story of Butler's Rangers.* Toronto: Macmillan, 1954.

Sheffe, Norman, ed. *Many Cultures, Many Heritages.* Toronto: McGraw-Hill-Ryerson, 1975.

The Great Migration (1815-1914)

In 1815 the Napoleonic Wars, which had plagued Europe for twenty-five years and had spread to North America and North Africa, finally drew to a close. In the century between the end of these wars and the beginning of the First World War in 1914, a huge number of people — probably over forty million (or almost twice the present population of Canada) — left the continent of Europe.

The majority of the emigrants went to the United States. Many others went to South America, particularly to Brazil. But over two million of them came to Canada. Their importance to our growth as a country can be seen in the charts on page 8.

The population density graphs opposite show clearly how Canada changed with their coming.

- Find out when the first settlement started in your own area. (Your school library or local public library will have books on local history.)
- Visit your local cemetery to find the oldest tombstones. Make a list of those from the time of the Great Migration. Try to tell from their names where these settlers came from in Europe. Are any of your own family among them?

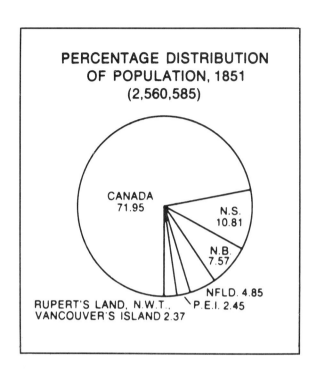

PERCENTAGE DISTRIBUTION
OF POPULATION, 1851
(2,560,585)

CANADA
71.95

N.S.
10.81

N.B.
7.57

NFLD. 4.85

P.E.I. 2.45

RUPERT'S LAND, N.W.T.,
VANCOUVER'S ISLAND 2.37

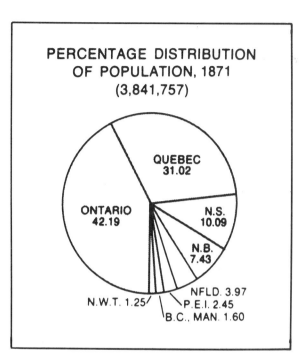

PERCENTAGE DISTRIBUTION
OF POPULATION, 1871
(3,841,757)

QUEBEC
31.02

ONTARIO
42.19

N.S.
10.09

N.B.
7.43

NFLD. 3.97

P.E.I. 2.45

B.C., MAN. 1.60

N.W.T. 1.25

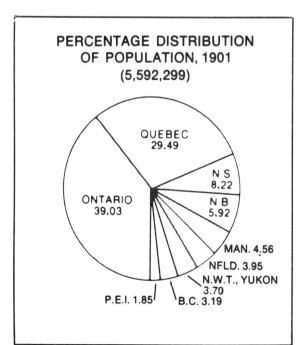

PERCENTAGE DISTRIBUTION
OF POPULATION, 1901
(5,592,299)

QUEBEC
29.49

N S
8.22

N B
5.92

ONTARIO
39.03

MAN. 4.56

NFLD. 3.95

N.W.T., YUKON
3.70

P.E.I. 1.85

B.C. 3.19

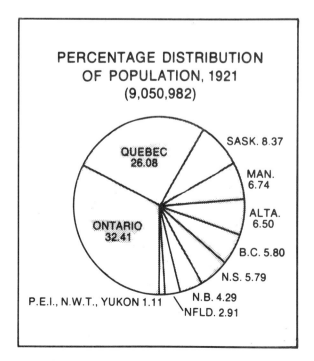

PERCENTAGE DISTRIBUTION
OF POPULATION, 1921
(9,050,982)

SASK. 8.37

QUEBEC
26.08

MAN.
6.74

ALTA.
6.50

ONTARIO
32.41

B.C. 5.80

N.S. 5.79

P.E.I., N.W.T., YUKON 1.11

N.B. 4.29

NFLD. 2.91

Why They Left Home

You already know that immigrants to Canada before 1800 had a variety of reasons for coming. Some, like the Frenchman Poutrincourt, came partly from love of adventure, partly to make their fortunes. Others had first come to North America as soldiers and later were given land grants by the French or British governments as payment for military service. Others came as missionaries or as nuns or priests. Still others, such as the Scottish settlers, came because of very bad living conditions at home, or, in the case of the Loyalists, because of civil war.

Very few of the forty million persons who left Europe during the Great Migration wrote about why they decided to give up their homes, their friends, and their country, and come to a completely new land. We know, however, that a great many of them felt *driven* from their homes: by a lack of opportunity, by fear of the government in power, by poverty caused by unemployment, or even by fear of starvation.

Through the following three quotations, we learn directly from those who lived at the time something of the harshness of the lives of many people.

A farmer in Scotland is forced by his landlord to leave his home:

> Our family was very reluctant to leave and stayed for some time, but the burning party came round and set fire to our house at both ends, reducing to ashes whatever remained within the walls.[1]

In an imaginary scene from Disraeli's novel *Sybil* a hand-loom weaver talks with his wife about his fear of the future:

> "Is that Harriet?" said his wife, moving in her bed.
>
> The Hand-Loom weaver was recalled from his reverie to the urgent misery that surrounded him.
>
> "No!" he replied in a quick hoarse voice, "it is not Harriet."
>
> "Why does not Harriet come?"
>
> "She will come no more!" replied the weaver; "I told you so last night: she can bear this place no longer; and I am not surprised."
>
> "How are we to get food then?" rejoined his wife; "you ought not to have let her leave us. You do nothing, Warner. You get no wages yourself; and you have let the girl escape."
>
> "I will escape myself if you say that again," said the weaver: "I have been up these three hours finishing this piece which ought to have been taken home on Saturday night."
>
> "But you have been paid for it beforehand. You get nothing for your work. A penny an hour! What sort of work is it, that brings a penny an hour?"
>
> "Work that you have often admired, Mary; and has before this gained a prize. But if you don't like the work," said the man quitting his loom, "let it alone. There was enough yet owing on this piece to have allowed us to break our fast. However, no matter; we must starve sooner or later. Let us begin at once."[2]

A witness called to testify before a House of Lords Commission Hearing on Poverty in Ireland describes the state of the tenants who are farming the tract of land he has bought.

> I purchased it [3000 acres of land in Ireland], and gave £40 000 for it. I found an immense Number of Widows and poor Persons, Paupers, upon that Property; and I found it totally impossible to make any Progress in improving the Estate while I had such a dense Population of poor Creatures upon it; they were under a nominal Rent which they had never paid for Years. I was obliged to feed them, and therefore I determined, as being the best Means of improving the Property, to send them off at once. I never pressed one Individual to go, but I intimated to them that if they wished to go I would provide them with a free Passage, and give them Provisions for the Voyage.[3]

Life in Europe seemed to be changing in a very drastic way, bringing great opportunity to some and to others, terrible suffering. Although most people who lived at the time were unaware of what was happening, historians now believe that at least three very powerful forces were responsible for the immense changes taking place. These forces were:

(i) changes in food production;
(ii) changes in industrial production;
(iii) a population explosion.

Because these same forces are still bringing about immensely important changes today in our own world, it is worthwhile for us to begin to understand them.

I Changes in Food Production

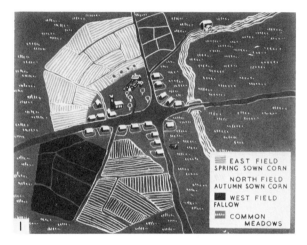

EAST FIELD
SPRING SOWN CORN

NORTH FIELD
AUTUMN SOWN CORN

WEST FIELD
FALLOW

COMMON
MEADOWS

The Village or Manor

In Canada today most of our farmers own their own farms. This was not true of Europe at the beginning of the nineteenth century. Most European farmers were still peasants or tenants, who worked land they rented from landowners, many of whom were wealthy aristocrats.

Farming methods had changed very little over the centuries. The homes of the peasants or tenant farmers were usually clustered together in a village, outside of which were three large fields. There was also an area called the common, where the peasants were permitted by their landlord to pasture their animals.

- Notice that each of the three fields is divided into strips, and that each farmer has several strips in each field. For the individual farmer what were the advantages and disadvantages of the strip system?
- Notice that in this English village some strips have been consolidated. Notice also that about 40 percent of the land is used by the landowner for sheep raising.
- What disadvantages might there be in having all of the animals of the village using the same pasture on the common?

Farm implements had changed little. You can find their counterparts in pictures carved on the walls of Egyptian tombs dating back five thousand years.

Because fertilizer was scarce, each of the three fields lay fallow (*i.e.,* without a crop) for one year in three. Throughout Europe a rotation system was in general use:

Threshing by using a flail

- Before the village can become more productive, what important changes will have to be made?
- After these changes, why will fewer labourers be needed?

Enclosures (The Creation of Larger Farming Units)

From time to time, some landlords had consolidated their land and had fenced in or *enclosed* some areas to enlarge their own acreage or to rent land to prosperous farmers in larger blocks. In Normandy enclosures were allowed by law. In England and Scotland a landlord wishing to enclose his land needed the consent of parliament. In Britain the enclosed land was often used for raising sheep since, when the price of wool was high, profits were excellent. Also, sheep needed few people to look after them.

Specialization of Crops

In parts of the Netherlands where land was in short supply, many farmers began to specialize in producing commercial crops such as flax (for linen), hops (for beer), and tobacco. They were also among the first Europeans to grow the potato on a large scale. Later the potato became a staple in many over-populated parts of Europe.

Some landlords were also tackling the problem of land wasted through crop rotation. Men such as Viscount Townshend began to experiment with the planting of turnips or clover as a third crop to replace the fallow year. These experiments in crop rotation were completely successful and had an amazing result. The new harvests of turnip or clover provided fodder to feed far more animals during the winter. It was no longer necessary to kill off almost all animals in the fall, keeping only a few for breeding in the spring. This increase in animals provided men not only with more meat and milk for their own use but with far more manure to fertilize the land and greatly increase its yield. A popular saying of the time sums up the relationship between crops and animals in this way: "No fodder, no beasts; no beasts, no manure; no manure, no crops."[4]

New Machinery

In the Netherlands the Brabant plough, the forerunner of the modern plough, was invented. In Great Britain, Jethro Tull invented a seed drill that could be used to plant seeds in rows to make hoeing easier and a second machine, a "horse hoe," to make it quicker. These were the first of a long series of machines that would eventually change agriculture completely.

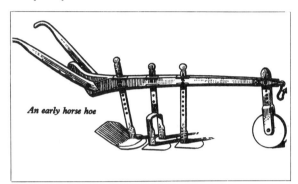

An early horse hoe

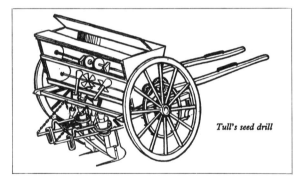

Tull's seed drill

- How would the use of machinery speed up the movement of enclosure?

Selective Breeding

The breeding of prize sports animals had been practised for centuries. Certain breeds of cattle, such as the Holstein, were famous in Europe. With the enclosures there was a new interest on the part of wealthy landlords in improving the quality of their animals for market. In England, Robert Bakewell began to produce prize sheep by selective breeding. He started a movement that spread quickly among other landowners and greatly improved the size and weight of farm animals.

Bakewell did not really understand the modern science of genetics. Jethro Tull did not understand why the exposure of roots to air improved plant yields. Nor did Townshend know that the roots of clover plants are actually nitrate factories, producing excellent fertilizer. All three men were practical innovators who seized on new methods simply because they worked.

Old breed of sheep

Bakewell's New Leicester

- Farming became far more efficient in Britain and parts of Europe after 1750. What, though, do you think would be the fate of many of the tenant farmers caught up in the change?

A popular proverb of the time of the agricultural revolution in Britain says: "The law locks up the man or woman who steals the goose from off the common, but leaves the greater rascal loose who steals the common from the goose."[5]

- What does the saying mean? What group of people in Britain kept the saying alive?
- With two other members of your class, develop a conversation between Jethro Tull, a landowner eager to improve his crop yield, and a small farmer in danger of losing his land.
- Reread the quotations at the beginning of this section (page 96). Explain the connection between these people's tragic situation and the changes we call the Agricultural Revolution.
- You are a visitor in a country whose people are largely poor farmers. Yet the area seems blessed with good soil and climate. What four basic questions might you ask your guide about farming in his country?
- Visit a farm in your area, or if you live on a farm, study it from a new point of view. What jobs do you see being done by machinery that previously were done by hand? Has the output of the farm increased greatly in the past twenty years? Why, or why not?
- Make a study of how *one* modern farm machine has developed over the past fifty years. Report your findings to the class.

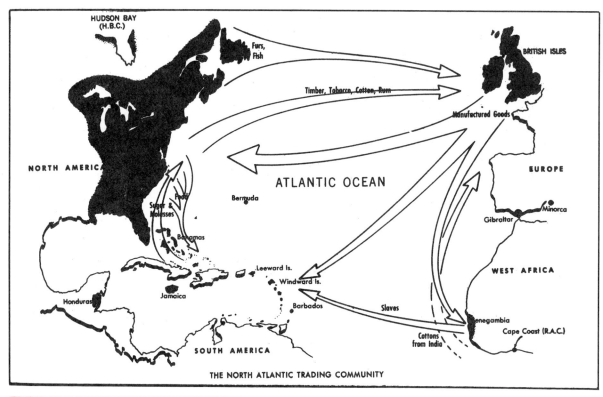

THE NORTH ATLANTIC TRADING COMMUNITY

Map labels: HUDSON BAY (H.B.C.); Furs, Fish; BRITISH ISLES; Timber, Tobacco, Cotton, Rum; Manufactured Goods; NORTH AMERICA; ATLANTIC OCEAN; EUROPE; Bermuda; Minorca; Gibraltar; Sugar & Molasses; Fish; Bahamas; WEST AFRICA; Leeward Is.; Windward Is.; Honduras; Jamaica; Barbados; Slaves; Senegambia; Cape Coast (R.A.C.); Cottons from India; SOUTH AMERICA

WALPOLE AND THE CABINET

Walpole has often been termed the first "Prime Minister" and the "founder of cabinet government". He was neither, but he did a great deal to establish both the Cabinet and the position of Prime Minister in the English system of government. There were several important differences between the cabinet system then and now: Walpole did not choose all his colleagues, although his word had great influence with the King. The members of the Cabinet did not necessarily, present a united front. The support of the King was more important to the Cabinet than the support of Parliament. The Cabinet did not resign as a unit when the government was defeated, as it would today.

THE BANK OF ENGLAND

The Bank of England, the most famous of world banks, was started in 1694. Until 1946 it was a private organization and for a long time was really the government's banker. In the last half of the eighteenth century many other smaller banks were established, thus making possible the rapid and easy flow of money and credit which was necessary to finance the great economic changes that were taking place. The Bank of England, however, remained the greatest bank in the country and its bank notes were the chief currency in London and in many other parts of England. By 1800 its notes were honoured throughout the world. Napoleon used it as a model when he established the Bank of France.

II Changes in Industrial Production

Today in North America we are part of the modern Technological Age. This simply means that we have discovered new methods (or mechanical techniques) not only for doing the work necessary for our survival, but also to make our lives easier and more pleasant. In most societies in the past, men created machines to help them perform their work. But the sources of *power* used to drive the machines were usually the same: men's own muscles and strength, and the power of animals, wind, and water.

Then in the 1750's in Great Britain a group of inventors created machines powered by a completely different form of energy: that of steam trapped under pressure. This kind of machine was not new — Leonardo da Vinci had created a working model in the fifteenth century, and Heron of Alexandria had invented novelties run by steam two or three centuries before the birth of Christ — but this was the first time in history that it was seen as something more than a curiosity or a toy. Almost overnight a number of inventions introduced its use into the textile industry. These were followed by a whole series of changes in the production and transportation of goods that have continued to the present time. As a result, our world today is completely changed from the one known to humanity for thousands of years.

Historians are sometimes asked why these great changes did not take place centuries earlier, or later, in some other part of the world. Some of the answers can be found in the pictures shown on the preceding three pages. Make a list of the clues you are able to find. Then try to relate them to each other to discover how each helped to bring about a tremendous expansion in production.

Confirm your answers by studying the following statements.

(i) By 1750 British merchants had already established worldwide contacts by trade in such basic products as timber, furs, tea, and spices. There were, therefore, within their reach, *markets* that would quickly absorb new British products if they could be cheaply made and had a wide use for many people. Cotton and woolen cloth, for example, was in great demand almost everywhere, but it was still relatively expensive, since yard or thread was spun by using a hand-operated spinning wheel and then hand-woven into cloth.

(ii) Britain had the largest merchant fleet in the world: ships were available to transport British products to world markets and to bring back the raw materials Britain did not have at home.

(iii) The government was stable enough to keep order in the country.

(iv) In Britain itself there were also all three of the *factors* (or essential ingredients) needed to manufacture the new products:

    (a) *raw materials:* Britain had good resources of coal and iron to make and drive the new machinery. She also had wool for textiles, while cotton could be transported by her merchant fleet from India and North America.

    (b) *capital:* The British merchant class and the nobility had money to invest in the new industries. Commercial banks were already established in Britain so that business transactions could be made quite easily.

    (c) *labour:* The new machines would require large numbers of relatively unskilled workers to tend them. The coal mines, similarly, would need many labourers to open them up, dig out the coal, and transport it to the surface. These workers were to be found, as you know, from among the farmers and farm labourers who had been forced from their villages by the enclosures and who now migrated to find work in the new industrial towns or mining areas.

- Why did the Industrial Revolution begin in the textile industry rather than in some other product?
- What sources of power, or energy, have largely replaced the steam engine in the twentieth century?
- Make a list of all the *benefits* we, as Canadians, gain from modern technology. Make a second list of the *problems* we face because of modern technology. Which list is longer?
- Make a list of all the things you do during an average day that require the use of electricity or petroleum products. Can you picture what your life would be like without them?

How Life Changed

(i) SOCIAL EVILS

Eventually industrialization would bring a much higher standard of living to most people. In the beginning in Britain, however, the common people suffered great hardship. Work in the coal mines was dangerous and unbelievably harsh. Since children could be paid low wages, and were more easily controlled than men, there would be work for them more often than for their parents in the new factories. One large group, the hand weavers and spinners, lost their means of making a living. They joined the ranks of those who had been evicted from their farms by the enclosures to form a great surplus of workers. At the beginning of the Great Migration, many of the people who came to North America were from these two groups.

- Reread the second quotation at the beginning of this section. Do you think that this family would emigrate? Why or why not?

(ii) URBANIZATION

The new industrial towns grew very rapidly. In the beginning they were completely unplanned. Men with capital built their factories where they could get cheap raw materials and power. People quickly congregated wherever work was to be found — in factories, mines, or shipyards. Later the cities created their own armies of workers, who built and maintained water and sewage systems, transportation systems, and many other services.

The Spread of Industrialization

The Industrial Revolution spread slowly from Great Britain to other parts of the world. For over a century after the first steam engines were used in Britain's textile factories, she was the world's leading supplier of manufactured products.

It was not until 1870 that Germany and the United States were strong competitors against Britain in world markets. Industry did not become an important part of the economies of eastern Europe or the Soviet Union until World War I. China's industrialization really began after World War II, and there are many parts of the world today where industrialization is now only beginning.

- Most Canadians today live in an *urbanized, industrialized* society. This means that our whole way of life is very different from that of people who lived, or are today living, in unindustrialized countries.
- Working with a group of students, make a list of ten machines or appliances you feel have most changed the life-style of Canadians.
- Reread the statement by the Indian working for a Native organization on page 19. Distinguish between culture and heritage.
- In what obvious ways is each of the parts of our culture being changed by modern technology?
- Contrast the North American Indian attitude toward the land (natural resources) with those of our technological society.
- In what ways do you think our life-style is (i) richer, (ii) poorer because of modern technology?
- It has been suggested that in the future all Canadians will belong to one *"homogenized"* culture, one in which all of us will be alike. Do you agree or disagree? Defend your answer.

III Population Explosion

For many centuries the population of Europe had remained almost unchanged as births and deaths cancelled each other out. By 1800 it stood at about 180 million people. Then, suddenly, within the next one hundred years, that number more than doubled to 460 million. Even more amazingly, by 1914 there were also more people of European origin in other continents than there had been in Europe itself in 1800.

Why was the explosion occurring? Not because more babies were being born, as many people imagine, but because far more children were surviving to adulthood and were themselves having children. We still do not know exactly why this was happening. The following reasons, however, have been suggested:

(i) An improvement in law and order: There were no terrible European wars between 1815 and 1914. Perhaps even more important, there were no large-scale revolutions that resulted in the massacre of great numbers of people.

(ii) The improvements in agriculture had greatly increased the supply of food: Generally speaking, there were fewer great famines in Europe. Also, a better-fed population was more resistant to the diseases that had plagued mankind from the beginning of time.

(iii) The Industrial Revolution, while creating terrible conditions during its early stages, did provide the population of those countries it reached with greater means of earning a living and, eventually, a higher standard of living.

(iv) The birth, toward the end of the nineteenth century, of modern medicine. The discoveries of bacteria and anesthetics, in particular, were applied to immunology (*e.g.,* vaccination) and to surgery, greatly reducing deaths. In our own century the improvement in medical and health care is probably the greatest single cause of the world population explosion.

(v) In the expanding cities the construction of water and sewage systems helped to reduce dangers of epidemics.

- Look back to pages 39 and 40 and study the birth and death rates in New France compared with Canada in 1973. Explain the differences.
- With the population explosion, the size of farms in many parts of Europe became dangerously small. Reread the third quotation (page 96) at the beginning of this section. Establish the connection between the information in the quotation and the material you have just read.
- Explain the statement, "Agriculture by plough gave way to agriculture by hoe."
- What products could be grown to make maximum use of the small amount of land available to each family in overpopulated parts of Europe?
- Today we talk about a new population "explosion." To understand the term better, make a bar graph using the statistical information given in the following statement:

The world's population reached 1000 million by about the year 1830. It was only 100 years later that the 2000 million figure was reached. The 3000 million figure was reached by about 1960 — just 30 years later. The over 3700 million world population of 1971 is expected to be doubled by shortly after the year 2000, if current rates continue.

- During Europe's population "explosion" in the nineteenth century, forty million people left for other continents. Where will the exploding populations of the twenty-first century migrate?
- You read the statement, "there were too many of us" in your study of the chapter on the Scots. Yet the population of Scotland today is much greater than it was then. Why were there "too many of us" in the 1760's and not today?

The Atlantic Crossing Under Sail

Imagine yourself, for a moment, as one of the thousands of persons planning to leave Europe for British North America in a sailing vessel between the end of the Napoleonic Wars in 1815 and the 1850's. (After this many passengers crossed in steamships or in steam-and-sail vessels.) Your mind is filled with questions about the Atlantic crossing: How much, for instance, will the voyage cost? How long will it take? What will life be like on board? and so on. The answers to your questions, given below, are based on information from persons who lived at the time and knew about conditions from first-hand experience. Some answers will surprise you. Remember that the information represents the knowledge of that time, not ours.

How much will the voyage cost?

It will cost anywhere from ten pounds (about fifty dollars) to fifty pounds if you are one of the three to

seven persons out of one hundred who will travel as a cabin passenger. If you travel in steerage (in the hold), as over 90 percent of passengers do, you will probably pay anywhere from twenty shillings (about five dollars) to just over four pounds. If you are borrowing money for the fare, you should know that most farm labourers in British North America earn about thirty shillings and board per month during their first year. Later their pay may be almost doubled.

The reason that prices for steerage passengers vary so much is that ships of every condition and size are leaving port each day during the spring and summer. Everything will depend, then, on your luck and your skill in bargaining.

Also, notice that these prices are for the Atlantic crossing to St. John or the Port of Quebec. We'll discuss the journey inland later.

Can I get any help to pay the costs of the journey and of establishing myself in North America?

There are a number of things you might try. Have you, for instance, a member of your family already established in North America? Perhaps he will send you money for your fare and give you help when you arrive. We know that this is the way that thousands of Irish, for example, have arranged for their passage.

Perhaps your own parish (or local municipality) will help you to leave. This will be true particularly if you are in an area where there is a great deal of unemployment and you might otherwise be accepting relief (welfare) payments from your local government. The taxpayers, you see, might find it cheaper to send you away than help you and your family at home.

If you are a farm labourer, your landlord may, perhaps, have you sent to North America at his own expense. We know of many cases where this has been done. Colonel Gordon of Cluny, for example, assisted over fifteen hundred of his tenants to emigrate.

If you have some capital of your own, you may prefer to settle in Canada through a land company. Colonel Thomas Talbot, for instance, has opened up large tracts of land in western Upper Canada by helping provide immigrants with good land. Under his system the settler must build a house, clear and sow ten acres of his land within three years, and help with opening a road fronting his property.

How long will the crossing take?

Anywhere from four weeks to three months. The average time is about six weeks. Remember that sailing ships are at the mercy of the Atlantic weather. For this reason you should avoid a winter crossing.

What will the sleeping quarters be like?

Most of the passenger ships are converted timber vessels, whose owners make additional profits by carrying a human cargo back to British North America rather than returning almost empty. Timber is the largest single export from British North America: it is estimated that one in seven of all British merchant ships are engaged in the North American timber trade.

The ships are usually converted to passenger vessels by laying a second temporary deck or floor across the hull about 5-1/2 feet below the first. This "between-decks" space is called steerage.

The hatchways are not only stairwells but also the only source of air and natural light. In bad weather they must be fastened down. There are often two decks of berths on each side of the steerage space and down the centre. Each berth, approximately 6 by 6 feet (2 by 2 metres), is usually shared by four adult passengers.

Passengers in the steerage share the responsibility for keeping the floor area clean. In good weather, mattresses can be taken to the upper deck for airing. During a storm, water may enter the steerage from the hatches or seep up from the hull. One covered light is kept burning during the night beside the main hatchway.

It must be emphasized that if you choose steerage accommodation, your comfort on the voyage will depend entirely on the condition of your vessel, its captain and crew, the weather, and the number of passengers travelling with you. If a large group from one parish or county decide to travel together to organize food supplies, assign space, and regulate daily routine, your trip may be relatively pleasant. Similarly, several families travelling together may be permitted by the captain to block off a certain amount of space for their own use. But if you travel in a crowded vessel in a "bad" year and with desperately poor families who have no adequate provisions, your voyage will be more horrible than anything you can imagine.

What will the food be like?

If you are a cabin passenger on a regular vessel, the food can be as good as you wish. A typical menu includes butter, fresh eggs, vegetables, roast meat, fowl, duck, ham, dried and fresh fruit, and a variety of fine wines.

If you travel steerage, you will usually provide your own food. Captains are required only to carry water and flour: fifty gallons of water and fifty pounds of bread for each passenger. You are advised to take with you provisions for at least sixty days. The following list, recommended by Mr. A.C. Buchanan, Immigration Officer with the Port of Quebec, should see five persons through the voyage at very low cost:[1]

48 stone (672 lbs.) of potatoes	50 lbs. fish (herring) in a small keg
2-1/2 cwt. of oatmeal or flour	1 gal. spirits
1/2 cwt. of biscuits	1 gal. molasses
20 lbs. butter	a little vinegar
20 lbs. bacon	

If you can afford more, try to include lemons, figs, apples, and tea. Carrots, turnips, and onions can be used in making broth. Salted beef will also keep well. Some passengers bring live poultry (for eggs and meat), but the fowl often sicken. Pigs seem to be hardier and usually can be left in a crate on the upper deck.

Food is cooked by the passengers at two large stoves on the open deck. Grills are laid over the coals for baking bread or boiling cereals or stews. Water is a special problem since it is often kept in large storage tanks, formerly used for oil or wine. You should therefore bring vinegar to add to the water to cover its taste and smell. Or, if you can afford it, bring bottled beer or bottled boiled milk as a substitute.

How much sickness is there?

Attacks of seasickness are to be expected. Oranges, soup, and gingerbreads will help to restore your appetite after an attack. On ordinary crossings there are always some fever cases and some deaths, usually among the very young and the old. Your vessel may or may not have a doctor on board. Captains' wives have also sometimes helped nurse the sick.

Two diseases, however, are greatly feared by all travellers, especially since we do not know what causes them. The first, typhus, is often called "ship's fever," or "black fever." Very few patients survive this hideous disease, which causes very high fever, delirium, and vomiting. The victim first develops a rash and later terrible sores, which may be infected with gangrene. The second disease, cholera, is very like typhus. The fever of cholera, however, reaches a peak and relapses. If the patient survives, the fever may return a third, or even a fourth time. The disease is therefore often called "relapsing" fever or, sometimes, "yellow" fever because of the colour of its victims.

Typhus and cholera spread very quickly among people who are crowded together, especially if they are weakened by lack of food and fresh air. In 1832, the cholera year, over fifteen hundred travellers died in the Port of Quebec during a few days at the height of the epidemic. Thousands of others died on the voyage across. One such death has been recorded by a cabin passenger on a vessel crossing the Atlantic in 1847, the year of the cholera outbreak in Ireland:

Passing the main hatch, I got a glimpse of one of the most awful sights I ever beheld. A poor female patient was lying in one of the upper berths — dying. Her head and face were swollen to a most unnatural size, the latter being hideously deformed. . . . She had been nearly three weeks ill, and suffered exceedingly. . . . Her afflicted husband stood by her holding a "blessed candle" in his hand and awaiting the departure of her spirit. . . As the sun was setting the bereaved husband muttered a prayer over her enshrouded corpse, which, as he said "amen" was lowered into the ocean.[2]

Who will my fellow passengers be?

Immigration officials at Canadian ports are required to keep records of all immigrants who enter. The following table contains a listing of the skills and trades of immigrants arriving at the ports of Quebec and Montreal, 1846-1859:

Most, as you can see, are either farmers and farm servants or labourers. Others are skilled workers. Very few professional persons are among them. You can also see that they are bringing to British North America many important skills and trades.

What arrangements should we make for our landing and transportation inland from Quebec?

Your vessel will have to undergo medical inspection on Grosse Isle. If there are no cases of ship fever aboard, you will not be detained for long. You will then be taken in your vessel to your destination at the Port of Quebec. Many immigrants do not realize how long the journey inland from Quebec

can be. You are therefore advised to study the map on the next page carefully.

You must first arrange passage up the St. Lawrence to Montreal. The trip usually takes between 1-1/2 and two days by river steamer. Prices by 1834 are about five shillings steerage or twenty-six shillings for a cabin passenger. In Montreal travellers can usually get inexpensive lodgings. There are also sheds at the entrance to Lachine Canal for poor immigrants.

Because of the rapids and heavy currents, the trip

Trades and Callings of Emigrants Arrived at Ports of Quebec and Montreal, 1846-59

	1846	1853	1854	1855	1856	1857	1858	1859
Bakers	14	35	51	36	65	19	16	14
Blacksmiths, tinsmiths, braziers	61	11	16	9	18	20	61	—
Bookbinders and printers	17	21	19	13	14	22	11	12
Bricklayers and masons	60	172	228	118	115	119	52	18
Butchers	15	21	23	18	35	35	9	8
Cabinet-makers and turners	7	—	20	9	10	25	10	2
Carpenters and joiners	162	322	617	239	308	478	205	113
Cart and wheelwrights	8	15	39	36	50	44	—	—
Coachmakers	1	2	8	2	7	5	10	—
Coopers	12	9	40	27	27	21	12	3
Curriers and tanners	2	2	2	4	4	11	1	—
Dyers	1	1	4	4	19	—	3	—
Engineers	4	40	76	21	35	124	18	11
Gardeners	14	19	37	24	49	32	24	—
Hatters	1	2	3	1	12	6	—	1
Merchants and clerks	—	74	156	89	104	327	192	331
Millers and millwrights	10	48	131	88	83	127	35	13
Miners	98	119	238	35	61	156	41	10
Moulders and foundrymen	—	3	24	13	9	21	7	3
Painters and glaziers	—	15	41	19	20	24	17	9
Paper-makers	1	1	4	3	2	1	—	—
Plasterers	5	—	5	9	13	1	3	—
Professional men	—	—	—	—	—	—	—	13
Ropemakers	—	4	6	1	5	—	—	—
Saddlers and harness makers	4	15	18	11	11	15	5	2
Sail makers	—	1	5	4	2	—	3	—
Sawyers	1	5	16	6	9	21	5	5
Ship-builders	2	2	17	2	—	—	—	—
Shoemakers	87	154	358	167	227	157	52	27
Smiths	—	199	354	127	216	201	24	49
Stone-cutters	2	17	67	13	13	27	10	3
Tailors	84	176	433	153	206	207	94	61
Watch and clock makers	6	9	43	21	51	31	4	2
Weavers	—	51	85	64	65	41	23	—
Wheelwrights	—	—	—	—	—	—	9	—
Wool and flax dressers	—	3	4	9	4	10	—	4
Unenumerated	—	84	163	159	189	184	178	266
House-servants	87	146	117	26	32	134	—	—
Farmers and farm servants	4831	3974	5632	2007	2342	3518	1651	1051
Labourers	6733	6667	10448	3722	4338	6279	1593	866
Total	12366	12455	19466	7309	8769	12443	4442	3081

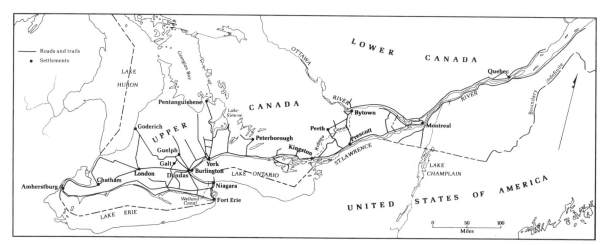

from Montreal to Prescott must be by bateau or Durham boat. A stagecoach also leaves fairly regularly, but it is expensive. By water the trip usually takes from six to twelve days.

As you can see from the map, Prescott is a junction point for settlers going north or west. There is a large camp there, established by the Government of Upper Canada, where some immigrants stay for weeks or even months.

From Prescott you may make the trip to York either by Lake Ontario or by the Rideau Canal (completed in 1832). Many travellers prefer this second route because it is usually shorter and cheaper.

If you go by way of the St. Lawrence and Lake Ontario, once more, as in Liverpool, you should bargain with the captain of the merchant vessel for the lowest fare possible.

Conditions Change

With the building of canals on the St. Lawrence in the 1840's, it became possible to go the whole distance from Quebec to any point on the Great Lakes much more rapidly. By the 1850's a steerage passenger could travel from Quebec to Chicago for 35 shillings. By the end of the 1850's the Grand Trunk Railway was providing cheaper, quicker service than by water.

- The Atlantic crossing would change greatly for the

better when clipper ships began to provide regular passenger service. The most famous of the clippers was the *Bluenose.* Try to find out about the career of this beautiful vessel. Every Canadian has seen her picture. Where?

- When steam vessels were introduced for Atlantic travel, the conditions under which passengers travelled were made more pleasant and much safer. Find out when the Canadian Pacific and Cunard steamship lines began regular trans-Atlantic service.

- Groups of concerned people tried to bring about changes in British law to improve conditions on board sailing vessels. Why were these measures largely unsuccessful?

- "Changes in technology may accomplish for the welfare of people what governments often fail in attempting to do." Discuss this statement as it applies to nineteenth century travel.

Early Years

Study the population graphs on page 95. When were the first European settlements in your part of Canada? What common problems do *all* pioneers have to face? Would these problems differ very much from one part of the country to another? Would they differ greatly from one century to another?

Sources of Information

The best way to study about pioneer settlement is by investigating your own local area. There are many *sources* to guide you. Some of these are pictured below:

- What special information do you think you might gain from each source? Make your own additions to these sources.

The document that follows is a description of the settlement at Nanaimo, British Columbia, written by G.M. Grant, who was secretary to Sandford Fleming's expedition across Canada in 1872. It is given to illustrate how a diary can be used to gain valuable information about your local area.

> . . . we rounded into the northern horn of Nanaimo harbour, called Departure Bay, and drew alongside

the pier where a lately organized Company is shipping coal from a new seam that has been opened, three miles back from the point of shipment. . . .

At Nanaimo proper, is a population of seven or eight hundred souls, — all depending on the old or Douglas mine. The manager informed us that they would probably ship fifty thousand tons this season, . . . They could give employment to fifty or sixty additional men at once, at wages averaging from two to three dollars a day. A new seam, nine feet thick, had lately been discovered, . . . The coal was of the same excellent quality as that of the old mine, which is the best for gas or steam purposes on the Pacific coast. . . .

It is provoking to know, however, that the agricultural settlements in the neighborhood, . . . are not able to supply the present population of Nanaimo with food; and that no steps are taken to bring in new settlers, . . .

Nanaimo does not look like a coal mining place. The houses are much above the average of miners' residences in Britain or in Nova Scotia. Scattered about, often in picturesque situations, with gardens, and not in long, mean, soot-covered rows, as if laid out with the idea that men who see nothing of beauty underground cannot be expected to appreciate it above. . . .

In the evening a concert was held on behalf of the Episcopal Church of the place. . . . The hall, which holds about two hundred was well filled, and the entertainment consisted of music, vocal and instrumental, and magic lantern views. . . . The Ontario papers that reviled the constituency that returned Sir F. Hincks, should send reporters to Nanaimo; . . .[1]

- The document is packed with information. What can you learn from it (i) about the economy of British Columbia in 1872? (ii) about the economy of Nanaimo itself? (iii) about the lives of the settlers?

Your teacher will have a number of things planned to help you to study your own area. Here are other suggestions:

- Find out what sources there are in your community that you can use. Have you a local museum? What materials are there in your school? In your local library? Is there a local historical society? Are there people who know the early history of your community? Is there a re-created pioneer village you might visit?
- Find out how the land in your community was first surveyed and how it was divided into separate lots. Try to find early settlement maps showing the names of the families who settled on the different lots.
- If you live in a new development, try to trace the ownership of the land on which your house or apartment building is located.
- As a major project you might create a photographic essay of some historical landmark; make an accurate model of a pioneer house, a grist mill, or pioneer tools; tape an interview with an older inhabitant about early life in your area; write a biography of one of the leading personalities in your community in pioneer times; write a history of the oldest newspaper in your area.
- Visit the oldest cemetery in your area. Gather as much information as you can about: (i) names of earliest inhabitants, (ii) possible ethnic origins of early families, (iii) the size of pioneer families, (iv) evidence of epidemics, (v) frequency of infant and child deaths, (vi) life expectancy for men and women, (vii) religious beliefs of different families.
- What did early settlers in your area do for recreation?
- Find out where the earliest schoolhouse was built. Try to find information about what students studied.
- Find a local history of your area. Relate the history of your local area to dramatic events in the history of your province.
- Try to gather pictures showing how buildings and roads changed during the first fifty years of settlement.

Representative Immigrant Groups

- Did your area grow very rapidly? Was this growth connected with any major change in *technology* (*e.g.,* the building of a railway)?
- Compare the growth of your community with that of another close by. Which grew more rapidly? Why?
- What natural resources, other than agricultural land, drew settlers to your area? What occupations did they follow?
- How did settlers of different ethnic and/or religious backgrounds relate to one another?

In the last section we suggested that you study the early or pioneering years in your local area. In many classrooms across Canada students are working with their teachers in making similar studies. If we could bring these studies together and arrange them in chronological order, we would have a fairly clear picture of the opening up of much of Canada during the century of the Great Migration. More than that, we would have a picture of the ethnic backgrounds of the immigrants who came, of their relationships with each other and with the Native peoples. We would learn about the kinds of work they did: on the farms, in the fishing villages, in lumber camps, and in mining towns. We would also learn about the growing impact of the Industrial Revolution on different parts of Canada with the building of canals and railways, and about the beginnings of secondary industry in our growing cities.

Construction gang at No. 5 Lock, Trent Canal, Ontario, 1889

We would discover too that there is a real break in the settlement of Canada: before Confederation in 1867 most immigrants settled in eastern Canada. Only with the completion of the Canadian Pacific Railway in 1886 did mass immigration flow to the Canadian West.

It is impossible for us to consider all of the different ethnic groups who came to Canada during the Great Migration. Those who came before Confederation were varied in background, but the great majority came from the British Isles and the United States. For this reason, the three representative groups we have chosen to consider are the English, the Irish, and the black slaves from the United States.

After Confederation a much higher percentage of the groups who came to Canada were "aliens" from eastern Europe and Asia. Among them were Finns, Jews, Hungarians, and many others. As our representative groups we have chosen the Ukrainians and the Chinese.

If you trace your own ancestry to another group who came to Canada during either the early part of the century (the so-called "Third Wave") or as part of the "Fourth Wave" of immigrants after 1867, we hope you will compare your family's experiences with those of the representative groups. We also hope you will share your information with other members of your class.

The English

The following two documents are excerpts from two letters contained in a pamphlet entitled *The Advantages of Emigration to Canada.* The author of the pamphlet, William Catermole, used the information contained in the letters in a lecture tour throughout the British Isles in 1831.

Read the excerpts critically. What particular groups of English people do you think would be attracted to come to Upper Canada (Ontario) by the letters?

> . . . I am satisfied that there is no country in the world in which industry of every description, is so well and so speedily rewarded. Among the host of emigrants who came out last year, there is not one

now to be found unemployed or in an unsettled state; those who brought money with them, and many who did not, are now comfortably and prosperously settled down on farms of their own, or in some other advantageous way of business, and labourers now appear to be as scarce and as much in demand, as if no emigrants had arrived.[1]

10 Octr. 1830. Port Talbot.
My Dear father I think God I am Got on the Land of Liberty and Plenty. — I arrivd hear on 9 of July. I had not a single Shilling Left when I got hear — But I met with Good frends that took us in and I Went to Worke at 6s Pr Dea and My Bord on to this Day, and Now I am goun to Work on My One frme of 50 Eakers wich I bot at 55£ and I have 5 years to pay it in. I have bot Me a Cow and 5 pigs. — I have sowed 4-1/2 Eakers of Wheat, and I have to more to sow, meaking 6-1/2. Ham Goin to bild me a house this fall, if I Liv and will; and if I had staid at Corsley I never should had nothing. . . .

So My Dear Father I most conclud, with my Love to you all Brothers and Relations, not forgetting my Duty to my Superiors who interseed in My Coming out.[2]

- What motives might each of the writers have for stating how good life is in Upper Canada?
- What does the spelling of the second letter tell you about its author?
- Who are the "Superiors who interseed in My Coming out"?
- Relate these letters to the listing of the occupations of the passengers on ships reaching Quebec in the 1840's and 1850's (page 107).

The Promise

The population of Upper Canada was very low in 1815. Because the government wished to encourage large numbers of immigrants to come to the province, it began to offer free or very cheap land as an incentive to settlers. It also granted large tracts of land to individuals or companies, who might make a profit by servicing an area, that is, building and maintaining roads and bridges, and then subdividing the land into lots for sale to settlers.

It was necessary to let people in Great Britain know what Canada was like and what opportunities there might be for immigrants. The most usual forms of advertising, and probably the most effective, were carefully chosen extracts from the thousands of letters written by recent settlers to their relatives or parish councils back home. Some of these letters might be published by British newspapers. The land companies also employed their own agents. Mr. Catermole, for instance, worked for the Canada Company, which had a million-acre tract of land running along the southeast shore of Lake Huron.

The following extract from Mr. Catermole's lecture illustrates the kind of information he gave about life in Upper Canada on Canada Company lands:

> Persons with families, who are inclined to work, will be able to take land, and pay for it from their labour, which is usually more profitable than free grants in townships not enjoying similar advantages. In addition to these advantages, the new settler will find good society, mills, stores, and above all, the means of educating his family, and enjoying places of worship; the payment for land is rendered so easy, that emigrants with 70£ to 100£ on getting to the land, may safely buy 100 acre lots, 1/5 of which is paid down in cash, and the rest in five annual instalments.[3]

- What facts about life in Upper Canada would you question Mr. Catermole about before emigrating?

The Reality

English settlers who came to Canada during the early part of the Great Migration have left a surprising number of descriptions of their first years in our country. Through their letters, diaries, and travelogues we can learn much about the hardships and achievements of pioneer days in eastern Canada. Experiences, of course, were varied.

The following account is an excerpt from the diary of John Howison, who spent 2-1/2 years travelling in British North America and the United States. He published his *Sketches of Upper Canada* in 1821 to inform "emigrants of every class" of what to expect.

The persons who may be inclined to emigrate to Upper Canada . . . are of three different descriptions, viz. the poor peasant or day-labourer; the man of small income and increasing family; the man possessing some capital, and wishing to employ it to advantage.

Persons of the first class never would repent if they emigrated to Upper Canada, for they could hardly fail to improve their circumstances and condition. . . . the poorest individual, if he acts prudently and is industrious, and has a common share of good fortune, will be able to acquire an independence in the space of four or five years. He will then have plenty to eat and drink, a warm house to reside in, and no taxes to pay; and this state of things surely forms a delightful contrast with those hardships and privations which are at present the lot of the labouring population of Great Britain.

Mechanics cannot fail to do well in Upper Canada; for, when not employed in clearing lands, they will find it easy to gain a little money by working at their professions; . . . Weavers, being ignorant of country affairs, and unaccustomed to bodily exertion, make but indifferent settlers at first, and their trade is of no use to them whatever in the woods. Married persons are always more comfortable, and succeed sooner, in Canada, than single men; for a wife and family, so far from being a burden there, always prove sources of wealth. The wife of a new settler has many domestic duties to perform; and children, if at all grown up, are useful in various ways.

But it sometimes happens, that emigrants are too poor to purchase the provisions, stock, and farming utensils that new settlers require, when commencing their labours. Persons so situated must hire themselves out, until they gain enough to make a beginning. They will be paid for their work in money, grain, cattle, or provisions; . . . The female part of the family may engage themselves as household servants, whose wages are always paid in money, and thus add a good deal to the general stock.[4]

- What groups of workers did the author feel would succeed? Why?
- Why was a weaver's trade of no use to him?
- Mr. Howison's account also included some stories

of individual failures and personal tragedies connected with illness or accident. On the whole, however, the settlers of southern Ontario in the 1820's and 1830's had an easier time than those who had first opened up the Maritime provinces and Quebec. State three or four reasons for this.

The Irish Immigration (1846-1849)

Introduction

In the middle of the St. Lawrence River, just thirty miles east of Quebec City, there is a beautiful island that was once used as a quarantine station for immigrants coming from Europe. All ships were required to stop at Grosse Island for medical inspection, and persons with a contagious disease were taken to the hospital there.

If you visit Grosse Isle today, you will find a monument bearing this inscription:

> In this secluded spot lie the mortal remains of 5,294 persons who, flying from pestilence and famine in Ireland in the year 1847, found in America but a grave. [1]

Very few Canadians are familiar with the tragic events behind the memorial. It does not make a pleasant or romantic story. Yet it mirrors many similar events in history. Our greatest enemies throughout time have been disease and hunger. For two-thirds of mankind they are still a menace today.

How Great Was The Disaster?

Beginning in 1821 a government census was taken every ten years in Ireland. The actual population, however, was probably larger than the official statistics shown below:

Year	Population (to nearest thousand)
1781	— just under 3 million (est.)
1821	— 6 802 000
1831	— 7 767 000
1841	— 8 175 000
1851	— 6 552 000
1861	— 5 765 000

- Plot the growth in population on a line graph. If the trend of growth had continued after 1841, what would you have expected the population to be by the census of 1851? Show this by a broken line on your graph.
- Does your graph show that almost two and a half million persons — more than one-quarter of the population — must either have died or left the country between 1841 and 1851?

Study this second group of statistics: [2]

Year	Percentage of Farms	Size
1841	93%	under 30 acres
1841	45%	under 5 acres
1851	22%	under 5 acres

- Compare the size of farms in Ireland in 1841 with those in your own area in its pioneer days. How large a farm was the English day-labourer able to buy in Port Talbot in 1830? (See page 112.) Nearly half the farms in Ireland in 1845 were under five acres. What does this tell you about the standard of living of the people?
- Why was the percentage of farms of under five acres greatly reduced by 1851?

Why the Disaster Occurred

Picture, for a moment, a typical Irish wedding in the year 1845 — the groom is eighteen, the bride, seventeen. Both come from families of six children. The boy's father has given them a small part of his fifteen-acre farm to cultivate. Their cottage, a one-room house without windows, was put together in a few days. They will start housekeeping with an iron pot, a stove, perhaps a bed.

Their major crop will be potatoes, the staple or basic food in their diet and in the diet of the poultry and pigs, and of the cow they may one day have.

Because the potato requires close tending only at planting and harvest, there will be little work for the man during the long winter. The family will be warm, though, since peat cut from the bogs is cheap and close by. It will also be relatively well fed. In the quantities that potato is eaten (probably about 2.7 kgs. daily for each adult!), it contains the essentials of a good diet if combined with milk and an occasional egg or meat. Family and friends are close by. Often in the evenings there will be dancing — in a neighbour's barn in winter, at the crossroads in summer.

But the situation of this young couple, and that of eight million other peasant farmers in Ireland in 1846, was extremely dangerous, for the Irish potato was a very highly specialized crop. It had a major advantage in that the plants could be grown close together; a farm of only 1-1/2 acres, for example, could more than feed a family of six for a year. This advantage, however, could lead to disaster. Unlike wheat, the potato could not be stored from one season to the next. When it ran out, it could not be replaced by another food so cheap or so easily prepared. It was also very susceptible to blight, a disease which periodically swept through Europe and the British Isles. Potatoes infected by blight might seem normal when dug up, but within a few days they were filled with black slime and unfit as food for either people or their animals. In 1845 the blight struck, and famine descended on Ireland.

We now know that blight was caused by a fungus which could remain in the soil from one year to the next. In 1846 no one knew.

> Wild suggestions were advanced. Had the potatoes become blighted by "static electricity," generated in the atmosphere by the puffs of smoke and steam issuing from the hundreds of locomotives* that had just come into use? Or was the disease caused by "Mortiferous vapours" [deadly gas or fumes] arising from "blind Volcanoes" in the interior of the earth? . . . From County Clare came a new theory; a field was partly covered with clothes laid out to dry, and the covered portion escaped the blight — "this," reported the *Nation,* "proves that the blow came from the air."[3]

---

* *The reference is to the steam engine used in all railway locomotives. The smoke was black.*

- With reference to the black smoke of the steam locomotives mentioned above, what similar fears are expressed about jet aircraft today?
- Blight today is controlled by the use of chemicals, one more benefit we have received from technological change. Find out whether there are any dangers in their use.

The Famine and Cholera

Briefly summarized, the course of the famine was as follows: the destruction of almost the whole potato crop in 1845 meant that by March of 1846 large numbers of poorer persons — those who had worked as day-labourers or who had very small farms — were already close to starvation. When the crop of 1846 was also destroyed by blight, starvation became more general. Eye-witness accounts are horrifying. The following letter, written by a member of the Society of Friends, or Quakers, who were attempting to bring relief, describes conditions in the County of Galway:

> . . . the population were like walking skeletons, the men stamped with the livid mark of hunger, the children crying with pain, the women, in some of the cabins, too weak to stand. . . . all the sheep were gone, all the cows, all the poultry killed. . . . at Clifton I was quickly surrounded by a mob of men and women, more like famished dogs than fellow creatures, whose figures, looks and cries all showed they were suffering the ravening agony of hunger.[4]

Death by famine was followed, as it always is, by death from disease in terrible forms: dysentery, typhus, and cholera. Perhaps because they had not developed immunity by earlier exposure to the diseases, the middle and upper classes suffered an especially high death rate. Hospitals were soon hopelessly overcrowded. Many persons died at home, untended by doctors; some were deserted by their families. Terror now filled the land:

> Before the potato failure, to leave Ireland had been regarded as the most terrible of all fates, and transportation [exile to one of the colonies] was the most dreaded of sentences. But now the people, terrified

and desperate, began to leave a land which seemed accursed. In a great mass movement they made their way, by tens of thousands, out of Ireland, across the ocean, to America, or across the sea to Britain.[5]

The Atlantic Crossing

Many people managed to escape by using money sent to them by relatives living in North America. Captains accepted far larger numbers of passengers than usual, and overcrowding was general. Some owners took advantage of the emergency to gain passengers for vessels in very poor repair. The following account was written by Steven de Vere, a writer who took a steerage passage in April of 1847 to discover for himself what conditions were like:

> Before the emigrant has been a week at sea, he is an altered man. . . . Hundreds of poor people, men, women and children . . . huddled together, without light, without air, wallowing in filth. . . . sick in body, dispirited in heart . . . washing was impossible; and in many ships the filthy beds were never brought up on deck and aired. . . . Spirits were sold once or twice a week, and frightful scenes of drunkenness followed . . . the voyage took three months, . . . many of the passengers became utterly debased and corrupted.[6]

The scene described by de Vere must have been repeated many times. Of the hundred thousand who left for British North America in 1847, perhaps seventeen thousand died on the voyage across, most from typhus, the dreaded ship fever.

Landing in British North America

During the winter of 1846-47 rumours about the famine reached British North America, and a large number of immigrants was expected. What no one imagined, however, was the condition in which many vessels arrived: the first vessel reached Grosse Isle on May 17 with eighty-seven cases of fever on board. On May 21, eight more ships arrived with a total of 430 fever cases. What followed was a nightmare: seventeen more vessels arrived in the next three days; all had fever cases. On May 26, thirty vessels with ten

thousand immigrants were waiting in line to clear their passengers. By the 29th the number of ships had increased to thirty-six, with thirteen thousand passengers awaiting to land.

By July more than twenty-five hundred sick were on Grosse Isle. Several doctors who were tending them were infected with the disease and died. Few nurses could be found. Supplies were completely inadequate.

In August, Bishop Mountain, the Anglican Bishop of Montreal, visited Grosse Isle.

> He saw people who had just been brought ashore and were lying opposite the church screaming for water. . . . In another tent was a dying child . . . no relatives could be traced and several other children were unidentifiable waifs. Under a tree was the body of a boy; he had been walking with some others, had sat down for a moment and died.[7]

Before winter closed in and Grosse Isle closed down, over five thousand others had died there. Of those who continued their journey, it is estimated that another twenty thousand died within a few months in the ports of Quebec and Montreal, Kingston, or Toronto. Of the sixty thousand who remained alive, many of the strongest probably entered the United States illegally through the Great Lakes. Others returned to Great Britain, but many of the destitute spent the winter wandering in the streets of Montreal and Toronto, dependent on charity from churches and individuals.

Some citizens complained to the governments, but they had neither the money nor the organization to cope with the disaster. In addition, as colonial governments, they did not have the power to refuse admission to immigrants from Great Britain.

- Imagine you are the farmer who wrote about his first days in Upper Canada in the letter on page 112. Write a similar letter to friends in England describing your reactions to the influx of Irish to Canada in 1847.
- Twenty years after the potato famine, in 1866, Canada was threatened with invasion by hundreds

of Fenians from the United States. The Fenians were members of a secret organization which planned to take over Canada and use it as a base to overthrow English rule in Ireland. You are a Fenian. After reading further about religious conflicts in Ireland after the time of Cromwell (*c.*1650), explain to the class why you hate the English so much.

- It is easy to assign blame to the Irish landlords, to the British Government, or to the Irish peasantry itself for the disaster. You have not been given enough information in this section to debate who was at fault. What *questions* would you need to find the answers to before reaching a decision?
- You are a concerned member of parliament from London in the autumn of 1847. You are taking part in a debate on the troubles in Ireland. Plan and deliver a speech urging the Cabinet to act.

Later Immigration

If you look once more at the statistics on page 114, you will notice that the census of 1861 showed another decline in population in Ireland. Having given up hope of finding security at home, many Irish abandoned their country during the 1850's. Most of those who left Ireland came to North America to join relatives who were able to send money for their passage. One historian has described this practice as one of "building a bridge of letters" to the New World.

In North America the Irish tended to congregate in the ports of entry from the British Isles or in other cities that could be reached relatively easily by water. Part of the panic created by the threat of a Fenian invasion of Canada in 1866 was the knowledge of heavy Irish populations in Toronto (30 percent), in

Irish emigrants leaving home. The priest's blessing.

Montreal (20 percent), and in Saint John (25 percent), who, it was felt, might join in an uprising against the British Government. The fear was probably groundless, but a rift remained between the Irish and other Canadians for some time.

In 1872 an Irishman by the name of Nicholas Davin visited Canada, and in 1875 he wrote a book entitled *The Irishman in Canada.* He later moved west to Regina where he published the newspaper *The Leader.* In his book he said that the Irish were to be found in every part of society: in city politics, as policemen, clerks, firemen. In rural areas, they were settled throughout the country:

> Men have come here who were unable to spell, who never tasted meat, who never knew what it was to have a shoe on their foot in Ireland, and they tell me they are masters of 1,000 to 2,000 or 3,000 acres.[8]

Other Irish found jobs not mentioned by Mr. Davin: many young girls became domestic servants; young men found jobs in canal building, lumbering and railway construction, as well as in general construction in the rapidly growing cities of Eastern Canada.

Today the Irish are one of the largest ethnic groups within Canada's population. On St. Patrick's Day many Canadians join with them in a celebration of all that they have brought to our country.

The Fugitives

While immigrants from the British Isles were making the dangerous Atlantic crossing, another kind of immigrant was making a shorter, but no less frightening, trip to find freedom and safety in British North America. The excerpts which follow were spoken by *fugitive* (fleeing) slaves who left the United States in the years before the American Civil War (1861-1865). Slavery had been abolished in British North America (1833) and was opposed by many in the United States, where it would be officially abolished in 1865. Until the middle of the Civil War, even Americans who opposed slavery had to obey the American Fugitive Slave Law which required them to return runaway slaves to their owners in southern states or face a heavy fine and possible imprisonment.

An Underground Railway or secret network of sympathetic people in free northern states such as Ohio and Indiana gave shelter and food to fleeing slaves and directed them to the next "station" or home. They did not dare stay in the free northern states because of the Fugitive Slave Law. Hiding by day, the fugitives travelled north by night following "The Drinking Gourd" (the Great Dipper) and the North Star. The goal was Canada West (Upper Canada or Ontario).

Benjamin Drew interviewed over one hundred ex-slaves in Canada West and published his findings in Boston in 1856 in a book entitled *The Refugee; or the Narratives of Fugitive Slaves in Canada.* He estimated that there were thirty thousand Blacks in Canada West in 1852. Nearly all the adults, he said, had been fugitive slaves.

The Fugitives Speak

> I look upon slavery as I do upon a deadly poison. The slaves are not contented nor happy in their lot. . . . My feet were frostbitten on the way North, but I would rather have died on the way than to go back.[1]

> My work is as hard here as it was in slavery. The hardest thing in slavery is not the work, — it is the abuse of a man.[2]

> I want to say to the colored people in the United States: . . . if you wish to be free men, I hope you will all come to Canada. . . . There is plenty of land here, and schools to educate your children.[3]

> I heard when I was coming that Canada was a cold and dreary country; but it is as healthy a place as a man can find.[4]

> The future prospects of the colored people of Canada are very favorable.[5]

> I came in without a shilling. I now own a house and one hundred and one acres of land. I have averaged about fifteen acres of land a year that I cultivated. . . . This enabled me to support myself and family.

. . . My wife belonged to another man. I sent on and bought her for $400.[6]

I have twenty-five acres of land, bought and paid for, — about eight acres cleared. I am often hired out, and never refuse to work where I can get my pay. . . . The colored people are industrious, and if any say they are not willing to work, it is a lie, and I'll say so, and sign my name to it.[7]

I have been about among the colored people in St. Catharines considerably, and have found them industrious and frugal. No person has offered me any liquor since I have been here; I have seen no colored person use it. I have been trying to learn to read since I came here, and I know a great many fugitives who are trying to learn.[8]

There are colored people employed in this city in almost all the mechanic arts; also in grocery and provision stores, etc. Many are succeeding well, are buying houses, speculating in lands, and some are living on the interest of their money.[9]

The laws here are impartial. We have access to the public schools here, and can have our children educated with the white children. If the children grow up together, prejudice will not be formed.[10]

Many of the whites object to having their children sit in the same forms with the colored pupils; and some of the lower classes will not send their children to schools where the blacks are admitted. Under these circumstances, it is unpleasant to the colored children to attend the public schools — especially if any of the teachers happen to be victims of the very prejudice which they should induce others to overcome.[11]

There is much prejudice here against us. . . . At one time, I stopped at a hotel and was going to register my name, but was informed that the hotel was "full." At another time, I visited a town on business, and entered my name on the register, as did the other passengers who stopped there. Afterward I saw that my name had been scratched off. I went to another hotel and was politely received by the landlady: but in the public room — the bar — were two or three persons, who as I sat there, talked a great deal about "niggers," — aiming at me. But I paid no attention to it, knowing that when "whiskey is in, wit is out."[12]

In regard to riding in coaches or [railroad] cars, I never had any trouble in Canada. . . . The amount of prejudice is small here.[13]

I like the country. . . . I like the laws, which leave a man as much freedom as a man can have, — still there is prejudice here. The colored people are trying to remove this by improving and educating themselves, and by industry, to show that they are a people who have minds . . .[14]

They say, too, that the colored people steal. It may be that a few are a little light-fingered. . . . What two or three bad fellows do, prejudice lays to the whole of us.[15]

The colored people usually attend divine service: some in the same societies with the whites; others maintain separate churches. But I do not think it advisable to have separate churches. In this place the door is open into all the churches of the denominations that the colored people profess . . .[16]

The colored people have also their separate churches here. . . . I asked him why they did not attend the churches of the whites of the same denomination. His reply indicated that they thought they would not be welcomed there . . .[17]

- What kinds of prejudice did the blacks whose statements appear above encounter in Canada West?
- In what ways did they consider their lives better than under slavery?
- What human rights legislation would prevent some of the situations they described from happening today?
- What similarities or differences can you find between their experiences and other immigrant groups you have studied?

The book *Roots* and the television program of the same name have given both blacks and non-blacks in North America a new appreciation of the original African cultures from which black slaves came to the United States. It is sometimes forgotten that slavery existed in New France and British North America until it was abolished in 1833. The first record we have of a black slave in New France is dated 1629. In

1759 it is estimated that there were approximately four thousand slaves in New France of whom possibly eleven hundred were blacks. The first great influx of both free and slave blacks came with the Loyalist migration after the American Revolution.

- For what reasons did slavery not develop on a large scale in New France and later in British North America?
- Research the development of free black communities in Nova Scotia and New Brunswick after 1783.

Although government authorities welcomed black refugee slaves from the United States in the 1840's and 1850's and had brought in black refugees from Jamaica earlier, government employees did not always make it easy for blacks to immigrate to Canada. In the period from 1896 to 1907 when over one million Europeans and Americans immigrated to the Canadian west, fewer than nine hundred American blacks were admitted. Canadian law did not bar them; immigration officials who reflected public attitudes frequently discouraged them because they could not stand the cold or for "medical" reasons.

There is not a single black culture or way of life from which blacks in Canada have come. Blacks have a common ancestral home in Africa but no common language or culture. The cultures from which they come may reflect many generations of Canadian-born ancestors, or a West Indian heritage, or an American heritage. Some may be the descendants of slaves; others are not.

- Study the census graph on page 4. Why would it be difficult to establish the number of blacks in Canada and their cultural origins?
- Use the model outline on page 187 to develop your own study of West Indian immigrants to Canada since World War II.

John Ware and family, c. 1896

Black colony, Athabasca Landing, Alta.

Opening the West

"That Company of Skins and Pelts"[1]

Up to this point we have considered only the opening and settlement of eastern Canada. In 1670 the vast lands of western Canada lying east of the Rocky Mountains were granted to a company of fur traders, the Hudson Bay Company. For two hundred years, from 1670 to 1870, the company dominated the trade of this huge territory.

> Charles the Second, by the grace of God, King of England, Scotland, France and Ireland . . . greeting: . . . we . . . do give, grant and confirm, unto the said Governor and Company . . . the sole trade and commerce of all those seas, straits, bays, rivers, lakes, creeks and sounds . . . that lie within the entrance of the straits commonly called Hudson's Straits . . . we do constitute the said Governor and Company . . . the true and absolute lords and proprietors of the same territory . . . yielding and paying yearly to us . . . for the same, two elks and two black beavers . . .[2]
>
> *Excerpts from the charter granted to the Hudson Bay Company in 1670*

- What rights and powers did the Hudson Bay Company have in western Canada?
- Why would the Hudson Bay Company discourage permanent agricultural settlers in the West?

Culture Groups

The approximately 35 000 Indians who inhabited the vast western plains had developed a remarkable culture by the late 1700's. Their technology had already been transformed by 1750, although their contacts with Europeans were still relatively few. They had domesticated the horses which were the offspring of those let loose in Mexico and Texas by the Spaniards in the 1600's. With the gun supplied by traders and with the horse they had perfected, their way of life centred on the buffalo. The Cree, who had pushed westwards from their woodland homes, became the great middlemen in the fur trade. For this role they had two key advantages: the early possession of the gun, and an Algonkian language which gave them contacts with many tribes from the Maritimes to the Rockies. This network of contacts may be seen on the map on page 14.

Another culture was also developing in the West — that of the Métis. The Métis were originally the descendants of European fathers and Indian mothers. Their heritage was that of the French *coureurs de bois* and of the Indians in whose environment they lived. Some Métis were the descendants of British traders who worked for the Hudson Bay Company. Although there were Métis in the East, it was only in the West that they developed a sense of their own special identity. There were differences such as religion and language among the Métis of British and French ancestry, but there were strong bonds as well: Indian origin, the fur trade, a common western homeland.

The Métis found themselves caught up in the fierce rivalry that developed after 1784 between the North West Company operating out of Montreal and the Hudson Bay Company. Many of them worked as voyageurs for the North West Company and supplied pemmican for the traders. They were encouraged by the North West Company traders to see themselves as a new nation, neither European nor Indian. Their sense of identity was stimulated by the attempt of Lord Selkirk to start a settlement at Red River in 1811. A farming settlement was a threat to their nomadic life-style.

- Re-examine what you have learned about Lord Selkirk's attempt to start a settlement at Red River. How does his attempt help us to understand more about cultural conflicts? What role did the Hudson Bay and North West companies play in the conflict that developed between the Métis and the Scottish settlers?

"The Métis Were Red River"[3]

After the death of Lord Selkirk and the merger of the North West and Hudson Bay companies in 1821, many Métis began to settle in the Red River area. As their own communities, their own leaders, such as Cuthbert Grant, and their own institutions, such as the Roman Catholic Church, developed, their sense of identity deepened. Their way of life was only partly dependent on farming. Their main activities were still those of a partly nomadic people. They hunted, trapped, carted freight, and acted as voyageurs for the Hudson Bay Company. The annual buffalo hunts became the focal point of their culture. They borrowed what they wished from both European and Indian cultures and in the process evolved a distinct culture of their own. The two excerpts below illustrate this process:

> With the guns of the Whites, the birch bark canoe of the Woodland Indians, the pemmican of the Plains Indians, and their own unique Red River cart they were key men in developing a fur trade empire in western Canada which successfully kept the aggressive Americans out of the new lands.[4]

> Dancing was a favorite form of recreation. The Métis learned the dances of the Cree from their Indian mothers, while from the Scots and French-Canadians they learned reels, quadrilles and other European dances. They combined the various forms and created new dances and dance steps. These they danced to the music of the fiddle. . . . they learned to make their own from maple wood and birchbark.

> The favorite dance of the Métis and Scottish settlers alike was the Red River Jig.[5]

With the merger of the two rival fur trading companies, the main transportation route in and out of the west became the Hudson Bay route. This tended to isolate the Prairies from the East. British Columbia remained isolated from both.

The Far West

The visit of Captain Cook to Nootka Sound in 1778 had revealed the fur trading possibilities of the far West. It has been estimated that there were approximately fifty thousand Native people living in the coastal areas and approximately thirty thousand inland in what is now British Columbia. This was the densest concentration of Native peoples anywhere in Canada. Alexander Mackenzie, working for the North West Company, reached the Pacific coast at Bella Coola in 1793. George Vancouver mapped the coast. Spain abandoned her claim to the area shortly afterwards.

The oldest continuous European settlement in British Columbia was established in 1805 by Simon Fraser, a Nor'Wester, at Fort McLeod. David Thompson furthered the interests of the North West Company through his explorations and building of trading posts. After 1821 the Hudson Bay Company took over the fur trade of the far West, and Fort Victoria on Vancouver Island became its headquarters in the 1840's when the international boundary was established at the 49th parallel. Vancouver Island became a British colony in 1849, but in 1855 the white population was under eight hundred. Small groups of traders operated on the mainland. The discovery of gold on the Fraser River drew thousands to the area in 1858. The mainland was proclaimed a British colony later that year.

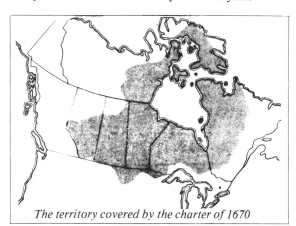

The territory covered by the charter of 1670

- A study of one of the coastal tribes of British Columbia before and after Cook's arrival in 1778 will illustrate the cultural exchange that took place when European and native cultures first met. What effects did the later gold rush have on the native cultures in the area? What role did Native peoples play in the explorations of the Mackenzie, Fraser, and Thompson rivers?

British North America in 1859

"Canada" in 1859 meant southern Ontario and Quebec. Britain's Atlantic colonies were Newfoundland, Prince Edward Island, Nova Scotia, and New Brunswick. Her Pacific colonies were British Columbia and Vancouver Island. Also British was the vast area controlled by the Hudson's Bay Company.

A traveller recalled:

> When I came to this country, in 1859, Canada was practically confined to the country watered by the great River St. Lawrence, and Lakes Ontario, Erie and Huron; and the town of Pembroke, north of the city of Ottawa, Owen Sound and Collingwood, north of Toronto . . . were regarded as the frontier towns of civilization, or, as they were called, "jumping off places." Beyond these lay the civilization of the Indian, the trapper and the buffalo, the whole . . . dominated by that company of skins and pelts — the Hudson's Bay Company.[6]

A Trip to Red River

A traveller to Red River from the British Isles in 1859 might take a ship to York Factory on Hudson Bay. From York Factory to Red River the journey might be made on a York boat. A traveller from "Canada" might find the journey a little more complicated. Here are two possibilities:

(i) From Toronto to Collingwood (154 kilometres) by railroad. From Collingwood to Fort William by lake steamer (851 kilometres). From Fort William by wagon and boat to Red River (720 kilometres). Some travellers took the lake steamer to Duluth and made their way to Red River from there.

(ii) From Chicago to St. Paul by railroad. By Red River cart or steamship to Red River.

The transportation revolution based on the railway and steamship (which was already changing the East) would soon end the isolation of the prairies and British Columbia from eastern Canada.

Confederation

Between 1867 and 1873 a number of other far-reaching changes occurred. The first of these was the union in 1867 of the colonies of Canada (Ontario and Quebec), Nova Scotia, and New Brunswick to form a new nation — the Dominion of Canada. There were a number of reasons for their union. Among these were the desire to have better trade among themselves, a common defence system, and a united stand against the possibility of American expansion.

The political leaders of the eastern provinces were particularly eager to bring the western areas — British Columbia and the Hudson Bay territory — into the new nation. Some of their reasons are given in the quotations which follow.

> If Canada acquires this territory . . . The wealth of 400,000 square miles of territory will flow through our waters and be gathered by our merchants, manufacturers and agriculturalists . . . If we allow the North West to slip from our grasp and to pass into the possession of the U.S.,. . . Our ultimate absorption would be a foregone conclusion.[7]

> Almost any week from May to October inclusive, a splendid steamboat may be seen at Fort Garry discharging her cargo of goods, and taking off packages of furs for the St. Paul, Boston, or New York market: whose boat is this? American . . .[8]

> If the United States desire to outflank us on the West [by the acquisition of Alaska], we must accept the situation, and lay our hand on British Columbia and the Pacific Ocean. This country cannot be surrounded by the United States.[9]

> Try for one moment to realize China opened to . . . commerce, the new gold fields in our territory to the extreme west . . . also within reach. . . . Try to realize . . . a main through railway from the shores of the Atlantic to the Pacific.[10]

> . . . a union of the provinces . . . will . . . bring to our shores a stream of immigration greater, and of better class, than we ever had before. . . . The larger our population, the greater will be our productions, the more valuable our exports, and the greater our ability to develop the resources of our country. . . .

Fill up our vacant lands, double our population, and we will at once be in a position to meet promptly and effectively any invader who may put his foot . . . upon our soil. . . . recognize the immediate necessity of those great [western] territories being brought within the Confederation and opened up for settlement.[11]

- What economic benefits did the people of the 1860's believe Confederation would bring?
- What evidence is there to suggest that fear of American expansion was a strong motive for union?
- Why would a transportation system based on an Atlantic to Pacific railway be essential to the success of Confederation?
- Why did George Brown believe that Confederation would encourage immigration? Why did he believe immigration was desirable?
- George Brown, in the last quotation above, refers to "vacant" lands. How might a Métis or Indian have responded to this comment?

"From Sea to Sea"

In 1869 the new Dominion of Canada purchased the huge territory held by the Hudson Bay Company for $1,500,000 and a grant to the company of one-twentieth of the land of the Northwest. Manitoba (1870), British Columbia (1871), and Prince Edward Island (1873) became part of the new nation.

Approximately ten thousand Métis and twelve hundred white newcomers lived in Red River in 1869. Two life-styles — that of the hunter and that of the farmer — were about to clash. Large numbers of farmers from the East and new roads and railways would drive away the buffalo, which was the mainstay of both the Métis and the Plains Indians. Many Roman Catholic French-speaking Métis feared that a government representing the new life-style would be forced upon them. It would be dominated by English-speaking Protestants. The words of Archdeacon Cochran in 1865 seemed to sum up the fears of both Métis and Indians: "The English are destined to spread all over North America. . . . The

white man is destined to exercise dominion, but the red man will make an excellent servant.[12] Canadian government surveyors used the square township method of dividing up lands. Although the government promised to respect Métis land claims, the Métis feared for their strip farms with their irregular boundaries along the Red and Assiniboine Rivers. Under the leadership of Louis Riel the Métis demanded and got favourable terms of entry into Canada for the province of Manitoba in 1870. Today they look with pride on their part in the formation of Manitoba.

- Research more fully the reasons for the Red River Uprising in 1869-70 and the role of Louis Riel and the Métis in the founding of Manitoba.
- What were the terms of entry for Manitoba into Canada as outlined in the Manitoba Act (1870)?
- Find out the terms of entry into Canada for British Columbia and Prince Edward Island.
- Many French Canadians hoped that the transfer of the Northwest to Canada would open up that area to them. For several decades population pressures had been driving them out of Quebec into New England and Ontario. To what extent were they able to settle in the West after 1870?

Opening the Doors

The Canadian government offered settlers free homesteads of 160 acres in the West. Surveyors began to plot the orderly settlement of the area. The Royal North West Mounted Police were formed to establish law and order. Beginning in 1871 the Canadian government made a series of eleven treaties with the Native peoples of the Northwest. The process would continue until 1921. In return for the surrender of their claim to the land, Native peoples received reservation lands and other rights as outlined in each treaty. The map on page 127 shows the areas covered by these treaties.

Homestead Requirements

(i) Any male of 18 or a widow who was head of a

family was eligible for a free grant of 160 acres.
(ii) Settlers had to live on the homestead for 6 months in each of 3 consecutive years.
(iii) Settlers had to break 10 acres each year and build a house.
(iv) Settlers had to pay an entry fee of $10.00.

In 1878 the government of Sir John A. Macdonald embarked on an ambitious plan to develop the economy of the new nation and to tie its scattered parts together. Macdonald's National Policy included protective tariffs to encourage the development of manufacturing industries in the East, the encouragement of immigration to the West to develop its agriculture, and a transcontinental railway to bind the regions together. Ports on both the Atlantic and the Pacific would stimulate trade. The completion of the Canadian Pacific Railway in 1885 seemed to make the "national dream" come true. "Thus the doors of this sealed territory were opened," said an observer who watched the first daily passenger train leave Montreal for Vancouver in 1886, "with an unbroken iron road of two thousand nine hundred and six miles stretching out before it." Canada would now become important in the "enterprise and trade of the world."[13]

- Why did the observer describe the West before the coming of the railway as a "sealed" territory?
- What facilities besides railroads were essential for large-scale wheat exports?
- Examine the causes of the Northwest Rebellion of 1885. What changes had occurred for the Métis and Indians of the West after 1870?
- In 1867 the Indians of Ontario, Quebec, Nova Scotia, and New Brunswick became the "responsibility" of the Canadian government. The Indians of British Columbia (1871) and Prince Edward Island (1873) followed. Examine the terms of the Indian Act of 1880. Why do many feel that this Act gave them an inferior status? What grievances do the Indians who signed Treaties have at the present time?

Metis hunting the buffalo

Salteaux Indians

Metis, Maple Creek

Indian camp, Dog's Head Lake

Indians hunting the buffalo

Metis traders

- The Métis were not included in the Treaties or under the Indian Act. The census of Canada in 1971 did not list them as an ethnic group although many of them do indeed feel themselves to be a distinct group: "We, as Métis people, recognize the fact that we are the product of two cultures. Therefore, we are not "White," nor are we "Indian" — we are Métis and request to be regarded as such."[14]

Examine some of the difficulties the Métis have encountered in identifying their place in Canadian society.

"How is it that things do not come together?"[15]

Most observers agreed that the West had the makings of a great wheat-growing area. The first shipment of wheat from the Winnipeg area had been made as early as 1876 by steamboat and rail to Duluth and then by lakeboat to Toronto. The first overseas shipment was made in 1884.

The completion of the Canadian Pacific Railway in 1885 and the building of feeder lines provided the transportation needed. Farm machinery such as the mechanical drill, the plough with chilled steel mouldboard, the steam thresher, and the self-binding reaper were available. New milling processes allowed the hard spring wheat to be made into a high-grade flour. Experiments were producing new strains of fast-ripening wheat which would mature during the short growing season. American experience showed that grain could be handled as though it were a liquid. It was easier to pour grain from cart to box car to ship's hold than it was to bag it and lift it by hand. Grain elevators were built at Winnipeg and the Lakehead.

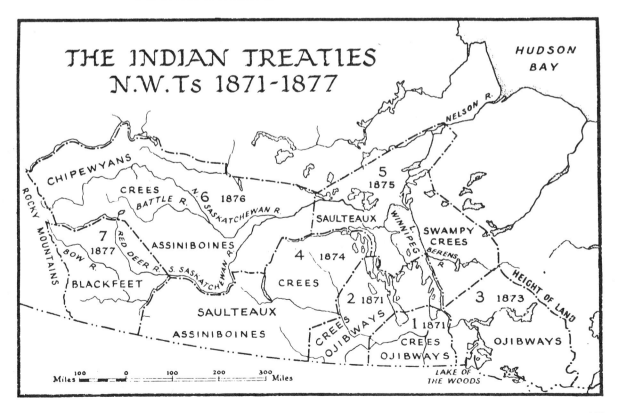

In spite of the "miles upon miles of glorious land waiting for the coming emigrant,"[16] the number of immigrants was disappointingly low as the following graph shows. A disappointed observer wondered: "How is it that things do not come together? There are thousands and tens of thousands in Great Britain crying out for land, and here is the richest land, I suppose, in the world crying out for men.[17]

IMMIGRATION 1880-1896

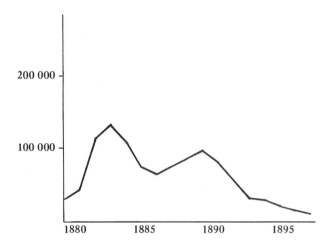

The Canadian government tried a number of advertising techniques to attract immigrants:

(i) Advertisements were placed in newspapers in Britain and other European countries such as Germany and Austria.
(ii) Lecturers gave talks and "lantern" shows about Canada.
(iii) Wheat samples were displayed at farm exhibitions.
(iv) Travellers' accounts were published.
(v) A Canadian lacrosse team played exhibition matches.

(vi) Shipping agents were paid a commission for each immigrant they booked.
(vii) Successful settlers were encouraged to write cheerful letters home to friends and relatives.

- What forces should have encouraged rapid settlement of the West after the completion of the Canadian Pacific Railway in 1885?
- Which of the advertising methods described above do you think would be most successful? Why?

Historians have identified some of the reasons for slow immigration in the early 1890's:

(i) The greater attractiveness of the United States. In 1890 it was estimated that a million ex-Canadians were living there. It was the destination of most European immigrants as well.
(ii) Brazil, Argentina, Australia, and New Zealand offered free or cheap land and help with transportation costs.
(iii) The West had a severe winter climate and a short growing season. On the average, 115 frost-free days are required to grow current strains of hard spring wheat.
(iv) Poor world economic conditions from 1891 to 1896. How would the following wheat prices affect immigration to the Canadian West?

Wheat Prices per Bushel — Fort William[18]

1880	$1.18
1885	$0.84
1890	$0.90
1895	$0.72

"It was Canada, Canada, Canada"

Immigration to Canada showed a great rise beginning in 1896. In one year alone — 1913 — more immigrants came to Canada than in the entire ten-year period from 1891 to 1900. Why did so many immigrants come to Canada in the period from 1896 to 1914? What reasons do the four lists which follow suggest?

City Populations[19]

	1871	1881	1891	1901	1911
Calgary	—	—	—	4 091	43 704
Montreal	107 225	140 747	219 616	267 730	467 986
Toronto	59 000	96 196	181 215	208 040	367 471
Vancouver	—	—	13 709	26 133	100 401
Winnipeg	241	7 985	25 639	42 340	136 035

Railway Mileage[20]

1885	10 773
1890	14 004
1895	16 091
1900	17 824
1905	20 601

Wheat Prices per Bushel — Fort William[21]

1896	$0.66
1900	$0.75
1905	$0.77
1910	$0.94

Freight Rates for Wheat per Bushel Regina to Liverpool[22]

1895	$0.27
1900	$0.27
1905	$0.20
1910	$0.21

What incentive was there for farmers who wished to start a farm on the prairies? (Page 124) Other reasons for increased immigration were:

(i) Good free land was no longer available in the United States.

(ii) Improved strains of wheat could be grown in the short growing season.

(iii) The Canadian government under its new Minister of the Interior, Sir Clifford Sifton, stepped up the campaign to attract immigrants. An English immigrant said that everyone talked about Canada. "It was Canada, Canada, Canada."

(iv) Between 1850 and 1890 many passenger ships sailing from Europe were of the "steam and sail" variety. By the 1890's steamships dominated. The journey became faster and cheaper.

(v) A tremendous rise in the output of gold encouraged new industries and provided jobs.

- What gold strike occurred in Canada in the late 1890's? How did it help to promote other jobs and industries?
- How important is wheat to the Canadian economy at the present time?

Immigrants skipping on the
S.S. Empress of Britain c. 1910

The Fourth Wave

Historians call the great immigration wave between 1896 and 1914 "The Fourth Wave." The first wave had been French, in the seventeenth century. The second wave was the Loyalist movement of the eighteenth century. The third wave was the Great Migration from the British Isles in the first half of the nineteenth century.

During the fourth wave over two million immigrants entered Canada. More than a million came from the British Isles. Between 1904 and 1914, 811 368 Americans settled in Canada. For the first time massive numbers came from central and eastern Europe. The impact of these immigrants was enormous. The populations of eastern and western cities increased greatly. The prairies were settled and two new provinces — Alberta and Saskatchewan — were formed in 1905. Population growth stimulated new industries, and a wheat boom brought increased prosperity. Established Canadians had to come to terms with a rich but bewildering variety of cultural traditions. Fierce debates raged about what a "Canadian" was and how or if the newcomers could be "Canadianized." Working and living conditions in the growing cities were studied as the problems of poverty, poor health, crime, and inadequate services were revealed.

People from over twenty-five ethnic groups came to settle in Canada during these years. Only two groups — the Ukrainians and Chinese — are discussed in the next section.

- Why would large numbers of American farmers be attracted to the Canadian West during this period?
- From 1896 to 1914 immigrants from the British Isles were the largest group. Why would this be so?
- What improvements in transportation and communication made it possible for more immigrants from eastern and southern Europe to come to Canada?
- On page 187 there is an outline which may be used by individuals or groups to study the arrival of any

immigrant group to Canada. At this stage you may want to consider an in-depth study of one of the groups that arrived in Canada in the period after 1867. The immigration list below provides a guide.

Origins	1871	1911
British—	No.	No.
English	706 369	1 823 150
Irish	846 414	1 050 384
Scotch	549 946	997 880
Other	7773	25 571
Total British	2 110 502	3 896 985
French	1 082 940	2 054 890
Austrian	—	42 535
Belgian	—	9593
Bulgarian and Rumanian	—	5875
Chinese	—	27 774
Czech (Bohemian and Moravian)	—	—
Dutch	29 662	54 986
Finnish	—	15 497
German	202 991	393 320
Greek	—	3594
Hebrew	125	75 681
Hungarian	—	11 605
Indian	23 035	105 491
Italian	1035	45 411
Japanese	—	9021
Negro	21 496	16 877
Polish	—	33 365
Russian	607	43 142
Scandinavian	1623	107 535
Sarbo-Croatian	—	—
Swiss	2962	6625
Turkish	—	3880
Ukranian — Bukovinian	—	9960
Galician	—	35 158
Ruthenian	—	29 845
Ukranian	—	—
Various	1222	20 652
Unspecified	7561	147 345
Grand Total	3 485 761	7 206 643

The Men in Sheepskin Coats

A great number of Galician agriculturalists of Ruthenian nationality desire to quit their native country, due to over-population, subdivision of land holdings, heavy taxation, and unfavourable political conditions.

The question therefore arises to find a country with ample good, free land for settlement, willing to accept thousands of farmers. . . .

The representatives of the Brazilian Government are conducting intensive propaganda with the aim of directing the flow of emigration towards Brazil, promising the immigrants, apart from a free homestead and material assistance for the beginning, free transportation from Italy to Buenos Aires and to the place of settlement as well. . . .

. . . we would prefer Canada as . . . it is a country with a stable form of government and safe living conditions.[1]

The man who wrote this letter was Dr. Josef Oleskow. It was addressed to the Canadian Department of the Interior in Ottawa. The year was 1895. Dr. Oleskow was a professor of agriculture at Lviw in Galicia.

- In 1895 in what country were the regions called Galicia, Ruthenia, and Bukovina? What other countries had borders along these regions? During and after World War I (1914-1918) Galicians, Ruthenians, and Bukovinians developed a national consciusness of themselves as Ukrainians. What is the status of the Ukraine today?
- What reasons did Dr. Oleskow give for Galician immigration to Canada in 1895?
- What was the policy of the Canadian government in regard to immigrants at this time?
- Why did Dr. Oleskow feel that Canada would be a more suitable country for Galician immigrants than Brazil? Can you suggest another reason not given in the quotation?

In 1895 Ukrainians did not have a country of their own. They identified with the region where they lived. Some of them lived in provinces of the Austro-Hungarian Empire. Others lived under the government of the Tsar of Russia. Their rulers spoke languages and followed customs that were not theirs. Many small farmers in Galicia felt crushed by the Polish landlords who were their social superiors.

Dr. Oleskow calculated that the average peasant family of five people farmed about 7-1/2 acres of land. If such a farm were subdivided between two sons, each son would have less than four acres of land. It would be almost impossible for them to raise their families on such a small amount of land. Some families were trying to farm as little as one acre. Land was very expensive. The average price per acre in Galicia was eighty dollars. How could a farmer hope to earn enough money to buy land? A labourer who worked on a large estate earned about five cents a day.

"About Free Lands"

In July 1895 Dr. Oleskow published a pamphlet about Canada called *About Free Lands*. In it he said:

> . . . in the provinces where there is free land available, the climate is very much like that of our country, only the winters are as a rule more severe. . . . There are all kinds of roads. . . . Railways are everywhere where settlements are situated. This is simply because railways are built first and people settle along the lines afterwards. . . .
>
> The whole country is divided into squares, sections of 640 acres each. A settler can obtain a quarter of such a section.[2]

For those who wished to emigrate Dr. Oleskow had this advice:

> The best time to emigrate to Canada is in the early spring, because this will enable the settler to put in some potatoes and to sow some grain on his ploughed areas. Towards the summer, only those who intend to work during harvest time to earn some

additional money to start farming should emigrate. *Nobody should venture to Canada in the late autumn or early winter,* because he will have difficulty in finding work and will have to spend his money, perhaps his last cent, to live through the winter.[3]

Dr. Oleskow recommended that no one with less than four hundred dollars should try to emigrate. Immigrants should travel in groups. He noted that the ocean voyage was about five days. Extra travelling time was needed to reach Hamburg and to travel to the interior of Canada.

A TYPICAL TOWNSHIP

A township was subdivided into 36 sections. Each section contained 640 acres. A quarter section was 160 acres.

- ■ .... quarter section
- **S** .... reserved for schools
- **HB** Hudson Bay Company Land
- **R** .... Railway Land

- Why would Canada seem attractive to the Galician peasants who read Dr. Oleskow's pamphlet?
- What part of Canada contained the "free lands" he described?
- Why did he recommend that only those with a fair amount of money try to emigrate?
- How might a peasant raise the money he needed to emigrate?
- Why were jobs hard to find in the wintertime? Is this true today?
- Why would he recommend that the Galicians travel in groups?

The Journey Begins

Dr. Oleskow visited Canada in the summer of 1895. When he returned to Galicia, he wrote a pamphlet entitled *O emigratsii (On Emigration)*. Canada became a topic of daily conversation in hundreds of peasant villages.

The journey from Galicia to the Canadian West is approximately 9500 kilometres. We shall now re-create the journey through the eyes of three families who made it in the years 1896 and 1897.

Our journey begins with the family of sixteen-year-old Ivan Nimchuk in the village of Dzhuriv. Ivan had been to school for five or six years. He had read Dr. Oleskow's pamphlet *O emigratsii* to his family. The long-awaited moment had arrived. At nine o'clock in the evening of February 1, 1897, Ivan and his family were ready to board the train. Their crying relatives crowded the platform. Ivan and his father broke away and entered the coach just as the impatient conductor called "all aboard." The relatives were pushed back. The door closed. Suddenly, Ivan realized that his mother and the baby were still outside. Her two sisters would not let his mother go. The furious conductor opened the door and hoisted them onto the train.

The train stopped at various stations to pick up more passengers. More sad farewells. More tears. For the first time in his life Ivan saw gaslights and an electric trolley car. The train continued to Krakow. At the larger stations government officials came aboard. Emigrants were fearful. The government did not want to lose a source of cheap labour. Some passengers were not allowed to continue.

The busy port city of Hamburg was noisy and frightening. The Nimchuks felt lonely and isolated amid the bustling crowds. At the shipping agent's they paid their fares and exchanged their remaining money for Canadian dollars. The passage across the Atlantic from Hamburg to Quebec and then to Edmonton by train cost seventy-two renskys (twenty-eight Canadian dollars) for each adult. "My father left the blood and sweat of his and his father's years of toil" at the shipping agent's, said Ivan. Their ship was ready to sail three days later. "We shuddered," recalled Ivan, "but what could we do — we had to keep on."[4]

- What changes and improvements in transportation made it possible for Ukrainians and other inhabitants of central Europe to emigrate?
- What did Ivan mean by "My father left the blood and sweat of his and his father's years of toil" and "what could we do — we had to keep on"?

The Ocean Voyage

In 1897 the Romanchych family set out on their voyage across the Atlantic. Dmytro Romanchych, who came with his father and sisters and settled near the Dauphin district in Manitoba, describes their voyage:

> After a short wait in Hamburg, one and a half thousand Ukrainian emigrants were loaded into a very old but not very large ship. . . . It was a boat that had steam engines as well as sails which were hoisted when a favourable wind was blowing. . . . Below water level, under the third and fourth decks, there were no cabins, only one big space with rows of iron bedsteads, three or four storeys high. In the lower beds the women and children slept. . . .

> We stopped over at Antwerp, in Belgium . . . for five days. Nobody was permitted to leave the boat. . . . it was unbearably hot. . . .

> When we left the English Channel and entered the open sea, the weather was beautiful for the first few days . . . . whole herds of dolphins accompanied our ship . . . . about half way across the Atlantic . . . a storm broke out. . . . One moment we were on top of those foaming mountains and the next we were thrown into what seemed a bottomless abyss. . . . The seamen . . . herded us all below deck and closed the hatches. . . . Garlic, onions, whiskey . . . were good remedies against seasickness. . . . terrible smells developed below deck during the storm. . . .

> . . . somehow we survived it without great losses. Only two persons died, an old man and a child. . . . the storm stopped. . . . Suddenly, during the night, a loud blast and a shock which rattled our iron bedsteads woke us up . . . . the boat was surrounded by ice. . . . The siren was blowing all the time to prevent eventual collision with some other boat, because it was foggy. . . .

> We were ordered, when the whistle blew, to run from one side of the boat to the other as fast as we could, and back again. We repeated this manoeuvre many times. The boat began to sway, broke the ice which surrounded it, and began to move forward. . . .

> . . . we finally reached Quebec and Canada. We had been at sea twenty-one days.[5]

- What similarities and differences do you see between the Romanchych's voyage in 1897 and that of Marc Lescarbot in 1607?

The Trip West

A journey of nearly 3200 kilometres by rail awaited the Ukrainian immigrants who landed at Quebec. Theodore Nimirsky was sixteen when his family left their native village on April 6, 1896. He describes the train trip west:

> . . . the CPR took us over Ontario's rocky mountains. . . . Each asking the other what was to be if there were no better soil. . . . the heart froze in not a few men . . . as the train bumped on day and night without stopping . . . because not a few think, what if they get into something like this?[6]

The Nemirskys and their party were more confident when they reached Winnipeg. They spent a few days at the Immigration House and then set out for Strathcona, the Edmonton railway station. Here they were told that their "promised lands" were about sixty miles away by wagon trail.

> We selected from among us a couple of the more knowledgeable men to go ahead, look over the lands and select the farms. A . . . land-guide . . . was assigned to us by the Land Office, and an interpreter. . . . These went together, while the rest . . . remained in the Immigration House in Strathcona. . . .
>
> Our people returned . . . having . . . selected farms. . . .
>
> All threw whatever each had into the wagon and left for the farms. . . . My farm happened to be good, but some were not so fortunate.[7]

- Why were the immigrants afraid as they crossed Ontario by train? What part of Ontario were they seeing?
- What services did the government provide for immigrants?
- What did the immigrants have to provide for themselves?

The New Home

The Nimchuks, our first family, who had begun their journey in Dzhuriv, reached the colony of Star near Edmonton in the spring of 1897. Star was a great disappointment — one lonely log building. They stayed with the Melnyk family for several weeks while they tried to get used to the new country.

> Their first two or three days brought the Nimchuks to a realization of how badly mistaken they had been in their conception of the Canadian frontier, a revelation that faced all the earlier Ukrainian immigrants. . . . They had expected villages similar to those in the Ukraine, where several families built their homesteads side by side and went out from these to cultivate the land. It was hard for them to conceive of a country, where the old-world type of village was not practical because every family had 160 acres, and therefore, lived in isolation sometimes half a mile or more from the nearest neighbour. Being a gregarious people, they found it hard to imagine one family living by itself.[8]

- What "culture shock" awaited the Nimchuks and other Ukrainian families in the Canadian West?
- Why would established Canadians seem unfriendly to them?

Typical Galician home, Alta.

The First Years

In 1898 C.W. Speers reported to the Commissioner of Immigration about the progress of Ukrainian immigrants. Here are the assets he listed for Ivan Pylypow whose family of eight came in 1894 with capital amounting to $200.[9]

Comfortable house	$100.
Stables, Outbuildings	$150.
Good granary	$ 75.
75 tons of hay	$150.
6 horses.	$300.
14 cattle	$400.
80 acres under cultivation	240.
1300 bushels of wheat in granary	——
New Binder	$150.
Mower and rake	$ 80.
Wagon	$ 50.
Discs, harrows and ploughs	——
Two good wells.	$100.
12 hogs	$ 60.
Two sheep	——

Two years later, in 1900, Speers recorded that Pylypow had buildings worth $1000 and 320 acres of land valued at $1600. He had acquired a share in a steam thresher and flour mill.[10]

- Ivan Pylypow and Vasyl Elyniak are considered to be the earliest Ukrainian pioneers in Canada. Have members of your class present the play *Westward to Canaan,* which is based on the experiences of Ivan Pylypow.[11]

"These People Are Desirable Settlers"

The following words were written by C.W. Speers in 1898:

> . . . much of the ill feeling in the district of Edmonton held by certain people with reference to the advent of the Galicians into that district is becoming slowly, but surely dissipated, and that evidence of prosperity, with the other redeeming qualities of the people, is largely changing the sentiment in that locality. And I am persuaded the day is not far distant when all will concede that these people are desirable settlers. They are all producers and in looking over the short time they have been settled, have made as much progress to do them justice as any other nationality could be expected to do.[12]

In 1901 the Commissioner of Immigration in Winnipeg reported that there were 27 036 Ukrainians in farm settlements in Manitoba and what are now the provinces of Saskatchewan and Alberta. The largest concentrations were at Dauphin, Manitoba (5000), near Edmonton, Alberta (9000) and Yorkton, Saskatchewan (4500).[13] They were mainly settled in "blocks." Speers visited Rosthern in Saskatchewan in 1903 and stated that he was "astonished at the progress of these people. . . . Their adaptibility to our customs, both in manner and dress, their anxiety to acquire the English language . . . make them most desirable settlers."[14]

- Why does Speers believe the Ukrainians are desirable settlers?

The typical Ukrainian immigrant of the day was portrayed as a hard-working farmer in a sheepskin coat. The following statements made in 1908 by J.S. Woodsworth, a Methodist Minister in Winnipeg, remind us that some Ukrainians were settling in the cities. He also gives us his picture of those who became farmers.

> Much of the rough work of nation-building in Western Canada is being done by the despised Galician. The unskilled labor for which contractors and railway builders have been loudly calling is supplied principally by the Galician. In the cities and towns, where new works are being pushed to rapid completion, or out on the farthest stretches of the prairies, where the steel is being laid for the coming settler, can be found the grimy, stolid Galician. . . . But the Galicians are not all to be found herded together in cities or working in contract gangs; an astonishingly large number have taken to the land. . . .

Ukrainian women cutting logs, Athabasca, Alta., c. 1930

As farmers they are not particularly enterprising, and yet their worst enemies must admit that since coming to Canada they have made progress, and that to a considerable degree. . . . They are purchasing modern machinery, and are gradually adopting Western methods. Those of the younger generation are adopting our customs, and are beginning to intermingle with the peoples of other nationalities.[15]

- What similarities and differences do you see in the accounts of Speers and Woodsworth? Which of the two accounts, in your opinion, is fairer? Why?
- What "Canadian" ways do both men see the Ukrainian immigrants adopting? What standards are Speers and Woodsworth applying?
- Pick out the words which illustrate the prejudice Ukrainians encountered.

"They Have Made Progress"

The early years of settlement before 1914 witnessed the rapid development of schools and churches in the Ukrainian settlements. The first Ukrainian newspaper was established in 1903. "First" homes were replaced by more substantial homes, and more land was acquired. Community organizations and groups were formed to ease the loneliness many felt in the new land and to preserve and develop traditional arts, crafts, and music. Difficulties were encountered among the immigrants and with neighbours. Painful adjustments were made. World War I, which broke out in 1914, brought this first wave of Ukrainian immigration to an end. No accurate count of the number of Ukrainians who came to Canada between 1891 and 1914 was made. Ukrainians were listed under a variety of names: Galicians, Ruthenians, Bukovinians, Poles, Russians, Austrians. The number of people of Ukrainian ancestry in Canada in 1921 was about 100 000.

- World War I brought difficulties for Ukrainians who had come from such "enemy" countries as Austria-Hungary. The Wartime Elections Act (1917) took away the right to vote from Canadian citizens born in "enemy" countries or naturalized since 1902. After considering the political situation in Europe, explain why many Ukrainians felt bitter about this. Find out what contributions Ukrainians made to Canada's war effort in World War I.

- A second wave of Ukrainian immigrants arrived in Canada in the 1920's. A third wave arrived after World War II (1939-1945). In what ways were these second and third waves different from the first? Is it difficult for Ukrainians to immigrate to Canada today?
- Draw a graph showing people of Ukrainian ancestry in Canada, using the following figures: 1901–5682; 1911–75 432; 1921–106 721; 1931–225 113; 1941–305 929; 1951–395 043; 1961–473 337; 1971–580 660.
- Why is January 22 an important date for many Ukrainians?
- Ukrainians are proud of the economic contributions they made to the development of western Canada. In agriculture they brought millions of acres into production, and they did much of the heavy construction work on such projects as the railways. Find other examples of their economic contributions in such fields as business and the professions.

- Over 130 place names of Ukrainian origin have been recorded in western Canada. Locate some of these on a large map of Canada.
- As Scots revere the poetry of Robbie Burns, so do Ukrainians admire their great poet Taras Shevchenko. Read some of his poetry.
- Pioneer women in Canada have always shouldered a heavy burden. Find out more about the work of

Plum Ridge School, first school for Ukrainians in Manitoba

The Chinese

Ukrainian pioneer women. Include in your study household articles and equipment.
- Find specific contributions that Ukrainians have made in the fields of politics and the arts.
- Find examples of Ukrainian newspapers published in Canada. Is Ukrainian taught in any of the schools in your area?
- The vast majority (over 75 percent) of Ukrainians now live in urban areas. Consult the latest statistics you can find to determine which ten cities have the largest numbers.
- Christmas and Easter are very important celebrations for many Ukrainians. Find out how they prepare for and celebrate these holy days.
- Canadians of many backgrounds appreciate Ukrainian folk dances, food, and crafts. Ask someone to your class to demonstrate the decorating of Easter eggs. Try to visit a display of wood carving, embroidery, pottery, costume, and musical instruments — or put together your own. Find recipes for foods such as borsch and pyrohy. Watch a performance by a Ukrainian choir, orchestra, or folk dance group.
- Keep a list of Ukrainian words, such as *pyrohy,* that you learn.

The following two descriptions were written within two years of each other. One was written by a white Methodist minister, the other by a Chinese scholar. Each writer is astonished by what he considers the outlandish customs and appearance of the race to which the other belongs.

These passages are taken from a study of "Chinatown" written by the Rev. J.C. Speer in 1902. The author did not intentionally reveal his attitudes toward the Chinese and, like most of us, was probably unconscious of his own prejudices.

> The average Chinaman comes to this country with no intention of remaining longer than the time when he can save a little cash, and therefore, as it is with many others when settling but for a brief period of time, the Chinese are in no way particular as to the locality or the character of the dwelling. The result is that while Chinatown is generally in the heart of the city it is the most unattractive, squalid and forlorn of all the places one can find.

> For the most part, the Chinese are transients, and such as these do not bring their families to our shores. It is always a disaster for men to congregate together, whether for a longer or shorter period without the blessed influences of a home in which there are women and children. . . .*

> Here and there in Chinatown one meets the tottering form of a woman, picking her way to the house of a neighbour. She is the victim of a custom which has been an unmitigated curse to millions of little children and women . . . that of foot-binding . . . she wears tiny shoes, most beautifully embroidered, with the sole tapering almost to a point, so that the foot rolls as on a rocker as the wearer walks. . . .

> Passing the windows one sees the cobbler at work on the paper-soled shoes, using the most primitive implements for his work. Next door will be the butcher of the town, who sells to all and sundry from the animal which has been roasted whole in his great oven. This saves the necessity of every cook in the

* Contract labourers could not bring their families to Canada with them. If they decided to remain in Canada, they could not gain admission for their wives and children since they could not become citizens.

Chinatown, Keefers Station, B.C., during construction of the C.P.R. main line, c. 1881-1885.

town cooking a small piece for each meal. Then one comes to the bric-a-brac dealer, and is bewildered by the accumulation of thread, needles, matches, punk-sticks, red paper, bird-kites, tumbling toys and fire-crackers; but time and space would fail me to write down all that John the merchant has in his little corner store for the curio hunter or for his fellow countryman.

One is puzzled at the variety of strange foreign vegetables for sale. Some of them are imported, and some are grown in our own soil — long roots like those of the golden or white pond lily, turnip-like roots, peculiarly formed cabbages, and a preparation of what is known as beancurd, which may not be toothsome [tasty] and nutritious to a Canadian. . . .

As we wander through Chinatown we come across the theatre, where the Chinaman finds much of his amusement. . . . To the ordinary listener it is one tumult of conflicting sounds. . . .

Passing an uncurtained window one sees a dozen men around a great dish of boiled rice, and with a dex-terity which is positively bewildering these clumsy men are feeding themselves with chop-sticks. It is as near to the proverbial 'supping gruel with a knitting needle' as it is possible to get.

The screech of a Chinese fiddle, or a number of them, is not just like any sound known to the ears of men. . . . But over against these we must place the sound of the bells which are touched by the soft hammer in the hands of the Confucian worshipper. Soft and liquid are these notes, like spirits lost among the discord of the drums and fiddles. . . .

The dead walls are the places for the announcements of the various society meetings, and the notices are in the form of a red strip of paper upon which stand out the curious Chinese characters. Several societies have their headquarters in every Chinatown. Before these billboards there is to be found a crowd of people reading not only the notices of meetings of secret societies, but also many other items of interest which the writers keep posted for the information of the people. They have few, if any, books and no newspapers, and they read and discuss the notices by the hour.

One cannot leave Chinatown without seeing the Joss House. Victoria, B.C., has two or three, and they stand for heathen worship transplanted to this Christian land. . . . An outer court, which has at its entrance a few smoking, ill-smelling punk-sticks; an aged caretaker who with the utmost politeness, admits his visitors, many of whom are not over-considerate of the feeling of the "heathen Chinese", into a large square room, which is shrouded in semi-darkness and filled with the vile odour of the incense which is ever burning or smouldering on the altar. . . . Depression of feeling to those who visit such places is an almost universal experience, and one there for the first time realizes the delights of worshipping in the Christian forms, where congregations gather as friends, and where to the power and sympathy of numbers are added the inspiring themes of sacred praise and sermonic instruction.[1]

The following description was written by the Chinese scholar Hwuy-Ung during a trip to Europe in 1899. You will notice that he is as startled by Western society as Dr. Speer was by Chinatown.

What a strange manner they have here of fixing their speech on paper — no pencil [brush], no ink slab, none of the variety seen in our characters. They have slit pieces of metal to hold the ink which is kept liquid in small glass vessels. Will my honoured elder brother believe me when I say that there are only twenty-six different signs! And we have twice as many thousand! These simple signs are formed into group of infinite variety, and then they correspond to ideas. But what a poor language it must be, with only twenty-six signs! . . .

The people here [do] not open their mouths; they whisper through their lips, which makes it difficult to discover variety in the sounds. . . .

There are no emphases, no tones. Just as their language has the sameness of the desert of Gobi, so is their appearance. They all look alike, though differing in height; some being very tall. My present idea of them is ugliness and stiff angular demeanor, perhaps due to ungainly garments. Their eyes have a peculiar look in them; they lie on a straight line, and are green and blue, sometimes brown. Their cheeks are white and hollow, though occasionally purple; their noses like sharp beaks, which we consider unfavourable. Some of them have thick tufts of hair, red and yellow, on their faces, making them look like monkeys. . . . Though sleepy-looking, I think they have intelligence. Their garments are tight-fitting and very uncomfortable in hot weather, as it is now. . . . Truly a wonderful people! They do everything in a manner contrary to us.

Chopsticks are unknown; instead they make use of a thin-bladed knife with rounded end and a three-pointed implement like that we use for candied fruit — but larger, which serves to hook their meat and thrust it into the mouth. In the beginning I wondered how they did not wound their lips and tongue with the sharp point. When I used this instrument I was careful not to hurt myself; now I am expert.

They have a great number of slits in their clothes leading into small bags, a most curious device for retaining objects such as coin, a cloth for the nose, a watch, papers, tobacco, pipe, matches and many other things. I counted as many as five in my jacket, four in my little undercoat and three in my trousers, making in all, twelve! . . .

The streets are to me an endless subject of admiration and amusement. The center is intended for wheeled traffic and is often crowded with vehicles drawn by horses or by machines, like the steam horse, but using oil instead of steam. . . . All vehicles moved by oil machines are supplied with noisy trumpets to warn people to keep out of the way, for they have no right on the road unless the street-surety waves his hand for them to pass. These trumpets are unluckily of many kinds; whereas they should be all the same when a person would immediately know what the noise was for, and so not be in doubt. Some sounds are like those from a horn; some make harmony so pleasing that a man may stand entranced in the roadway and be crushed, for the owners are proud of their speed.

I went a moon before with my instructor to the game they call Foo-poh. [It] is played in winter heaven for it requires top endurance and activity. Within [the arena] were three ten thousand men and women. These young, strong, quick men, what [do they] do? Men [on] one side try to kick a goose-egg pattern ball between two poles that represent a gate or entrance. They run like hares, charge each other like bulls, knock down one the other rushing in pursuit of the ball to send it through the enemy's poles. . . . Men and women mad with excitement yell and scream at the players.

The demeanor[behaviour] of many youths in this country shows want of respect for their parents and their elders. . . . I have heard youths contradict fathers and be pleased in showing them in error. I have seen girls reading foolish books while mothers are preparing food or washing clothes. . . . Fathers and mothers frequently complain — sometimes before a magistrate — and say that their children are beyond their control. . . . Our great Sage, Meng, taught that "If each man would love his parents and show due respect to his elders, the whole empire would enjoy tranquillity." And the Prince of Men had already said same before his time: *"From the loving example of one family, a whole State becomes loving, and from its courtesies, a whole State becomes courteous."* [our italics]

What is respected in this land is Power, in all forms — Money, Authority, Bodily strength, Skill, Endurance. If you[*do*] *not have one of these you* [*do*] *not find much respect or consideration.* [our italics][2]

- Make lists of the things that each of the writers finds (i) amusing or (ii) objectionable in the society that is *foreign* to him. Compare the lists.
- If the two writers had been able to talk with each other, which of their objections to the other's way of life might have been explained away? (You and another student might pretend to be Dr. Speer and the honoured scholar Hwuy-Ung. Explain to each other what accomplishments and customs of your society you are most proud of.)
- Each of the two writers was guilty of prejudice: of pre-judging a society very different from his own. Have you any prejudices? *E.g.,* do you like bagpipes? Riopelle's paintings? lobster? (If you answered "no" to any of these, have you really tried more than once or twice to enjoy them?)
- Both men are also biased in favour of their own group. This is particularly true of their tendency to give all the credit for great developments to their own society. Give examples of this from the two readings.

The Two Societies Meet

When societies that are different from each other first meet, there is often conflict. You have probably read about a number of these conflicts in Canada's history: the destruction of the Beothuk Indians of Newfoundland, for example, or the rebellion of the Métis in Manitoba. The troubles in British Columbia can partly be explained by the special conditions under which the Chinese entered Canada. The following passage illustrates the opinion of many white persons in British Columbia in 1907. The author, Mr. J.S. Woodsworth, had shown great sympathy for immigrants from eastern Europe.

> British Columbia has an immigration problem peculiarly its own and a perplexing problem it is — the Oriental question. It is difficult for the rest of Canada to really appreciate the seriousness of the problem, although it was realized to some extent when the news of the Vancouver riots of some months ago was flashed over the wires . . . . it is not to be wondered at that the people of that province, especially white labour, took alarm at the hordes pouring in by the steamer load. If this were to continue, the millions of the far East, would soon swamp the country west of the mountains.[3]

- Why did Mr. Woodsworth fear immigration from the Orient?
- What are visible minorities? Why are they often the victims of inter-group conflict?

Background in China

The civilization of China is one of the oldest on earth. By the middle of the nineteenth century, however, the Chinese government had become very weak. The country had also undergone a heavy population explosion, and poverty was widespread. Famine periodically caused many deaths and deep suffering. In the coastal cities, whole sections were controlled by European and American companies, who also controlled much of China's outside trade.

Under these circumstances it was relatively easy for agents of railroad and mining companies to enlist large numbers of labourers — or coolies — to work in North America for a period of several months for very low wages. Under this system of contract labour, thousands of Chinese had come to the United States. After their contracts had expired, many stayed on; by 1880 it was estimated that there were a hundred thousand Chinese living on the American West Coast.

In 1881 when cheap and dependable labour was needed for the building of the Canadian Pacific, the federal government permitted Chinese contract labour to be used. Some general histories of Canada contain short references to Andrew Onderdonk and his imported army of seventeen thousand Chinese coolies who blasted and dug their way through the Rocky Mountain barrier. During the building of the railway, the Chinese were almost invisible to the general population. After it was completed in 1885, it was expected that most would return to China with their earnings. Many could not. Instead they settled in Vancouver and Victoria, creating their own "Chinatowns" in the older sections of these cities.

From the beginning the Chinese were generally feared or looked upon as inferior by the white settlers in British Columbia. Many people shared the opinion of Mr. Woodsworth that the Chinese could never become part of the white, Christian society. Still others felt that the whites would themselves be swamped by hordes of immigrants from the Far East. In addition, many workers resented the competition of Chinese workers, who were often forced to accept much lower wages than others. In Victoria a Workingman's Protection Association was formed to protect white workers. In Ontario the Knights of Labour included as part of their program the exclusion of Chinese workmen from Canada.

Government Response

Canadian governments responded to the pressures put on them by many citizens. In 1886 the British Columbia legislature successfully appealed to the federal government to place a head tax of fifty dollars on all newly arrived Chinese immigrants. By 1903 it had reached five hundred dollars.

In 1923 the Chinese Immigration Act successfully cut off the legal immigration of almost all Chinese. Until its repeal in 1947, under fifty Chinese legally entered Canada. This was a tragedy for the Chinese who had entered before 1923 because they were prevented from having their families join them

After the end of World War II, government policies changed. In 1947 an act was passed giving the Chinese rights of citizenship — including the vote — for the first time. As citizens they could sponsor their wives and children, who could now come to Canada.

Finally, when the "point system" (see p. 173) was adopted in 1967, the Chinese could enter Canada on the same basis as all other nationalities. Many have entered Canada from around the world: from Viet Nam, Taiwan, North China, Singapore, the Philippines, India, the West Indies, and Hong Kong. They have come as students, businessmen and businesswomen, teachers, doctors, skilled workers.

The Chinese Community Today

With this new group of immigrants, the Chinese experience in Canada has turned full circle. In contrast to the extreme poverty of the early workers on the railway and in the mines, there are today large numbers of well-to-do Chinese in Canada, and more than a few who are very wealthy. These new groups are adding great strength to the Chinese community. At the same time, their communication with other Canadians is very open. This means two things: (i) ordinary Canadians are being helped to become more familiar with the Chinese way of life, and (ii) the Chinese community is becoming more "Canadianized."

Some examples of this process are revealed in the pictures and short pieces of information that follow.

Photo John Reeves

Simmy Lui is the managing director of the International Chinese Restaurant in Toronto. It is the largest Chinese restaurant in North America and employs one hundred people. Her father is a wealthy Hong Kong businessman.

The Flying Horse of Kansu is the work of an unknown Chinese sculptor from nearly two thousand years ago. In 1974 the Flying Horse was part of a great exhibition of Chinese art brought to North America by the Chinese government.

Sik Yee Wong and his wife Margaret. He is a calligrapher and painter recently from Hong Kong.

Photo John Reeves

Fred Kan came to Canada to study in 1959. He is a graduate from the University of Toronto in mechanical engineering. In an interview for *Toronto Life* (December 1976) he said:

> When you are a student, for the first year you want to go home. By the second year, you start to get used to Canada. After the third year, you don't want to go home at all and by the fourth year you have adopted Canadian attitudes and it is very difficult to go home. . . . By the time I graduated, I had become very Canadian.

FOR FURTHER READING

Addy, John. *The Agrarian Revolution.* London: Longmans, Green and Co. Ltd., 1964.

Batten, Jack. *Canada Moves Westward 1880/1890.* Canada's Illustrated Heritage. Toronto: McClelland and Stewart, 1977.

Brown, George, ed. *Canada and the Commonwealth.* Toronto: J.M. Dent & Sons (Canada) Ltd., 1953.

Bruce, Jean. *The Last Best West.* Toronto: Fitzhenry & Whiteside, 1976.

Burke, Marguerite V. *The Ukrainian Canadians.* Multicultural Canada Series. Toronto: Van Nostrand, 1978.

Catermole, W. *Emigration: The Advantages of Emigration to Canada.* London: Simpkin and Marshall, 1831 (Coles Canadiana Collection) (pp. 79-84).

Chamberlin, E.R. *The Awakening Giant.* London: B.T. Batsford Ltd.

Doughty, Howard. *British Roots.* Toronto: Wiley Publishers, 1978.

Fairborn, Douglas H. and Brown, Graham L. *A Nation Beckons: Canada, 1896-1914.* Canadiana Scrapbook. Toronto: Prentice-Hall, 1978.

Gilbert, J. and Read, D.P. *Pioneers: Pioneer Life in Upper Canada.* Toronto: Collier-Macmillan Canada Ltd., 1972.

Guillet, Edwin C. *Pioneer Days in Upper Canada.* Toronto: University of Toronto Press, 1963.

Hall, E., comp. *Early Canada: A collection of historical photographs by officers of the Geological Survey of Canada.* Ottawa: Queen's Printer, 1967.

Hardwick, F.C., ed. *To the Promised Land.* Canadian Culture Series. Vancouver: Tantalus Research Ltd., 1973.

Harney, Robert and Troper, Harold. *Immigrants: A Portrait of the Urban Experience, 1890-1930.* Toronto: Van Nostrand, 1975.

Howison, John. *Sketches of Upper Canada.* Edinburgh: Oliver & Boyd, 1821 (Coles Canadiana Collection) (pp. 2-12).

Lehr, John. "The Ukrainian Presence in the Prairies." *Canadian Geographic* (October/November 1978), pp. 28-33.

Marshall, Dorothy. *English People in the Eighteenth Century.* London: Longmans, Green and Co. Ltd., 1964.

McLeod, Joan, ed. *We Are Their Children: Ethnic Portraits of British Columbia.* Vancouver: Comm Cept Publishing Ltd., 1977.

Pratt, K. *Visitors to China.* Toronto: Macmillan, 1968.

Radley-Walters, Maureen and Watson, Peter. *Canada: Land of Immigrants.* Toronto: Thos. Nelson & Sons, 1973.

Richer, J.C. and Saywell, J.T. *Europe and the Modern World.* Toronto: Clarke, Irwin & Co. Ltd., 1969.

Robertson, Heather. *Salt of the Earth: The Story of the Homesteaders in Western Canada.* Toronto: James Lorimer, 1974.

Sealey, D. Bruce. *Cuthbert Grant and the Métis.* Toronto: Book Society of Canada, 1976.

Sheffe, Norman, ed. *Many Cultures, Many Heritages.* Toronto: McGraw-Hill, 1975.

Williams, David. *Early Days in Upper Canada: Experiences of Immigration and Settlement, 1790-1940.* Toronto: Gage Educational Publishing, 1972.

Immigration After World War I

Study the line graph on page 8.

- Why was there such a drop in immigration in 1915?
- Estimate the total number of people who came to Canada between 1919 and 1930.
- Why does immigration drop off so steeply after 1930?

Almost all of the nearly 1-1/2 million people who came to Canada between 1919 and 1930 were from Europe. Two out of every three were from the British Isles. Others came from many parts of Europe, including the Scandinavian countries, Russia, Finland, Poland, Hungary, and the Ukraine. After 1923, when immigration regulations against enemy aliens were changed, Germans and Austrians were also admitted.

The motives of the immigrants are not hard to discover, particularly if you compare a map of Europe in 1913 with one after the war.

Some immigrants came as political refugees: Jewish immigrants from Rumania, for example, or Ukrainian soldiers who had fought a losing battle for their country's independence. Most, however, were attempting to escape from the terrible hardships of life in postwar Europe.

Why They Chose Canada

Immigration Policies

Some people deliberately chose to come to Canada as a way of entering the United States "by the back door," since the American quota system (page 147) prevented them from entering directly from their own countries. We know, for example, that this must have been true of British immigrants. A comparison of census figures for 1921 and 1931 shows a smaller increase in the number of British Canadians than the records of immigration officials would indicate.

Immediately following the war, Canada suffered a short depression as war industries closed down and returning soldiers looked for work. By the early 1920's, however, Canada was experiencing an economic boom, for world demand for her natural resources created large export markets. Workers were needed in the industrial areas of southern Ontario and Quebec, in the mining and lumbering towns of British Columbia and northern Ontario and Quebec, on construction sites across the country, and in road and railway construction.

Not all persons who applied for admission to Canada were now permitted to enter. Before the war it had been the government's policy to encourage the immigration of farmers, farm labourers, and female domestic servants. Even during years of very heavy immigration, however, the federal government had attempted to keep out of Canada three groups of persons:

(i) the mentally, physically, or morally unfit;
(ii) those belonging to nationalities "unlikely to assimilate";
(iii) those who, because of their background or occupations, would be likely to crowd into cities.

Immigration policies were carried out through (i) acts of parliament; (ii) orders-in-council; and (iii) treaties with foreign powers. Each of these needs further explanation:

(i) The Immigration Act of 1906 *consolidated* (brought together) a number of earlier regulations, and many of its clauses remained unchanged until the 1960's. It was also an *enabling* act. This simply means that the government or cabinet was permitted to make any regulations its members thought necessary to carry out the "intent of the act."

(ii) These regulations agreed to by cabinet are called orders-in-council. They have the full force of law. When they are recorded, they are numbered beside the letters P.C., the abbreviation for Privy Council (or cabinet).

In 1923 three very important orders-in-council were introduced:

P.C. 182 restricted the admission of Asiatic immigrants to farmers, farm workers, female domestic workers, and a wife or child under 18 of a person legally resident in Canada.

P.C. 183 restricted immigration of other groups to the same classes as above, excepting citizens of the United States, Great Britain, Newfoundland, New Zealand, Australia, and the Union of South Africa.

The Tipple crew, Coal Creek, B.C., 1913

P.C. 185 introduced a formal passport requirement. Passports were granted only to persons recommended by a Canadian immigration officer in Europe, or a British diplomatic officer in other parts of the world.

(iii) In 1923 Japanese immigration was limited to 150 persons yearly by a treaty or "gentlemen's agreement" between the Canadian and Japanese governments.

- What are the advantages of enabling acts as opposed to other laws? What are their disadvantages? dangers?
- What groups of people would be prevented from entry into Canada by P.C. 183? by P.C. 185?
- Which of the three orders-in-council would you have supported? Which would you have opposed? Defend your position on each.

- The American quota system limited the immigrants from any country to 2 percent of the number of persons of that nationality living in the United States in 1890. What was the purpose of the quota system? Should Canada have introduced a similar system after World War II? Why or why not?
- Obviously P.C. 183 did not prevent many European immigrants from working in the mines or forest industries or from finding jobs in the industrial cities. Why was the order-in-council ineffective?

Speaking in support of the government's immigration policies, the Hon. R.B. Bennett, later prime minister of Canada, made the following statement in the House of Commons in June, 1928.

Read the history of the United States, read what is written in every magazine in that country by thoughtful men, and you will find that the principle of the melting pot has failed; and they are quite apprehensive. Every thoughtful man in the United States, every keen observer, every man who travels, every author, everyone who shapes and moulds public opinion in the universities and in the great foundations — all these are bewailing the fact that uncontrolled immigration has been permitted into that country, to such an extent that there is now in the United States a polyglot population, without any distinctive civilization, and one about which many of them are in great despair. . . . it is because we desire to profit by the very lessons we learned there that we are endeavouring to maintain our civilization at that high standard which has made the British civilization the test by which all other civilized nations in modern times are measured. . . .

These people [continental Europeans] have made excellent settlers; they have kept the law; they have prospered and they are proud of Canada, but it cannot be that we must draw upon them to shape our civilization. We must still maintain that measure of British civilization which will enable us to assimilate these people to British institutions, rather than assimilate our civilization to theirs. That is the point; that is all that may be said with respect to it, and it is the point I desire to make at this time. . . . That is what we desire, rather than by the introduction of vast and overwhelming numbers of people from other countries to assimilate the British immigrants and the few Canadians who are left to some other civilization.[1]

- What institutions was Mr. Bennett referring to?
- Attack or defend Mr. Bennett's statements.

Governments in Canada do not often act against public opinion. There is evidence that in the 1920's most Canadians supported the government's immigration policies.

A fourteen-year-old coalminer, Manitoba, 1912

Immediately following World War I, as we mentioned, there was a brief depression period. Antagonisms between groups quickly came to the surface. This occurred during the Winnipeg General Strike in 1919. Winnipeg's population had grown from 8000 in 1881 to 136 000 in 1911. There were a large number of new Canadian workers, including many — the Ukrainians, for example — from eastern Europe. Their wages were very low, hours long, housing poor. In 1919 unemployment was high, particularly among returned soldiers.

The strike started among skilled workers in one or two industries, then quickly spread to include most of the city's workers, among them transportation and delivery workers and firemen. A citizens' committee, made up of people not involved in the strike, was organized to carry out essential services. Soon the rumours spread that the "foreigners" were supporters of the Russian government and were plotting revolution in Canada. In early June the *Manitoba Free Press* carried the following warning:

> There are some 27,000 registered alien enemies in Winnipeg district. . . .
> The alien has had four years of safe work at high wages while Canadian boys were fighting in France and Flanders.
> The soldiers are now home; the vacant jobs are theirs by right; and they must get them.
> Choose between the
Soldiers who protected you
and the
Aliens who threaten you!
— Citizens' Committee of One Thousand[2]

For six weeks the situation in Winnipeg was very dangerous. At one point a workers' parade turned into a riot when a group of strikers clashed with the Mounted Police. Long after the strike was over, bitterness remained.

- Look again at P.C. 183. Establish one reason for the regulation.

In other, less dramatic, ways the eastern European immigrant was made to feel an outsider. In his book, *Under the Ribs of Death,* John Marilyn records the feelings of a young Hungarian-Canadian boy living with his family in Winnipeg's North End. In the following scene Sandor tries to explain to his father why he has been involved in a fight:

> "Everywhere I go," he cried, "people laugh when they hear me say our name. They say 'how do you spell it?' The lady in the library made fun of me in fronta all the people yesterday when I took your book back and she hadda make out a new card. And the school nurse . . . everybody . . . even the postman laughs. If we changed our name I wouldn't hafta fight no more, Pa. We'd be like other people, like everybody else. But we gotta change it soon before too many people find out."
>
> "So?" his father laughed, "and who are all these people?" . . . "The English," he whispered. "Pa, the only people who count are the English. Their fathers got all the best jobs. They're the only ones nobody ever calls foreigners. Nobody ever makes fun of their names or calls them 'bologny-eaters', or laughs at the way they dress or talk. Nobody," he concluded bitterly, " 'cause when you're English it's the same as bein' Canadian."[3]

Sandor's dream was to cease to be foreign by becoming what he believed a successful Canadian to be. He therefore deliberately tried to assimilate into Anglo-Saxon culture. This dream has been common among the sons and daughters of immigrants. Their children — third-generation Canadians — often want to re-establish ties with their ethnic group and help to preserve its culture. In a later chapter we shall learn how our governments today are assisting in this.

- Many immigrants changed their names in the past because it was "practical" to do so. Why was it "practical"? Should this be necessary today? Why or why not?

The Hutterites

One group of people who came to Canada after World War I refused assimilation. These were the Hutterites, who have created a way of life very different from that of most Canadians. As you read the information in this chapter, you will discover what basic beliefs and values have led the Hutterites to separate themselves from the rest of our society.

A Typical Colony

Today over fifteen thousand Hutterites live in just over two hundred communities scattered throughout western Canada. The diagram below shows a typical Hutterite colony or *Bruderhof*. It is located in the centre of a large farming area of from six thousand to nine thousand acres. It contains anywhere from fifty to 150 persons, or eight to twenty-five families.

Almost every building in the diagram tells you something about Hutterite life. As you study the diagram, work out your own hypothesis about what the daily lives of the people in the community might be like.

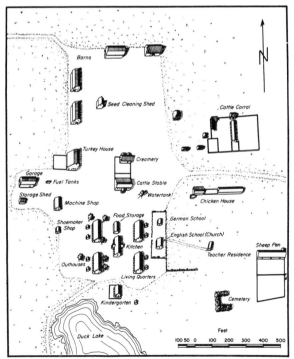

- Why are there only four buildings used as living quarters? Why is the kitchen in a separate building?
- Does each family have its own separate fields? its own separate barns?
- What different sources of income does the community have?
- Why do you think there are two schools? Why does the teacher of the English school have a separate residence?

To find out how accurate your hypothesis was, read the following description by an outside observer of the start of a typical day in a Hutterite community:

> On a summer morning the colony bell wakes everyone at 6:15 A.M. "Like everyone else," says a Hutterite girl, "I roll out of bed and get dressed, then go down on my knees to thank the good Lord for protection and to get a blessing for the day.
>
> The bell calls the adults to the communal kitchen for a breakfast of prunes, cheese, smoked ham, bread, jam and coffee. Quickly and in order the men file in, hang their hats on a rack extended from the ceiling, and take their assigned places on benches around a long table. All are dressed in black work trousers and colored shirts, and all of the mature men are bearded. Uniformly garbed women with identical hair styles enter next, wearing polka-dotted head scarfs, long, patterned aprons and dresses. They sit at a second long table separate from the men. The last are scarcely seated when a man gives the audible signal to pray. Instantly everyone raises folded hands and a man mutters a short prayer. . . . No children or babies are present; they have been left in the apartments and will eat separately. The highest official of the colony, the preacher and his assistant, eat in the preacher's apartment, where food has been brought to them from the central kitchen.
>
> Silence prevails during mealtime. Everyone eats quickly, and breakfast is dismissed with another prayer. Each person carries his own dishes to the kitchen. Women quickly finish clearing the tables and begin washing the dishes. In seven minutes the job is completed.
>
> The bell rings again, this time signaling the children from ages six to fourteen to their dining room. Those

from two and one-half to five years go to the kindergarten for their breakfast and will remain there for most of the day. The men gather in the shop, where every day begins with each person receiving an assigned responsibility.[1]

- How important does religion seem to be to the people of the community?
- In what ways are the Hutterites similar to the early Puritans in Britain? How are they different?
- What information does the description give you about the organization of a Hutterite community? Why, for instance, is there a bell?
- Who has authority in the community? What seems to be the role of women? Of children?

A Community of Sharing

The Hutterites are attempting to live their lives in imitation of those of very early Christians. Believing that they must "hold [own] everything in common," individual members refuse to claim any possessions as their own. Instead, each family receives a share of the total income "according to its needs." Food is shared by having members of the community eat together. Clothing, similarly, is distributed to each family by the tailor, who keeps a record of the materials given to each family. Before the colony buys its material, the tailor will agree to price and quality. The householder (or colony accountant) must agree to the cost, and the preacher to the colours chosen.

Each family is assigned sleeping rooms or apartments according to its size. A family is also given a storage box for its share of fruit and beer. Wine is made by the colony from grapes and rhubarb, and each adult is given a ration.

Education

Did you notice the two schools in the diagram of the Hutterite community? All children of school age attend the English school for the number of years required by their provincial governments. The Hutterites provide the building and, if the community

Hutterites strongly oppose the spending of money on luxuries.

is isolated, a house for the teacher. English school is considered important since there the children learn their second language and also mathematics and science. The teacher, who does not belong to the community, teaches the regular provincial curriculum, but is also subject to certain community regulations: radios, television, and phonographs are forbidden; the walls must be left bare each evening, since the school is also the Hutterite church; the blackboard must be erased; and any pictures must be taken down.

Hutterite children also attend their own German school for a year before starting English school, and later for an hour and a half each day before and after English school and throughout the day during summer vacation. Here their teacher is a highly respected male leader of their own community. They study the German language, which has always been the first language among the Hutterites, who are descended from a number of different nationalities in Europe. They learn Hutterite history and memorize parts of the New Testament. They are also taught to be obedient to the rules of their community and to work together as a group.

- Why do you think the Hutterites forbid the use of radios and television in the English schools?
- Hutterites do not generally continue in school after the compulsory eight or ten years. Very few attend college or universities. Why do you think this is so?
- What other ethnic or religious groups have special classes for their members after regular school hours?

Relations with Governments

The Hutterites originated during the sixteenth century in what is today Czechoslovakia. Because their beliefs and way of life seemed strange and dangerous to outsiders, they were forced to emigrate from country after country in Europe to escape persecution from governments and neighbours. One of their leaders, Jacob Hutter, was burned at the stake in 1536. Many others died with him. The story is told that as they went to the stake, they encouraged each other by singing hymns loudly enough for all to hear. Today the Hutterites preserve in their strong, harsh music the memory of that time.

One hundred years ago, after three centuries of persecution and war, only eight hundred Hutterites survived. In the 1870's the entire group applied to come to the United States and were admitted. When the United States entered World War I, a number of Hutterite men were put in prison for refusing to join the army. Since the Canadian government had earlier promised the Hutterites exemption from military service if they came to Canada, representatives from several communities immigrated to Canada in 1919 to establish new colonies. Canadian public opinion, however, was strongly against a people who not only spoke German as their first language, but who also refused to participate in the war. Reacting to this pressure, the federal government denied entry to Canada to other Hutterite groups. Until the regulation was withdrawn in 1921, those Hutterites who had remained behind to close down their colonies in the United States could not enter Canada.

Because of the fear of Alberta farmers that the Hutterites would buy up the best land in the province, in 1947 the legislature passed a bill limiting the total land held by the Hutterites to that owned in 1944. The Hutterites were therefore forced to buy land for new colonies in Saskatchewan or in the United States. In the early 1970's this law was changed to comply with the Alberta Bill of Rights. Hutterites can now apply to a government board for permission to buy new sections of land within Alberta, provided that colonies are at least twenty-four kilometres distant from each other.

In Manitoba the Hutterites have made private agreements with a number of municipal governments. They have agreed to limit the number and size of their colonies in any area and to space them at least 16 kilometres apart.

- Did you notice that all *three* levels of government have negotiated with the Hutterites? Why are all *three* concerned?

Relationships with Neighbours

Because the Hutterites suffered persecution from their neighbours in Europe, most of the colonies today still deliberately cut themselves off from close contact with outsiders. One of the leaders of a colony in the United States gives this explanation:

A good neighbour is one we never see, talk with, or help back and forth, or that never comes to the place. . . . We don't mind favouring them [neighbours] with help, but then they want to favour our boys by taking them into their homes, letting them listen to the radio, television, taking them to shows, and then our colony rules are broken. When we tell our neighbours not to do this, they just get mad, and then there is friction.[2]

Another source of tension between the Hutterites and their neighbours arises from the growth in the Hutterite population, which has doubled in the last sixteen years. Since each community cannot easily support more than one hundred persons, money is carefully put aside to buy land and machinery for new colonies. In Canada six to eight of these new colonies are established each year. The Hutterites have been accused of buying up some of the best land on the prairies. From time to time, groups of farmers have petitioned the government to act.

Because they do not value material things, the Hutterites buy only essentials from the merchants of the nearest town. It is therefore claimed that they are not good customers. Since their children help with farm work from a very early age, they do not have to pay high sums for their hired labour. They can, it is claimed, afford to undersell their neighbours and bring down the price of farm products in an entire district.

- If you were a Hutterite, what answer might you make to each of these charges?

Are Hutterites Good Citizens?

Those who do not feel that the Hutterites are acceptable members of the larger Canadian community emphasize that they do not perform the duties we associate with good citizenship: their religion forbids them from fighting in any war, no matter how just; they seldom vote, and do not hold public office; they appear to be uninterested in all public issues, national or local.

Those who feel that the Hutterites make a worthwhile contribution to Canadian society emphasize that they are excellent farmers. They also pay all taxes required of them, including income and public school taxes. Most do not accept family allowances from the government. Hutterites do not claim unemployment payments or other forms of welfare. They look after their members when they are sick or grow old. Although they do not accept the values of most Canadians, they have obeyed provincial education regulations. Also, although they believe that a child reaches adulthood at fourteen, they permit their children to remain in school as long as the provincial law requires.

- The future of the Hutterites is uncertain. What problems do you think the future holds for them?
- The only private possession each Hutterite is permitted is a small chest for gifts and letters. Each member of the community also receives a very small allowance. What functions do you think the chest and allowance serve?
- What part of Hutterite life would you find it most difficult to adapt to? What parts do you find most attractive?
- Not many young people break away from the Hutterite communities. Can you suggest why this is so?
- What basic values have led the Hutterites to separate themselves from the rest of society?
- How are these values related to their religious beliefs?
- Debate the resolution: "Hutterites are valuable members of Canadian society."

Japanese Canadians

After the Japanese attack on Pearl Harbor (Dec. 7, 1941) and Japan's formal entry into World War II, the Canadian government found itself facing the problem of what to do with its Japanese-Canadians.

The question needed careful thought because many Japanese-Canadians had been settled along the Pacific Coast for many years and had brought up their children as Canadians.

The final decision was to move all these Japanese-Canadians away from the coast to inland centres. At the same time, new regulations restricted their movements and activities.

The government did this for two reasons: (1) to prevent spying, which could lead to a possible Japanese attack on the B.C. coast, and (2) to prevent Japanese-Canadians from being harmed in possible anti-Japanese riots and demonstrations.

Many people said that the Canadian Government treated the Japanese-Canadians very unfairly. Yet, at the time the government felt strongly that it was doing the proper thing.

We shall look at some of the events leading up to this action by the government. It will be your job to decide whether the government was right or wrong to do what it did.

Japanese Immigration

Japanese immigration to Canada has always been small. They have settled mostly in British Columbia — because it is near, and in some ways similar to, Japan.

The first Japanese settlers were brought to Canada in the 1870s to work on the railroad. They hoped to make their fortune here and then quickly return to their homeland as wealthy men. As a result, most of them made little effort to learn the language or to become part of the community. Many of their Canadian neighbours disliked them for this.

By 1900 there were 5000 Japanese working mainly in railway building, fishing, and mining. British Columbians were disturbed by the swift increase in the Asiatic population and a protest riot occurred in Vancouver in 1907. The government responded by restricting the number of Japanese immigrants to 400 yearly.

Even so, by 1921 the Japanese numbered nearly 16 000 and possessed almost half of the fishing licenses in British Columbia. Again, under pressure, laws were passed to limit Japanese licenses and to limit Japanese employment in railroading and lumbering. Nor had the Japanese ever been allowed to vote in either federal or provincial elections.

In 1941, some 23 000 Japanese were living in Canada — all but 1000 in British Columbia. Two-thirds of them had been born in Canada; another 3000 had been accepted as Canadian citizens. Many worked small farms or set up their own businesses or service industries where restrictions were less severe. They continued to live close together and provided special schools so that their children could learn Japanese.

Pearl Harbor

On December 7, 1941, the Japanese forces launched a surprise attack on Pearl Harbor, dealing a crippling blow to the American Pacific Fleet. The Allies were stunned by the seeming treachery of the Japanese tactics, but were relieved that the U.S. was finally in the war.

Prime Minister Mackenzie King had long been suspicious of Japan's ambitions in the far East and the Pacific. Canada and Britain had been trying to avoid going to war with Japan without the U.S. on their side. While King may have been shocked by the suddenness of Pearl Harbor, he was certainly not surprised that it had happened.

In a meeting the day following the attack, he expressed concern that anti-Japanese demonstrations in B.C. might place the Japanese-Canadians in danger, and said that he had confidence in their loyalty. This statement was surprising considering that less than a year before he had called for the registration of "all persons of the Japanese race in Canada" over the age of sixteen.

After Pearl Harbor, the Americans quickly declared their West Coast states strategic areas and restricted their 110 000 Japanese to special camps for the next four years.

In early 1942, Canadian public opinion against Japanese-Canadians grew when reports of Japanese treatment of Canadian prisoners came from Hong Kong. At this point, the Canadian government made the decision to place special restrictions on the Japanese.

The Restrictions

The government took all Japanese-owned fishing boats, radios, and cameras into custody. They arrested a small group of "dangerous individuals," and closed the language schools.

These measures weren't extreme enough for many British Columbians. Public pressure soon forced the government to move all Japanese from a 100-mile-wide security strip along the B.C. coast. A further statement declared that all persons of Japanese origin, Canadian citizens or not, were to be considered aliens until the war ended.

The British Columbia Security Commission was created in the early months of 1942 to look after the details of relocating the Japanese.

In the first year, the 21 000 Japanese who were affected were registered by the RCMP and passed through various Security Commission centres. Over 2000 of the stronger men were sent to work on road construction in northern B.C. and Ontario. Some 3600 went to work in the sugar beet fields of Alberta and Manitoba. Another 3000 found jobs in communities "east of the Rockies,"

The federal government guaranteed that Japanese sent to other provinces would remain in agriculture, and would be removed after the war at the province's request. The government also said that their education and support would be paid for with federal funds.

The remaining 12 000 Japanese were taken to Interior Housing Centres in the centre of British Columbia. These consisted of four abandoned mining towns and two completely new communities. The Japanese were hired to help build the new units and remodel the old. They were paid from 22-1/2c to 40c per hour.

The government furnished utilities, and built and equipped schools and hospitals. The Japanese were given money to buy their own food.

Even before Japan officially became the enemy, Japanese-Canadians were no longer allowed to serve in the Canadian forces. The government also stopped any Japanese from buying or leasing property without a permit.

It should be pointed out that the crime rate in these new communities was extremely low. Also, the Government noted that "no Japanese in Canada has been suspected of, or linked to, an act of sabotage or espionage."

Security

Security arrangements for the centres were handled by the RCMP. The settlements were placed in isolated valleys with only a few roads connecting them to the outside. The Mounties set up checkpoints on these roads to control traffic into and out of the settlements. They also paid Japanese veterans of the first World War to watch over the settlements and report anything out of the ordinary.

Japanese were required to get travel permits from the RCMP if they were going on a journey of more than 50 miles or longer than 30 days, if moving, or if crossing a provincial boundary.

The legislation that set up the Security Commission also gave control of the property of Japanese-Canadians to the Custodian of Alien Property. Later, this power was widened to permit the sale or disposal of the property.

The Japanese had no say in the sale of their homes, farms, businesses or any other article that the Custodian wanted to dispose of. They often felt that the price they received was lower than it should have been.

Royal Commission

In 1943, complaints about low sale prices of property, living conditions in the housing centres, restricted job opportunities, and other matters were referred to a Royal Commission.

The Commission found unanimously "that the provisions made by the Government of Canada . . . for the Welfare of the Japanese . . . are, as a wartime measure, reasonably fair and adequate." The Spanish Consul, acting for the Japanese, and the International Red Cross both inspected the camps and found the settlements entirely satisfactory.

Considering the pressure put on Prime Minister Mackenzie King's wartime government, some observers find it surprising that much harsher measures weren't used. In fact, other allied countries placed severe limits on groups of people who had come from "enemy" countries. In 1940, the British had rounded up many German, Austrian and Italian citizens in Britain and put them briefly in a camp on the Isle of Man.

Nevertheless, other observers feel that the government showed racial prejudice when it ordered the registration of these people even though Canada was not yet at war with Japan. By contrast, they say, the government did not demand registration for people of German, Austrian, or Italian ancestry even during wartime. Also, they point out, these "white" groups were not subjected to the sort of restrictions the Japanese had to face.[1]

- Attack or defend the Canadian federal government's treatment of Japanese-Canadians during World War II. Give reasons for your position.

FOR FURTHER READING

Elliott, Jean Leonard, ed. *Immigrant Groups.* Toronto: Prentice-Hall, 1971.

Flint, David. *The Hutterites: A Study in Prejudice.* Toronto: Oxford, 1975.

Ito, Roy. *The Japanese Canadians.* Multicultural Canada Series. Toronto: Van Nostrand, 1978.

Patton, Janice. *The Exodus of the Japanese.* Toronto: McClelland é Stewart, 1973.

Schaffe, Norman, gen. ed. *Many Cultures, Many Heritages.* Toronto: MacGraw-Hill Ryerson, 1975.

Starbird, Ethel. "The People Who Made Saskatchewan." *The National Geographic,* Vol. 155, No. 5, May 1979.

Troper, Harold and Palmer, Lee. *Issues in Cultural Diversity.* Toronto: Ontario Institute for Studies in Education, 1976.

Immigration after World War II

From 1946 to 1970 approximately 3 500 000 immigrants came to Canada. This great postwar wave of immigrants is shown in the graph on page 8.

- Why did the number of immigrants coming to Canada go down sharply in 1931?
- Why did the Canadian government restrict the number of immigrants between 1931 and 1945?
- How many members of your class are from families who came to Canada in this post-World War II wave?

The information below shows the origin of the twelve largest groups of immigrants who came to Canada between 1946 and 1970.

ORIGIN OF CANADIAN IMMIGRANTS, 1946-1970[1]	
Britain	923 930
Italy	448 104
The United States	311 911
Germany (Federal Republic)	308 297
The Netherlands	172 942
Poland	105 050
Greece	101 219
France	101 020
Portugal	80 249
West Indies	68 912
China	68 796
Austria	65 464

- The table above shows that immigrants from the British Isles still form the largest group of immigrants. Why would you expect this?

Where Did They Settle?

About one-half of the immigrants who have come to Canada since 1946 (about 1 800 000 people) settled in the province of Ontario. About one-fifth (about 700 000) settled in the province of Quebec. In 1975 immigrants to Canada listed their intended destinations as follows:

IMMIGRANTS TO CANADA, 1975 Intended Destinations[2]	
Ontario	98 471
British Columbia	29 272
Quebec	28 042
Alberta	16 277
Manitoba	7 134
Saskatchewan	2 837
Nova Scotia	2 124
New Brunswick	2 093
Newfoundland	1 106
Yukon and Northwest Territories	290
Prince Edward Island	235
Total	187 881
	Information Canada

- Why is Ontario the single most popular destination of immigrants?
- Why do the Atlantic provinces attract very few immigrants?

Toronto: The Magnet

More than half of the immigrants who have come to the province of Ontario (about 900 000 people) have settled in Metropolitan Toronto. In 1971 approximately one in every three residents of Toronto was born outside Canada. The graph below gives a breakdown of Toronto's population in 1971, showing the four largest ethnic groups. It also gives similar information for Montreal and Vancouver — Canada's two other largest cities.

CANADA'S THREE LARGEST CITIES:
Largest Ethnic Groups 1971

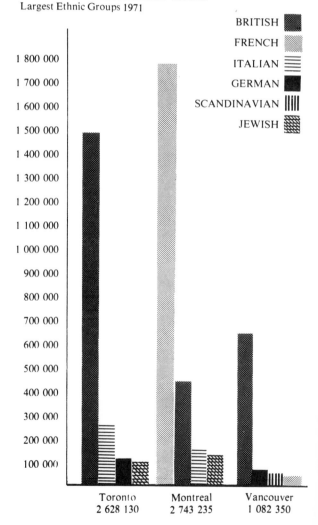

BRITISH	■
FRENCH	▦
ITALIAN	≣
GERMAN	■
SCANDINAVIAN	⦀
JEWISH	▨

Toronto 2 628 130   Montreal 2 743 235   Vancouver 1 082 350

Why Did They Come?

- Is Bill 101 (p. 52) likely to have an effect on the number of immigrants settling in Montreal and the province of Quebec?

Toronto has become the fastest growing city in North America. In the ten years from 1961 to 1971 Canada's overall growth was 18 percent. Metropolitan Toronto's overall growth was 44 percent.

THE AVERAGE METRO TORONTO AREA FAMILY...

SIZE OF FAMILY - 3.4

INCOME OF FAMILY - $12,933.00

ETHNIC ORIGIN OF FAMILY - 56.9% BRITISH ... GAD SUH!

PAY OFFICE

- How does the cartoon above show that Toronto's growth is due to immigration rather than natural population increase?
- How has the ethnic composition of Toronto's residents changed as a result?
- Why are Canadians as well as immigrants drawn to the city of Toronto?

Each immigrant had his own reasons for wanting to settle in Canada. The case studies that follow will suggest some reasons for the immigration of Americans, Italians, Germans, and Dutch.

Covered wagons from the United States in southern Alberta, c. 1893

Case Study no. 1: The Americans

Canada shares a long boundary line with the United States. During the past two hundred years this boundary line has been crossed millions of times by Canadians immigrating to the United States and by Americans immigrating to Canada.

The number of Canadians who have gone to the United States will never be known. In the early days no one thought to count people who were *leaving*. Thousands of French Canadians left for the New England states. During the peak years of immigration to Canada before 1914, it is estimated that forty to fifty thousand Canadians a year left for the United States. Similar movements occurred after World War I and World War II. Many immigrants have entered Canada only as a "stop over" on their way to the United States. The "brain drain" to the United States has caused concern for many years.

The movement north to Canada began with the Loyalists. Later the "post Loyalists" arrived. Fugitive slaves are another example of those who left the United States to settle in Canada. Thousands of American farmers, some of them former Canadians, came north during the great wave of immigration before 1914. The table on page 157 reminds us that many Americans have immigrated to Canada since 1945.

An American Family in Toronto

The Hill family lived in Detroit until 1969.

Mrs. Hill
I wouldn't consider going out at night in Detroit — there are over 700 murders a year. . . . Even in the daytime I kept my money in my pockets, so if anybody snatched my purse all he'd get was dirty handkerchiefs! After our son Lincoln was born, seven years ago, and I had to go outside a lot, I'd always be sure to get home before it got dark.

Mr. Hill
The riots of '67 took place right on our street. There was a tank in our front yard part of the time and I tell you I was happy to see it there. . . . You couldn't show yourself at the windows during the worst of it, so we crawled on the floor. . . .

It wasn't a good place to live, but we couldn't afford to move out. We had a baby, I was going to law school at night . . . and working at an advertising agency during the day . . . I was determined to finish my law degree which I did at the end of '69. But by that time I was doing well at the ad agency as a copy-writer and I loved the work, so I've never practiced law.

In 1969 the Hills moved to Birmingham, a suburban town near Detroit. In 1973 they moved to Toronto.

Mrs. Hill
Life was pleasant. . . . But it was time to move. For one thing, we'd always lived right there within a 100-mile radius, and we wanted to extend our horizons. Birmingham was . . . familiar and comfortable but totally unexciting.

Mr. Hill
In Detroit, if you're in advertising, you're in cars. After seven years of only cars, I'd had it, so I started looking around. . . . Then a friend called and told me an agency in Toronto was looking for a copy-writer. I'd never been to Toronto, but I'd heard only good things about it. . . . The three loneliest months of my life were the first three up here. . . . Trudi . . . and the boys stayed on in Birmingham. I lived in a boarding house. . . .

Mrs. Hill
I couldn't believe the place when I first came here. It was so fantastic, so beautiful, so alive. . . . One of my favorite parts of town . . . is the Portuguese section. It's filled with old row houses which have been painted in incredibly bright colors, terribly tidy, with lovely little gardens in front. I get over there when I can to shop in the open-air stalls in the Kensington Market. . . . Old Toronto, the old English families, have gone underground, . . . and the immigrants have taken over. But there are no real slums and no ghettos, just neighborhoods. . . . We got a terrifically warm welcome. . . . People went out of their way to entertain us and introduce us. . . . We met people much more quickly than back in Birmingham — perhaps because there are so few homegrown natives in Toronto. Even the Canadians come from Halifax or Winnipeg.

Case Study no. 2: The Italians

Mr. Hill

Toronto is not an inexpensive place. Salaries are lower here. Property taxes aren't too bad, but income taxes are maybe 10 percent higher than in the States. . . . Food is high, probably higher than at home. I figure it costs us much more to live here, but it's worth it.

Mrs. Hill

It's *clean.* That's the first thing that strikes you here. On top of that, . . . it's safe. You relax here. . . . You can feel free to prowl and poke on foot anywhere, any time.

Mr. Hill

My mother . . . says Toronto is just like Detroit when she was growing up. . . . I'm definitely an American, but I feel Canada is at an exciting stage, and I want to be part of it. If we try, we can avoid the mistakes other big cities and countries have made. . . . Toronto isn't a stop along the way for us. . . . It's where we'll stay. . . . It's the quality of life that really matters, right? And it's just plain pleasanter here.

- Why did the Hills decide to move to Toronto?
- Why did they find it easy to adjust to Canadian life?
- Why are American immigrants such as the Hills generally "invisible" in Canada?
- Try to interview another American immigrant to Canada to see if his or her reasons for coming to Canada are similar to or different from those of the Hills. Some suggestions for conducting an interview appear on page 186.

Perhaps you will be surprised to learn that John Cabot was neither French nor British, but an Italian from Venice. His Italian name was Giovanni Caboto. It may also surprise you that the first Italians came to Canada when it was still New France and that an Italian was rewarded for service to the king of France by being made governor of Trois Rivières. There were also Italian officers in Montcalm's army at Quebec, and later Italian *mercenaries* (career soldiers) fought in North America on the British side in the War of 1812.

At the time of Confederation there were only about one thousand Italians living in Canada. Many others came during the next fifty years. They were usually single men who came to find work on the railway, in construction, or in the mines. Many were migrant workers rather than immigrants, returning home to Italy each fall.

By far the largest number of Italians have come to Canada since World War II. Most are still first-generation immigrants, settled primarily in our large cities, particularly in Toronto and Montreal.

The following interviews reveal the experiences of one family in the Italian community. In the first interview a secondary school student in Mississauga, Ontario, talks with her father, an Italian immigrant to Canada. In the second interview the same student talks very openly with her teacher about her own experience as an Italian Canadian.

1. An Interview with my Dad

Q: Can you tell us a little about your background and your reasons for coming to Canada?

A: I was born in a little town east of Rome in Italy. After World War II I decided to come to Canada to try to find a better standard of living. By selling a large part of the harvest from our farm, I made enough money to pay my boat fare of $320. I made the trip alone. In late October 1951, I started my journey from Naples, Italy. After twelve days, I arrived at Halifax.

Q: Tell us about your first impressions of Canada.

A: I came with fifty dollars in cash and two suitcases of clothing. Everything was very new to me, but I was determined to make the best of what I had. With no special training or skills, little knowledge of the language, and only five years of education, I started my search for employment. In 1951 Canadian society was not helpful. Social services did not seem concerned with a struggling immigrant.
From Halifax I went to Niagara Falls where I lived with relatives. I got a job in a greenhouse for fifteen dollars a week. Then I transferred to Hamilton where I looked for a better job. I worked for a steel company and then a bakery. I stayed in Hamilton for two years, but when the bakery was shut down I moved to Toronto. This was in January 1954. In June of the same year I sent for my wife in Italy. I worked in another bakery until 1957. Then I started at the steel company where I still work.

Q: Describe your position in today's Canadian society.

A: After almost twenty-five years in Canada, I would say I have come a long way. I have kept my general moral standards, although some of my ideas and views have changed. As a family we have held onto some Italian customs, like wine-making and preserving each fall. I have a small garden. It is my pride, and the children appreciate the fresh vegetables.

Q: What advantages do you feel you have found by living in Canada?

A: Well, I have accomplished what I set out to do. My standard of living is better than I ever expected. Society has educated me. I think, though, if I lived in Italy, my health would be a lot better because of the fresh air and the simple life that is led by everyone in my village.

Q: Would you like to return to live in Italy?

A: No, not to live. It's just a great place to visit. My life in Canada is too advanced compared to that of Italy.

- What *five* adjectives come to your mind to describe Maria's father?
- What similarities do you see between Maria's father's experiences and those of any other earlier immigrants to Canada? How were his experiences easier? Harder?
- If you were to use this conversation as a model to guide you in conducting your own interview with a recent immigrant to Canada, what other questions would you ask?

2. **An Interview with Maria**

Q: What advantages do you think you have in being an Italian Canadian?

A: I feel I couldn't have been blessed with a greater advantage than that of being the daughter of an immigrant. I have developed several qualities that make me, as an individual, different.

Q: Do you speak Italian?

A: My first language was Italian. When I started school, I learned English. At the start I was a little behind, but now being bilingual is a great advantage. It also helps me in learning other languages.

Q: Your father doesn't say much about his life in Italy. Have you learned what life was like in the little town where he grew up?

A: My parents sometimes talk about the "old country." Their way of life, by Canadian standards, was very primitive. Their village had

one doctor and a few stores. If they needed a dentist or a hospital, they travelled quite a distance. Local transportation was usually by mule.

Q: How did your father's family earn its living?

A: The family lived on the farm products they grew. They would slaughter their own animals, cook, and then eat them on the same day. They grew most of their other food and bought little. It was from this rural background that many Italians moved to Canadian cities to face situations they did not even dream existed. That was my father's start.

Q: Your father must have had great courage and capacity for work.

A: From my interview with him you learned that when he first came to Canada, he lived with relatives. He earned a little money and after three years sent for my mother. After four years here they had their first baby. Over the next five years there were three more children born. Sacrifice, hard work, and very troubled times followed. My father saved every cent he could, and after fourteen years we moved to Mississauga. We lived quite comfortably in a bungalow, but my father still kept his habit of saving. He soon had enough money to buy the house we presently live in and to rent the other. Now, after almost twenty-five years in Canada, my father is very successful.

Q: Can you tell me a little about your mother's life in Canada?

A: Because she has no special training or skills, my mother works in a factory. She depends on us to help her get through the English language. She works with English-speaking people, but once she returns home she goes back to speaking Italian.

My mother says she can't complain about her present life-style. But she says memories of the early years in Canada are better forgotten. She almost shudders when she thinks of the great change that has come over her in Canada. Her life in Italy was simple. Like the other women of her village, she was brought up to be a housewife. She remembers few worries. A lack of money meant there would be no luxuries, but basics such as food were always available. She says that in Canada if one doesn't have money, it can mean real suffering. My impression is that she has, at times, bitterly missed the security of her life in Italy.

Q: Has being the daughter of immigrants made your life difficult in any way?

A: My parents' difficulties in adapting to a new life-style had an effect on us. It is very hard to grow up facing society's pressures when your parents are not willing to adapt to Canadian customs. I am thankful that we moved to an Anglo-Saxon area in Mississauga. If we still lived in the Italian section of Toronto, we would have kept more of our parents' views. I also think that teachers sometimes do not help immigrant children to strive for worthwhile goals. Girls are often not discouraged from taking a very basic education, and the boys from taking up a trade.

Q: You said that your parents have had problems in adapting to Canadian life. Is this still so?

A: I think it is now too late for my parents to adapt completely to Canadian life. If they were going to, they would have long ago. The children of immigrants must learn to handle society at a much earlier age because their parents will not.

Q: Yet you feel that being an immigrant's daughter has been of great advantage to you?

A: Yes. As a group the children of immigrants are very independent. Our determination is our greatest asset. We are eager and vivacious and feel that we have great opportunities ahead of us in Canada. This is the priceless heritage we have received from our parents.

• After reading Maria's conversation with her teacher, has your impression of her father changed? If so, how?

- Why is it natural for Italian immigrants to settle in a particular section of a Canadian city?
- Why was Maria glad her family had moved to an Anglo-Saxon area?
- Why is adjustment to a new life in Canada sometimes hardest for the mother of an immigrant family?
- What, to your mind, are the major contributions of this particular family to Canada?
- What do you think Maria meant by the sentence, "This is the priceless heritage we have received from our parents"?

Check the information given by Maria and her father, and the opinions they expressed, against the data given in the "information bank" which follows.

- Is any of the information contradictory?
- Do you think Maria's family's experience has been typical of that of other Italian immigrants?

Information Bank on Italian-Canadians

For numbers of Italians in different provinces of Canada, study the charts on pages 6 and 7.

Ethnic Origin and Selected Male Occupations (1961)[1]			
	British	Italian	Total Labour Force
Professional & Financial	10.6	3.4	8.6
Clerical	8.2	3.7	6.9
Personal Service	3.4	7.2	4.3
Primary and Unskilled	7.7	21.5	10.0
Agriculture	10.7	2.7	12.2
All others*	59.4	61.5	58.0
Total	100.0	100.0	100.0

* The category "all others" includes self-employed persons, e.g., owners of businesses or companies.

— Almost 80% of Italian immigrants come from the south of Italy or from the islands of Sicily and Sardinia. Most come from rural rather than urban communities.[2]
— In a survey of the Italian community in Toronto, 24% of immigrants interviewed said that finding work was the major problem faced; 22.4% mentioned language as the major difficulty.[3]
— An estimated 15% of the 500 000 Italians who came to Canada between World War II and 1972 returned home.[4]
— A tile-setter who had returned to Italy after working in Hamilton, Ontario, said, "Here if I make a hundred dollars, I take it easy for a few days. In Canada if you make a hundred dollars today, you still have to go to work tomorrow."[5]

Percentage of Over- and Under-Representation in Occupation by Ethnic Group[6]			
	British	French	Italian
Professional & Financial	+2.0	-1.9	-5.2
Clerical	+1.3	-.2	-3.2
Personal Service	-.9	-.2	+2.9
Primary and Unskilled	-2.3	+2.8	+11.5
Agriculture	-1.5	-1.4	-9.5
All others	+.4	+.9	+3.5

[Interpretation: There were 5.2% fewer Italian males in professional and financial work than the national average of all ethnic groups.]

— The Italian Immigrant Aid Society (I.I.A.S.), a non-profit organization to help Italian immigrants adapt to Canadian life, was founded in 1952.[7]

Ethnic Origins and School Attendance of Males, 5-24 years old (by percentage)[8]				
	British	French	Italian	Jewish
1961	+4.0	-4.2	-7.1	+16.5

[Interpretation: There were 7.1% fewer Italian males attending school than the national average of all ethnic groups.]

The sources of the information given above are not all equally reliable. Also, the bank contains some statements of fact and others of opinion. Separate the two types of statements. Then

  (i) Using a scale from 1 to 5, grade each fact for accuracy. Use 1 for lowest accuracy.
  (ii) Grade each opinion from 1 to 5.

Compare your ratings with those of other students in your class. Be prepared to support your rating.

SUGGESTIONS FOR INDIVIDUAL OR
GROUP RESEARCH

(i) *Our Heritage from Italy*
A group of students plans an itinerary for a seven-day tour of historical cities in Italy:

• Gather materials, including filmstrips or slides of the places you will visit in each city.

(ii) *The Italian Community in Canada*
A group of students investigates the Italian community in its local area:

• Visit one of the shopping areas or markets which cater to the Italian community. Record your impressions on paper or through photographs.

• Tape an interview with a first- or second-generation Italian Canadian. Compare the interview with those at the beginning of this section.

• Identify the resources, industries, and businesses in your area that may have attracted Italian immigrants. What sources could you consult to find what businesses Italian Canadians have established?

• What religious and community organizations exist in your area for Italian-Canadian families? Are there Italian newspapers? television programs? movie theatres?

As you can see by the graph below, people of German ancestry form the third-largest ethnic group in Canada after the British and French.

About six in every hundred Canadians (1 317 300 people in 1971) are of German origin. Although people of German ancestry have settled in Canada for over two hundred years, about one-quarter of them have come to Canada since 1950.

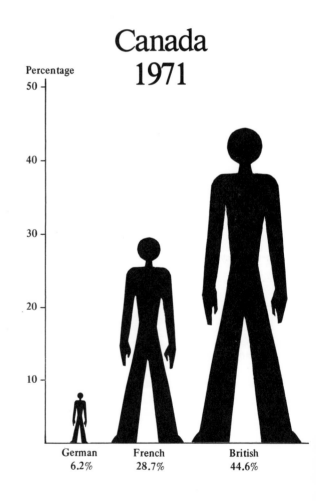

Canada
1971

Percentage

German	French	British
6.2%	28.7%	44.6%

Why Did They Come?

In 1951 the government of West Germany asked those who wished to emigrate why they wished to leave. The reasons most frequently given were:

  (i) difficulty of earning a living or actual unemployment;
 (ii) desire to join friends and relatives overseas;
(iii) expulsion from their home country;
(iv) fear of war.[1]

German immigrants at Quebec, c. 1911

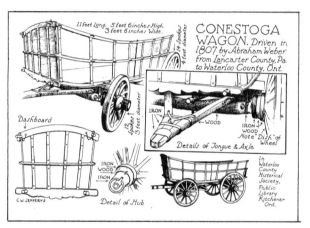

Conestoga Wagon
Among the Loyalists who came north to Upper Canada after the American Revolution were pioneers of German ancestry.

German-speaking Mennonites began to settle in Upper Canada at the end of the American Revolution. Successful Mennonite farm communities were established in the Canadian West during the latter part of the 19th century.

Leaving Germany for Canada

Case Study no. 4: The Dutch

- Try to interview a postwar immigrant from Germany. Find out why he came to Canada and what difficulties, if any, he had in adjusting to Canadian life.
- Twice during this century, Canada and Germany have been on opposite sides in a war — World War I (1914-1918) and World War II (1939-1945). Try to find out what problems this created for recent immigrants of German ancestry.
- "Germans living in Ontario are annoyed over the number of World War II movies and TV shows that depict everyone of Germanic origin to be a Nazi. . . . A Germany community organization . . . claimed that many Canadians of German origin have renounced their native language and culture and assimilated [for] fear of being identified, ridiculed and/or persecuted."[2]What other ethnic groups feel sensitive about the "image" that is presented of them?
- Immigrants of German ancestry come from a wide variety of backgrounds. Find out more about the Mennonites by consulting a good encyclopedia or reference book.
- Investigate the contributions that people of German ancestry have made in politics, business and science. You might start with John Diefenbaker, J.M. Schneider, and Adam Beck.
- German Christmas customs have become part of many Canadians' celebration. Find out what customs are of German origin and how they came to Canada.
- Oktoberfest, a popular German celebration, has now become a popular event for many Canadians. Find out how and where this celebration started.
- Investigate the contributions of the "Pennsylvania Dutch" who came to Canada in the early 1800's.
- What contributions have Germans made to the development of western Canada?

People of Dutch origin have been established in Canada for approximately two hundred years. However, the largest group has come to Canada since the end of World War II.

The story which follows is based on fact, although the names are fictitious. It is the spring of 1951.

Margaretha was tired. The nine-day trip across the Atlantic was longer than she expected. At first, it had been exciting. Her friends envied her family's good fortune. A Canadian farmer, Mr. Brown, who lived near London, Ontario was sponsoring her family's move to Canada. Her mother had cried the night before they had left their town and again as they had said their final good-byes to friends and relatives on the dock at Rotterdam.

Just one more day to Halifax! She'd be glad to get off the ship and leave the hot, noisy cabin where the family slept. The roll of the ship and the rumble of the engines made her feel sick at times. Last night she'd started to cry. Her mother had comforted her.

"Remember how bad it was when the Germans occupied our town?"

"I was just little then." Her mother always forgot that she'd been only one when the Germans came.

"Well, you remember the Canadian soldiers who helped to drive them out." Margaretha did remember them. One of her friends had an older sister who had married one of them. They'd called her the "war bride." The Canadian soldiers had made Canada sound like a wonderful place to live. There was farm land for everybody. There just wasn't enough land in Holland. The war had left a lot of damaged homes and flooded land in their town.

"Mother, will cousin Piet come to Canada too?"

"Perhaps. Your uncle can't go back to Indonesia. If we can get a farm of our own, he'll probably decide to come out."

"When will we get our own farm?"

"In a few years, when we save some money."

"We have the money now. Father said so. Why can't we get one right away?"

"Yes. Yes. But we can't take our money out of the country — only a few hundred guilders."

Mr. and Mrs. John Tamming of Strathroy, Ontario, in traditional Dutch costume

"Are the Russians really going to come to Holland? Father said . . ."

"Your father worries a lot. This new NATO organization will stop them. Hush now and go to sleep. We'll be safe in Canada."

The next day it was all noise and confusion when they landed. Somehow they found all their belongings and had their papers checked. The immigration man saw that they boarded the train and had food for the journey westward. Margaretha couldn't believe how big the country was, and the rocks and the trees! They slept in their seats and ate cold food.

The farmhouse where they would live was old and dirty. No one had lived in it for years. She helped her mother scrub and scrape away every speck of dirt. It looked a lot better when they got their things unpacked and set out.

Mr. Brown took them to town and showed them how to get to church. The minister spoke Dutch, and they met other families from Holland. Margaretha enjoyed the weekly lessons at church where they read the text in English with the Dutch right beside it. Perhaps by the time she started Canadian school in September, she wouldn't feel so strange.

The tobacco harvesting was hard work. Her father was exhausted at night, but he was earning seventy-five dollars a month cash, and they had the house to live in. Her father said that Mr. Brown was a pretty good boss, not like some he'd heard of. He let them have all the milk and potatoes they needed. Pretty soon they'd save enough for their own farm.

Dutch immigrants, c. 1911

The Dutch established settlements in North America over three hundred years ago. Among the Loyalists who came to Canada at the end of the American Revolution were people of Dutch origin. In what other parts of the world did the Dutch establish colonies?

- Holland is a small country, about half the size of New Brunswick. The population density is the highest in the world. Consult a good reference book to find out the number of people per square mile in Canada as compared with Holland. How has the Dutch government reclaimed large areas of land from the sea?
- What economic and political reasons were there for Dutch immigration at the end of the World War II?
- What special ties exist between Canada and the Netherlands as a result of World War II?
- Why did the Canadian government consider the Dutch to be very desirable immigrants after 1945?
- Try to interview a recent Dutch immigrant to Canada.
- What contributions did the Dutch make as pioneers in western Canada? What economic and agricultural contributions have they made?
- Investigate the work of individuals of Dutch ancestry such as Cornelius Kreighoff, Martine von Hamel, Egerton Ryerson, Petra Burka.
- What special Christmas customs have the Dutch brought to Canada?

FOR FURTHER READING

Burns, Florence M. *William Berczy*. The Canadians. Toronto: Fitzhenry & Whiteside, 1974.

Damania, Laura. *Egerton Ryerson*. The Canadians. Toronto: Fitzhenry & Whiteside, 1975.

Horst, Mary Ann. *My Old Order*. Mennonite Heritage. Kitchener: Pennsylvania Dutch Craft Shop, 1970.

McLeod, Joan, ed. *We Are Their Children: Ethnic Portraits of British Columbia.* Vancouver: Comm Cept Publishing Ltd., 1977.

Sheffe, Norman, ed. *Many Cultures, Many Heritages.* Toronto: McGraw-Hill, 1975.

Sturgis, James. *Adam Beck..* The Canadians. Toronto: Fitzhenry & Whiteside, 1978.

Who Can Immigrate To Canada?

Through the Department of Manpower and Immigration our federal government regulates the flow of immigrants to our country.

Imagine you are a Canadian immigration official. Read the following family histories, and write a short report on each. Include in your report your reasons for (i) rejecting, (ii) accepting, or (iii) being undecided about each family's application for admission to Canada. When you have finished, you will be able to check your recommendations against our present government regulations.

JOSIP BROZ

Mr. Broz is forty-three years old. He is married and has five children who range in age from two years to sixteen years. He was born near Zagreb, Yugoslavia. He has had ten years of formal education. Two of these were spent as an apprentice. He is a qualified typesetter. He has no relatives in Canada. He speaks and reads English with extreme difficulty. He hopes to settle in Montreal. Since he is without contacts in Canada, he has been unable to arrange for a job. His oldest daughter, who is fourteen, has asthma and requires frequent medical attention. His wife has eight years of education equivalent to grade eight in a Canadian elementary school. She has no specialized training. His father and mother are living with him at the present time in Zagreb. His wife's family were killed during the war. His wife has a cousin living in Philadelphia.

KATHY LEE

Dr. Lee is twenty-eight years old. She was born in Hong Kong and now lives in London. She has had nineteen years of formal education. She is a medical doctor with a specialist certificate in geriatrics. She is single. She has an aunt and uncle living in Toronto. Her mother has remarried and also lives in Toronto. She has a job offer from the Faculty of Medicine at the University of Saskatchewan in Regina at a salary of thirty-two thousand dollars a year if she passes the Saskatchewan medical examination. She speaks and reads English fluently and speaks and reads French moderately well.

PABLO MARTINEZ

Mr. Martinez is twenty-three years old. He is married with two children. He was born near Seville where he now lives. He has had seven years of formal education. He is a gardener and has had seven years' experience in this field. He has a brother living in Hamilton who thinks that he can get him a job working in the Royal Botanical Gardens. He speaks French reasonably well but has trouble reading it. He speaks broken English but cannot read English. He has three younger brothers who he hopes will come to Canada.

Our Present Regulations

The Selection System

In earlier chapters we have examined Canada's immigration policies in various periods of history. Our present immigration regulations were established by the Immigration Act of 1976. Different in many ways from earlier acts, its most important provisions are the following:

— It states, for the first time, that there will be no discrimination against particular groups.
— It links the numbers of immigrants admitted to Canada to labour market needs.
— It provides for consultation between the federal government and the provinces to forecast the number of immigrants that can be absorbed.
— It requires immigrants and visitors to obtain visas or authorization before entering Canada and prohibits visitors from applying for immigration while within Canada.
— It establishes a new "refugee class" of immigrants.

• Discuss with your teacher the reasons for each of the provisions.

Persons who wish to immigrate to Canada must apply for admission through the Canadian Immigration Offices in their own countries. They will be required to fill out application forms giving detailed information about their qualifications and personal histories. They must include birth certificates, educational record, and technical or professional certificates.

Immigrants are selected under three classes:

(i) *Independent and Others:*
Most members of this class are covered only by the general guidelines for selecting immigrants; but certain categories are given special consideration: *entrepreneurs* — businessmen who expect to employ five or more Canadians; self-employed persons, those assisted by relatives in Canada, and retired persons.

(ii) *The Family Class:*
This class includes all persons who are sponsored by a close relative who is a permanent resident or citizen of Canada. The relative must prove that he or she has the financial ability to provide for the care and maintenance of the applicant.

(iii) *Refugees:*
Refugees are persons caught in a political crisis or others who are displaced or persecuted. They are assessed on their general ability to adapt to Canadian life and/or the amount of settlement assistance available to them in Canada.

So that every candidate can be fairly assessed against the many thousands of others who wish to enter Canada, the point system establishes certain criteria for selection.[1]

FACTORS	CRITERIA	MAX. POINTS	self-employed	entre-preneurs	assisted relatives	others
			APPLICABLE TO:			
1. Education	One point for each year of primary and secondary education successfully completed	12	●	●	●	●
2. Specific Vocational Preparation	To be measured by the amount of formal professional, vocational, apprenticeship, in-plant or on-the-job training necessary for average performance in the occupation under which the application is assessed in item 4.	15	●	●	●	●
3. Experience	Points awarded for experience in the occupation under which the applicant is assessed in item 4 or, in the case of an entrepreneur, for experience in the occupation that the entrepreneur is qualified for and is prepared to follow in Canada.	8	●	●	●	●
4. Occupational Demand	Points awarded on the basis of employment opportunities available in Canada in the occupation that the applicant is qualified for and is prepared to follow in Canada.	15	●		●	●
5. Arranged Employment or Designated Occupation	Ten points awarded if the person has arranged employment in Canada that offers reasonable prospects of continuity and meets local conditions of work and wages, *providing* that employment of that person would not interfere with the job opportunities of Canadian citizens or permanent residents, and the person will likely be able to meet all licensing and regulatory requirements; *or* the person is qualified for, and is prepared to work in, a designated occupation and meets all the conditions mentioned for arranged employment except that concerning Canadian citizens and permanent residents.	10				●
6. Location	Five points awarded to a person who intends to proceed to an area designated as one having a sustained and general need for people at various levels in the employment strata and the necessary services to accommodate population growth. Five points subtracted from a person who intends to proceed to an area designated as not having such a need or such services.	5	●	●		●
7. Age	Ten points awarded to a person 18 to 35 years old. For those over 35, one point shall be subtracted from the maximum of ten for every year over 35.	10	●	●	●	●
8. Knowledge of English and French	Ten points awarded to a person who reads, writes and speaks both English and French fluently. Five points awarded to a person who reads, writes and speaks English *or* French fluently. Fewer points awarded to persons with less language knowledge and ability in English or French.	10	●	●		●
9. Personal Suitability	Points awarded on the basis of an interview held to determine the suitability of the person and his/her dependants to become successfully established in Canada, based on the person's adaptability, motivation, initiative, resourcefulness and other similar qualities.	10	●	●	●	●
10. Relative	Where a person *would* be an assisted relative, *if* a relative in Canada had undertaken to assist him/her, and an immigration officer is satisfied that the relative in Canada is willing to help him/her become established but is not prepared, or is unable, to complete the necessary formal documentation to bring the person to Canada, the person shall be awarded five points.	5	●	●		●

Refugees

- Measure the qualifications of the three applicants described at the beginning of this section against the point system. What chance does each applicant have to be admitted to Canada? Does this assessment correspond to your earlier one? What differences did you find?
- Turn to page 162. Find out what Maria's father's rating would have been on the point system.
- In a group of six or eight students, discuss each of the clauses in the point system. Attempt to reach a consensus on which of the criteria you support.
- Have you personal experience of families who have come to Canada under the point system? If possible interview one of their members.
- Why does our government warn applicants that they cannot be helped to gain admission to Canada by agencies in their country charging fees?
- Visitors to Canada who decide that they wish to remain permanently cannot apply from within but must return to their own countries. Why?

Canada's 1978 Immigration Act uses the United Nations definition of a refugee. A refugee is anyone who is unwilling or unable to return to his homeland because he fears persecution because of his race, religion, nationality, political ideas, or social group. During the last two hundred years, Canada has opened her doors to many refugees. The Loyalists, about whom you read in an earlier section, are the first major example of a people who sought safety and a new life in Canada.

Mennonites, Doukhobors, and Hutterites came to Canada to avoid persecution for their religious beliefs. Canada admitted Hungarian refugees in 1956-7, Chileans who fled when the government of President Allende was overthrown in 1973, and Russian Jews in 1974. American "draft dodgers," Ugandans from Africa, Tibetan Buddhists, and fleeing black slaves are among those who have sought freedom and security in Canada. Approximately 10 percent of the 3 500 000 people who have come to Canada since 1945 have been refugees.

Refugee woman and her children arrive in Canada after fleeing Viet Nam. Wide World

Refugees in Cheras Centre, Malaysia

Who Can Become a Canadian Citizen?

Late in 1978 the misery of the Vietnamese "boat people" received world-wide publicity. Canada admitted 604 people from the freighter *Hai Hong* and agreed to accept fifty thousand more. Many religious and civic groups volunteered to sponsor these refugees. Conditions on board the refugee ships are a vivid reminder of the hardships faced by earlier immigrants to Canada.

- Canada accepts only a small number of the many thousands of refugees who seek a home. First place is given to those with relatives in Canada and second place is given to those who seem likely to establish themselves successfully in Canada. Do you think the Canadian government should accept more refugees? Why or why not?
- What types of people, if any, do you think should be barred from settling in Canada?
- Investigate one of the refugee groups listed above and determine their reasons for leaving their homelands.
- Compared to most countries, Canada has a good record in her willingness to accept the victims of persecution. She has, however, been criticized in the past for her failure to admit more Jewish refugees from Nazi Germany. Investigate Canadian immigration policy and public attitudes toward refugees in the 1930's.

The Globe and Mail, Toronto

Citizenship Court

There are many people living in Canada today as *landed immigrants.* They have been accepted by our immigration officials and may make their living here indefinitely. After three years they may, if they wish, apply for Canadian citizenship. What privileges and obligations will this bring to them?

Our Department of Employment and Immigration has established certain conditions for citizenship. In order to qualify candidates must:

(i) Gain admission to Canada for permanent residence; this is known as "landed immigrant" status.

(ii) Live in Canada for three years after admission.

(iii) Speak either French or English — the two official languages.

(iv) Demonstrate good character. Members of the community where the candidate lives in Canada, such as his employer, bank manager, a community leader, or any other reputable citizen may testify on his behalf by providing a letter of reference or appearing before a Court of Canadian Citizenship to support his application to become a citizen.

Future Immigration Policies

(v) Possess some knowledge of Canada and of the responsibilities and privileges of citizenship.

(vi) Intend to live permanently in Canada.

(vii) Agree to take the Oath of Allegiance.

- Why is knowledge of *either* English or French required?
- Why are all persons required to take the Oath of Allegiance?
- Have there been any exceptions to this rule?
- Do you know what the Oath says?
- Should natural-born Canadians also be required to prove some knowledge of their responsibilities and privileges before they are granted citizenship at the age of eighteen?
- Should all high school students be required to make a study of Canada before graduation?

The present Immigration Act went into effect in April 1978. It appears that many Canadians are not yet fully aware of its full implications. In the future you may be required to reassess the policies it introduces. Should we:

(i) Continue to accept only those immigrants who compete successfully for entrance to Canada within the provisions of the present act?

(ii) *Lower* our standards to permit more immigrants to enter from countries that are overpopulated or cannot provide as many opportunities for their people as Canada can?

(iii) *Raise* our standards, refusing admission to Canada to all but a very few who meet new selection criteria?

(iv) Cut back on *all* immigration, allowing our country's population to grow much more slowly by natural increase only?

Before you make up your mind, study the arguments presented by the authors of the extracts below:

A small country cannot advance industrially, without getting into the world market at world prices, and in that market our prices just aren't competitive . . . . look at all the industrial goods we're importing — from shirts to bicycles to cars to color T.V. . . . with a static population we must also have a static manufacturing industry.[2]

Have we obligations as human beings to accept at least our share of people from underdeveloped countries?[3]

"I suppose you'd have to say that the point system for selecting immigrants is in ruins," the immigration officer said.

"When you set up criteria for choosing good immigrants, then over 20,000 people come in who don't meet the criteria (during an experiment by the federal government in allowing persons to apply for immigration while 'visiting' in Canada) and they turn out fine. . . . Then you have to look again at what you're supposed to be doing."[4]

"Employers want the unskilled immigrants; but if the economic situation changes in a couple of years, they'll cheerfully lay them off and we could have a nasty social problem on our hands."[5]

". . . the decisions about who you let into Canada will decide the kind of country we have 100 years from now."

". . . we know that up to a point, population increases can reduce the unit cost of consumer goods, et cetera, but we also know that social costs can increase . . . through pollution, urban renewal problems, even through the psychiatric services of a big city . . . but after a certain point of time, the costs increase faster than the benefits."[6]

FOR FURTHER READING

Canada and the World, February 1974 and October 1976.

Doughty, Howard et al. *Canadian Studies: Culture and Country.* Toronto: John Wiley & Sons (Canada) Ltd., 1976.

Hardwick, Francis C., ed. *The Helping Hand.* Vancouver: Tantalus Research Ltd., 1973.

New Directions: A Look at Canada's Immigration Act and Regulations. Minister of Supply and Services, Canada, 1978.

Canada: A Mosaic of Peoples?

An artist creates a painting by mixing or blending his paints on a palette. Usually almost no pure colours remain. A mosaic is very different: although the individual pieces used to compose the picture fit together to form a pattern, each individual piece is not melted into the other pieces, but remains separate.

We often hear Canada spoken of as "a mosaic of peoples" and the United States referred to as "a melting pot." At first thought the statements appear true. After all, we in Canada do have two official languages while the United States has only one. Also, our federal and provincial governments are trying to encourage what we call "multiculturalism" by helping different ethnic groups to keep their customs and arts alive.

But let us think about what we have already learned about the term "ethnic group." Because all share a number of things in common, its members feel *at home* with each other. These things include language, religion, customs and traditions, art and music, physical characteristics, and origins from a particular part of the world.

The question of the Canadian mosaic now becomes more complicated. Very few ethnic groups in Canada have kept all parts of their cultures. Most seem to have lost some parts entirely, replacing them by new ones borrowed from other groups. To test this statement, think of your own experience. Does your family still feel closely tied to its ethnic group's language? religion? customs and arts? geographic region outside Canada?

- Share your findings with two or three members of your class. Compare your backgrounds.

As Immigrants See Us

The experiences of newcomers to Canada are very varied. We do know, however, that many face a number of similar problems and adjustments. The following incidents and descriptions reveal what some of these are.

The scene is a Toronto hospital [1972]. A mother who speaks only Italian has taken her child to be treated for what she believes to be a minor ailment.

While the case is far from critical, a doctor feels that the child should be admitted for observation.

As soon as the child is taken from her, the mother becomes hysterical. In the rural area of Italy where she lived before coming to Canada, children were left in hospitals only when they were in danger of dying.

Nobody was immediately available on the hospital staff to explain to the distraught woman that her fears were groundless. This is a common scene in hospitals across Metro and a need that the Inter-Agency Council for Services to Immigrants and Migrants hopes to meet.[1]

The exploitation of immigrants is tragic. There are many thousands of them working in Metro far below the minimum wage and they are denied overtime. It is difficult to organize people who believe that if they join a union they will be deported. And if employers are caught no penalty is involved. They merely have to make restitution to the employee and that is hardly a deterrent.[2]

Cheddi Cato is 12 and black and often bewildered.

In Jamaica, his birthplace, his teacher might have taken the class out in the sunlight today. He'd be surrounded by dark-skinned schoolmates who talk and think and act as he does.

In Metro he's cooped up in a schoolroom. The others around him are white, and some of them jeer, "Hey, you black bastard."

His parents can only tell him he must learn not to react, he must be proud of his black heritage.

Mr. and Mrs. Canute Cato of Victoria Park Ave. aren't too worried about name-calling and childish fights. But Cheddi's schooling is another matter.

As they see it, Canadian teachers don't understand black immigrant children and the school system makes no special provision for them.

"If a kid has a school problem that has a language basis, he gets lots of help," said Cato. "If his problem has a cultural basis, there seems to be nothing done."

He complained that it's hard on the self-image of a black child to learn from school texts whose only heroes are white.

"He ends up with a slanted view of his own people. We think Cheddi's greatest education is the one he gets at home. We talk to him about black achievements. We take him around Toronto and expose him to black leaders, to people who have made it."[3]

Question: How do you react to Mafia stories?

Answer: In my job we're too close to the crime to pick out sinister patterns. If a jewelry store is robbed, we can't really say whether it's the work of a smart criminal or a syndicate. But on one aspect the Italian community is united: The Mafia legend has been over-exploited.

It's reached the point of absurdity. If we arrest a common purse snatcher who has an Italian name, the public assumes he's an agent of the local "family." The thief may strut a little at this, but I suspect it secretly worries him. After all, he's seen *The Godfather,* too.[4]

"Like the Italians," says Marlene, "West Indians are used to an extended family situation back home. But whereas the Italians often come to Canada with their families, West Indians more often than not come alone. As a result, they suffer from terrible feelings of isolation when they are first here."[5]

The Ugly Fact of Prejudice

- Which of the problems and adjustments faced by the immigrants in the examples above can best be solved by members of their own ethnic groups already established in Canada? Which need to be solved by government action? Which can be solved only by the general Canadian public?
- Write a handbook for new immigrants in which you explain some of the adjustments they will need to make to Canadian life.
- Talk with someone you know whose family has only recently come to Canada. How were their experiences similar to those revealed in the preceding descriptions? How were they different?

"Canada has a very serious problem. Though most Canadians aren't aware of it, every one of the 21 million people in this vast country of ours is prejudiced in one way or another. You may be prejudiced against blacks, or Indians or maybe you are prejudiced against someone who is of a different religious faith, but even worse, you may not even know you're prejudiced."

The writer of the above statements, Grant Farrer, a Grade 8 student in Scarborough, Ontario, was the winner of a provincial essay contest sponsored by the Canadian Council of Christians and Jews.

- Do you agree with Grant that we are all prejudiced? Why, or why not?
- Test your own reactions by answering the following questions. (You need not share your answers unless you wish to do so.)

  (i) Do I enjoy new experiences (*e.g.* dances, food, sports)?
  (ii) Do I have friends among members of other ethnic groups? If not, have I ever attempted to make them?
  (iii) Do I dislike any particular person belonging to an ethnic group other than my own? If so, why do I dislike this person?
  (iv) Can I write a list of words to describe the person I dislike? Do these words apply to some members of other groups as well? Why or why not?
  (v) Do I have a good feeling about my own ability and accomplishments?
  (vi) Am I aware that if I feel "put down" or have a low opinion of myself, I may look for others to blame for my lack of success?
  (vii) When I have felt bothered or in trouble, have I taken out my anger on those persons or situations that caused the trouble, or have I transferred it to some other person?
  (viii) Have I learned as much as I can about the background and values of other groups? Am I able to judge whether what I hear about them is true or false?

(ix) Do I put a person on the spot if he or she expresses open and unjustified dislike toward another group?

(x) Am I able to praise others — of whatever ethnic group — for their accomplishments?

The purpose of the questionnaire is to make you more aware of aspects of your personality which might affect your attitude towards persons from cultural groups different from your own. As the regulations of the new Immigration Act are applied, immigration patterns are changing. In 1976, for example, Europeans made up 34 percent of the immigrants to Toronto, while Asians, West Indians and Africans made up 59 percent. Very soon, therefore, Canadians will notice that our cities are changing, for there will be a greater intermixing of races, skin colours, and cultures. Some Canadians are obviously not ready for this change. You read earlier about the problem of "name calling" in our schools. "Visible minority" groups have also complained of discrimination in housing, of police indifference, of unprovoked attacks on city streets or on public transport.

Because the City of Toronto has attracted more immigrants than any other Canadian city, it has also experienced more violence in relations among groups. In 1977 a Task Force was created to study the problem. In its report, *Now Is Not Too Late,* it identified examples of violence:

> The Task Force found that there were instances of violence in parks and recreation areas, in public housing complexes, in school playgrounds, on the streets, in shopping plazas. Particularly vicious were the instances of continuous harassment of businessmen and repeated attacks on the homes of visible minority members.[6]

The report includes a *scenario* (script) describing a racial attack and the reaction of the victim to the attack. (Mr. Singhdil is an imaginary person, but his reactions are based on interviews with real persons.)

> Mr. Singhdil . . . no longer lives in the same world as that which most white Canadians inhabit. . . . Mr. Singhdil is extremely leery of having his wife ride the TTC now at all, and he will not allow his children to do so unaccompanied by an adult. Mr. Singhdil's children are not encouraged to use either of the public parks near their home — "Pakis" have had problems in both of them. Mr. Singhdil does not make a habit of taking his family shopping, or anywhere else, after dark, and he never, never takes them to quiet lonely places. Mr. Singhdil would not consider taking his family on an outing where other Sikhs were not likely to be present — he regards that as simply asking for trouble.[7]

- What action do you feel Mr. Singhdil and his friends should take?
- What role do you think each of the following might play to assist him?
  (i) the courts
  (ii) the police
  (iii) other community groups

Among the many recommendations made in the report were the following:

(i) Schools could help students to understand other people's lifestyle, culture, and religious practices.

(ii) Police should receive special training in working with minority groups.

(iii) Social service agencies might give training to their members in servicing visible minorities.

(iv) The media might be of greater assistance in helping Canadians to accept change.

- Read the following excerpts from a letter written by an angry citizen to the editor of the *Toronto Star,* January 6, 1979.

I fumed with anger when I read your front-page story "TV in 24 tongues coming for Metro's ethnic communities."

To make way for this drivel, you tell us that an American station will be "bumped" off basic cable service, and you add that if we wish to continue watching the station we lose, well, we'll have to buy converters!

And all for the sake of wistful foreigners who've never really left home and who seem to enjoy confusing themselves and their children by using their native tongues!

. . . when I came to this country I resolved to leave my native tongue behind and concentrate on English.

After all, I came to Canada, not Switzerland or Germany!

And I fail to see why the Canadian Radio-television and Telecommunications Commission (CRTC) finds itself constrained to pander to ethnic minorities by giving them their own shows and at our expense. . . .

By this outrageous decision . . . the CRTC has taken another gigantic step in its deplorable campaign of enforced multiracialism. Does it really expect us to keep quiet?

Finally, when I was last in Austria, I can recall no TV or radio programs that we designed for our own ethnic minorities — the Turks, the Yugoslavs, the Greeks, the Hungarians, the Italians, etc. — the reason being that all these people are busily mastering the language of their "host" country.

As it should be here.

- Write a letter to the editor in which you either support or attack the views of the writer.

Now is Not Too Late also considers what the ordinary person can do if he or she becomes part of a situation which might lead to violence:

It is the Task Force's view that everyone should be made aware of a series of steps which the average citizen can take to intervene with maximum effectiveness and with minimum risk to their own safety.

The United Church of Canada has produced a sign suggesting five steps any citizen can take:

1. Find out what is going on and offer the victim your assistance.
2. Loudly and clearly (but calmly) insist the attacker stop verbal or physical abuse.
3. Send for help (or if others are present enlist their support against attackers).
4. Stay with the victim. (Offer comfort and assistance.)
5. Report the incident to the police.[8]

- Do you agree with the steps suggested? Why or why not?
- How many of their traditional ways should immigrants to Canada change in order to be accepted by Canadians? Their clothing? Their cosmetics? Their food? Their language?
- How may each of the following contribute to friction between racial groups?

   (i) language
   (ii) ignorance of the other group's customs
   (iii) crowded housing
   (iv) competition for work

- Should advertisers on television be compelled to employ actors and/or models from different racial groups? Why or why not?

"Getting to Know Each Other"

Many of the recommendations of the Task Force emphasized the need for greater understanding among groups from different cultures. Between 1973 and 1975 the Ministry of Culture and Recreation of Ontario sponsored a series of workshops to bring different cultural groups together. In the following quotation, Dr. T.L. Samuel, an economist with the federal Department of Manpower, attempts to explain the background of emigrants from India to Canada:

> The country of the origin of . . . Indian immigrants has many faces. . . . A nation of about 600 million people, adding a Canada to its population every year, it is a land of contradictions. There live some of the poorest people in the world, and also some of the richest. India is atomic physicists in Bombay and Naga tribesmen in Assam. It is maharajas and street sweepers, Harvard or Oxford-trained scholars and unlettered farmers. . . . It wears turbans, Ghandhi caps, and no caps, the latest Paris fashion and simplest loincloth. It is palaces and huts, automobiles, and wooden ploughs. It is Hindus, Moslems, Christians (incidentally Christianity reached India before it reached Rome), Sikhs, Jews, Parsis, Buddhists, and atheists. . . .
>
> Indian migration to Canada makes very interesting reading. . . . As their numbers grew [after 1904] there were outbreaks of violence against them, as against people of Chinese and Japanese origins, and measures were taken to stop the "Hindu" immigration. A very effective one was the "continuous passage" rule of 1908, which said that an Indian could not change ships at any intervening ports on the way from India. But there were no ships from India visiting Canadian ports! In April 1914 a memorable episode, the *Komagata Maru* incident, took place. About 400 Sikhs from India chartered a ship and *did* come by continuous passage to Vancouver. The ship sat in Vancouver for three months before finally being turned away. . . .
>
> According to a study of the Department of Manpower and Immigration, Indian immigrants who came between 1969 and 1971 started to work an average 5-1/2 weeks after their arrival in the country.

> . . . After three years in Canada, the Indian immigrants who came in 1969 had an average family income of $9,056 a year. This compares with $12,237 for British immigrants, who were at the top, and $6,457 for Italian immigrants who were at the bottom. . . .
>
> Indian immigrants have not, generally speaking, established ethnic neighborhoods or residential communities. They are spread out in all residential districts from the posh to the poor. According to the study, in three years 29 per cent of them had bought their own homes.[9]

- What new information did you gain from this report about:

  (i) Canada's early immigration laws?
  (ii) the contribution of Indian immigrants to the Canadian economy?

- Why do you think Dr. Samuel emphasizes the financial success of the Indian groups in Canada?
- If you could interview Dr. Samuel, what questions would you ask him about the Indians in Canada?

Two Views of the Future

Read the following two views of Canada's future:

... although Canada has grown from Indian, Inuit, French and British roots, and although these roots have stood firm in the past, the new Canada — the Canada of the 21st century — will be a replica [copy] of the world with its many peoples, values, life styles and tongues. Its new branches and roots will be fused into a nation called Canada and a people labelled Canadian.[10]

We already live in the age of the faceless mass man, in North America at least. We look alike, eat alike, and talk alike thanks to Coca-Cola, television, and the standardized packaging both of our disposable goods and ourselves.[11]

- What evidence is there that the first view is realistic? unrealistic?
- How would your life in this kind of society be more interesting or exciting? How would it be more difficult? less satisfying?
- What evidence is there that the second view is the more accurate?
- Write an editorial in which you describe the kind of society you hope Canada will be by the year 2000.
- Visit parts of a Canadian city where ethnic groups come together, for example, the Kensington Market area in Toronto, Ontario.
- Invite representatives of one or more ethnic groups to come to your class to tell you about their relationships with other Canadian groups. Have they experienced discrimination? Stereotyping?
- Hold an Ethnic Day. In one school the day included the following:

Booths
The arts and crafts of the countries from which students' families originated were displayed in the resource centre.

Dances
In the gym students took part in dances from around the world.

Film
In the auditorium students saw a group of films depicting the experiences of different cultural groups in Canada.

Fashion Show
A number of students wore their native costumes throughout the day and later, in the fashion show held after the film, competed with each other for the most beautiful costume.

Lunch
This was the highlight of the day. Food of an amazing variety was served at a buffet set up in the school foyer. Many students contributed their families' favorite dishes. Recipes were exchanged.

- What are each of the following? *brothchan bruid, vichyssoise, lasagna, sauerbraten, shashlik, sukiyaki?* How many of these dishes have you eaten? Made at home?
- If your class were to have a Canada Day, what things would you exhibit in your booths? What foods would you serve? What films would you show? Have we our own dances? Our own special fashions?
- Discuss the statement: "Canada is neither a mosaic nor a melting pot, but a society in which a number of separate groups can share many common experiences and interests."
- Discuss the statement: "Home is where one chooses to live and is welcome to stay."

FOR FURTHER READING

Doughty, Howard et al. *Canadian Studies: Culture and Country.* Toronto: John Wiley & Sons (Canada) Ltd., 1976.

Hardwick, Francis C., ed. *When Strangers Meet.* Vancouver: Tantalus Research Ltd., 1972.

Spoule, Wayne et al. *Cultures in Canada.* Toronto: Maclean-Hunter Learning Materials, 1976.

Spoule, Wayne et al. *Minority Groups.* Toronto: Maclean-Hunter Learning Materials, 1971.

Troper, Harold and Palmer, Lee. *Issues in Cultural Diversity.* Toronto: Ontario Institute for Studies in Education, 1976.

APPENDIX I

A Guide for Interviewing a Representative of a Particular Ethnic Group

Before the interview find out as much as you can about the ethnic group to which the person belongs. If at all possible, make a tape or cassette recording of your conversation. You might have a practice conversation before the actual interview to test that the machinery is working properly and to put the person interviewed at ease.

The following questions are a guide only. Do not feel that you need to use them all. Be as sensitive as you can to the response of the person you are interviewing, and do not insist on answers to questions about things that are not of interest to the person, or things that he or she seems reluctant to discuss.

(i) *Life in the country of origin*
— location and size of place of birth
–- number in family
— occupations of family members
— special memories of what life was like

(ii) *The decision to leave*
— reasons for leaving
— reasons for choosing Canada
— contacts, if any, in Canada
— arrangements for emigration
— contacts with Canadian immigration officials

(iii) *The voyage to Canada*
— type of transportation to a Canadian port-of-entry
— cost of voyage
— length of voyage
— difficulties experienced

(iv) *First experiences in Canada*
— area of destination.
— first employment: how work obtained, type of work, conditions, hours, pay, relations with fellow workers

— first housing: type of housing, distance from work, cost, relations with neighbours or persons sharing accommodation
— difficulties experienced, for example, financial, language, possible discrimination, loneliness
— help received: from churches, ethnic organizations, relatives, schools, social services
— children's experience in school

(v) *Continuing ties with country of origin*
— family contacts
— financial help given
— visits home
— knowledge or experience of political situation

(vi) *Present identification with ethnic group*
— within the family: language spoken at home, types of food, religious observances, other customs preserved, family relationships
— within the ethnic community: relationships with the church, social or sports organizations, ethnic newspapers, theatres

(vii) *Integration within Canadian Society*
— within the family: relations between parents and children, possible intermarriage with members of other groups
— within the community: participation by children in after-school activities, membership by adults in non-ethnic organizations, attendance at night schools, awareness of or involvement in Canadian politics, possible move to a new neighbourhood

APPENDIX II

A Guide for Research into a Particular Immigrant Group

(i) When did members of this group first come to Canada?

(ii) Why did they leave their homeland?

(iii) Where did they settle when they first came to Canada?

(iv) What occupations did they follow?

(v) What difficulties did they have in adapting to the Canadian environment? to Canadian life?

(vi) Where do most of their descendants live today?

(vii) What occupations do they follow today?

(viii) Did the members of this group attempt to preserve their cultural heritage? If so, how? How successful have their attempts been?

(ix) What contributions have members of this group made to Canada in the past? What contributions are they making today?

(x) What parts of their culture have Canadians of other ethnic groups adopted?

(xi) Using the diagram of the roots of Canada's British heritage (p. 63) as a guide, consider other specific ways in which this group has influenced our Canadian life-style, for example, architecture, music.

(xii) Find out more about specific individuals who belong to this group.

(xiii) What *world contributions* has this group made throughout its history?

END-NOTES

THE FIRST PEOPLE

1. *Toronto Star,* April 1, 1974.
2. Adapted from E. Palmer Patterson II, *The Canadian Indian: A History Since 1500* (Toronto: Collier-Macmillan, 1972), pp. 37-41.
3. Emma La Roque, *Defeathering the Indian* (Toronto: Book Society of Canada, 1975), p. 8.
4. D. Bruce Sealey and Verna J. Kirkness, eds., *Indians Without Tipis.* A Resource Book by Indians and Métis. Project Canada West (Toronto: Book Society of Canada, 1974), p. 10.
5. LaRoque, *op. cit.,* p. 8.
6. Cited in Sealey and Kirkness, *op. cit.,* p. 55.
7. *Ibid.,* pp. 101-108.
8. CASNP, *Bulletin,* Vol. 18, Number 2, October 1977 (Ottawa: CASNP, 1977), p. 9.
9. Chief Dan George and Helmut Hirnschall, *My Heart Soars* (Hancock House and Clarke Irwin, 1974), pp. 36-41.
10. Canadian Association in Support of the Native Peoples, *And What About Canada's Native Peoples?* (Ottawa, 1976), pp. 8-9
11. Adapted from Sealey and Kirkness, *op. cit.,* pp. 156-7.
12. CASNP, *op. cit.,* p. 1.
13. *Ibid.,* pp. 1-3.
14. The Dene People. CASNP, *Bulletin,* Vol. 17, Number 3, December 1976 (Ottawa: CASNP, 1976), p. 8.
15. Ojibway-Cree Nation of Treaty #9 to the People of Canada. CASNP, *Bulletin,* Vol. 18, Number 2, October 1977 (Ottawa: CASNP, 1977), pp. 9-10.
16. Thomas R. Berger, *Northern Frontier, Northern Homeland.* The Report of the MacKenzie Valley Pipeline Inquiry: Volume One (Ottawa: Minister of Supply and Services, 1977), p. 36.
17. CASNP, *Bulletin,* Vol. 17, Number 3, December 1976 (Ottawa: CASNP, 1976), p. 25.
18. CASNP, *Bulletin,* Vol. 17, Number 4, September 1977 (Ottawa: CASNP, 1977), p. 5.

DID THE VIKINGS SETTLE IN NORTH AMERICA?

1. The Saga Tale (*c.* 995-996), quoted in Farley Mowat, *West Viking* (Toronto: McClelland & Stewart Ltd., 1965), pp. 117-18.
2. *Ibid.,* p. 118.

THE FRENCH IN CANADA

1. Marc Lescarbot. Cary F. Goulson, *Seventeenth-Century Canada Source Studies* (Toronto: Macmillan, 1970), pp. 39-40.
2. *Ibid.,* p. 36-37.
3. *Ibid.,* p. 42.
4. *Ibid.,* p. 44.
5. *Ibid.*
6. Samuel de Champlain. Yves F. Zoltvany, ed., *The French Tradition in America* (New York: Harper & Row, 1969), pp. 37-42.
7. Pierre Boucher. *Ibid.,* pp. 64-65.
8. Marie de l'Incarnation. Joyce Marshall, *Word from New France. The Selected Letters of Marie de l'Incarnation* (Toronto: Oxford, 1967), p. 330.
9. *Ibid.,* pp. 353-4.
10. Cameron Nish, ed. & trans., *The French Régime,* Volume I Canadian Historical Documents Series (Toronto: Prentice-Hall, 1965), p. 58.
11. Lahontan. Cited in Shortt, Adam and Doughty, G., gen. eds. *Canada and Its Provinces. A History of the Canadian People and Their Institutions by One Hundred Associates.* Vol. XV. Toronto: Glasgow, Brook & Company, 1914.
12. Nish, *op. cit.,* p. 157 and Marcel Trudel, *Introduction to New France* (Toronto: Holt, Rinehart and Winston, 1968), p. 131.
13. Nish, *op. cit.,* p. 58.
14. M.C. Urquhart and K.A.H. Buckley, *Historical Statistics of Canada* (Toronto: Macmillan, 1965), p. 54.
15. Minister of Industry, Trade and Commerce, *Canada Year Book 1975* (Ottawa: Statistics Canada, 1975), p. 152, p. 173.
16. Urquhart and Buckley, *op. cit.,* p. 54.
17. *Canada Year Book 1975,* p. 154.
18. *Ibid.,* p. 155.

[19] Trudel, *op. cit.,* p. 140.

[20] *Everything You Always Wanted to Know About the Census* (Ottawa: Dominion Bureau of Statistics, the 1971 Census), p. 6.

[21] Trudel, *op. cit.,* pp. 132-3.

[22] *Ibid.,* pp. 136-40.

[23] W.J. Eccles, *The Ordeal of New France.* Part I of a Four-Part History of Canada (The Canadian Broadcasting Corporation, 1967), p. 95.

[24] Champigny. Eccles, *op. cit.,* p. 55.

[25] Beschefer. *Ibid.,* p. 56.

[26] d'Auteuil. Virginia R. Robeson, gen. ed., *New France: 1713-1760.* Documents in Canadian History. Curriculum Series/23 (The Ontario Institute for Studies in Education), p. 65.

[27] Bougainville. W.J. Eccles, *France in America* (Toronto: Fitzhenry and Whiteside, 1972), p. 127.

[28] Franquet. Robeson, *op. cit.,* p. 68.

[29] W.J. Eccles, *The Government of New France.* The Canadian Historical Association Booklets. No. 18 (Ottawa: Public Archives, 1965), p. 13.

[30] Carleton. Eccles, *The Ordeal of New France,* p. 151.

[31] Eccles, *France in America,* p. 247.

[32] Robert Guy Sully, "To be French in North America," *Canadian Forum,* October 1975, pp. 6-9.

[33] The British North America Act, Section 133. J.H. Stewart Reid, Kenneth McNaught, and Harry S. Crowe, *A Source-book of Canadian History.* Rev. ed. (Toronto: Longmans, 1964), p. 264.

[34] *Canada Year Book 1975,* p. 173.

[35] Preamble to Bill 101. Charter of the French language. Assented to August 1977. Assemblée Nationale de Quebec.

[36] Thomas Wells. *Ontario Education Dimensions.* Summer 78. Volume II, Number 6 (Ontario: Ministry of Education), p. 8.

[37] *Toronto Star.* July 16, 1977.

[38] Jacques-Donat Casanova with the collaboration of Armour Landry, *America's French Heritage* (A Joint Publication of La Documentation Française and the Québec Official Publisher, 1976), p. 76.

[39] Department of Manpower and Immigration, *Living in Canada* (Ottawa: Information Canada, 1971), p. 25.

[40] Cited in N.E.S. Griffiths, *The Acadian Deportation: Deliberate Perfidy or Cruel Necessity?* Issues in Canadian History (Toronto: Copp Clar, 1969), p. 39.

CANADA AND GREAT BRITAIN

[1] Reprinted from E.A. Richardson and J.D. Thexton, *Footprints in Time* (Toronto: House of Grant (Canada) Ltd., 1963), p. 16.

[2] Reprinted from E. Lavender and N. Sheffe, *A Sourcebook for Ancient and Medieval History* (Toronto: McGraw-Hill Co. Ltd., 1963), p. 113.

[3] Reprinted from Richardson and Thexton, *op. cit.,* p. 26.

[4] S.T. Bindoff, *Tudor England* (Middlesex, England: Penguin Books Ltd., 1966), p. 306.

[5] Reprinted from G.M. Trevelyan, *History of England* (London: Longmans, Green and Co., 1952), p. 384.

[6] Reprinted from G.M. Trevelyan, *England Under the Stuarts* (Middlesex, England: Penguin Books, Ltd., 1960), p. 99.

[7] *Ibid.*

[8] *Ibid.,* pp. 135, 136.

THE SCOTS IN CANADA

[1] Canadian Boat-song. *Canadian Magazine* (Toronto: Southstar Publishers Ltd., 1974), p. 20.

[2] Charles W. Dunn, *Highland Settler, A Portrait of the Scottish Gael in Nova Scotia* (Toronto: University of Toronto Press, 1953), p. 12.

[3] Frederick A. Pottle, and Charles H. Bennett, eds. *Boswell's Journal of a Tour to the Hebrides with Samuel Johnson, LL.D 1773.* London: Heinemann, 1963, p. 243.

[4] *Ibid.,* p. 104.

[5] Cited in John Prebble, *The Highland Clearances* (Penguin Books,, 1963), p. 28.

[6] *Ibid.,* p. 106.

[7] *Ibid.,* p. 189.

[8] *Ibid.,* p. 102.

9 *Ibid.,* p. 79.

10 *Ibid.,* p. 61.

11 *Ibid.,* pp. 131-2.

12 *Ibid.,* p. 291.

13 James A. Roy, *The Scot and Canada* (Toronto: McClelland & Stewart, 1947), p. 83.

14 *Census of Canada 1971.*

15 Catharine Parr Traill, *The Backwoods of Canada* (Toronto: McClelland & Stewart, 1966), pp. 13-20.

THE UNITED EMPIRE LOYALISTS

1 Quoted in Eula C. Lapp, *To Their Heirs Forever.* Belleville, Ont.: Mika Publishing Co., 1977, p. p. 154.

2 G.M. Wrong, *Canada and the American Revolution* (New York: Cooper Square, 1968), p. 426.

3 Lapp, *op. cit.,* p. 227, 228.

4 *Ibid.,* p. 258.

THE GREAT MIGRATION: WHY THEY LEFT HOME

1 John Prebble, *The Highland Clearances* (Penguin Books, 1963), p. 79.

2 B. Disraeli, *Sybil* (London: Oxford University Press, 1950), pp. 118, 119.

3 Quoted in Charlotte Erickson, *Emigration from Europe 1815-1914* (London: Adam & Charles Black, 1976), p. 33.

4 Quoted in E.L. Daniher, *Britain and the Empire* (Toronto: Copp Clark Co. Ltd., 1947), p. 105.

5 *Ibid.,* p. 107.

THE GREAT MIGRATION: THE ATLANTIC CROSSING UNDER SAIL

1 Edwin C. Guillet, *The Great Migration* (Toronto: Thomas Nelson and Sons, 1937), p. 57.

2 *Ibid.,* p. 93.

3 Helen Cowan, *British Emigration to British North America: The First Hundred Years.* Toronto: University of Toronto Press, 1961, p. 304.

4 Cowan, *op. cit.,* p. 304.

THE GREAT MIGRATION: EARLY YEARS

1 G.M. Grant, *Ocean to Ocean* (Toronto: James Campbell & Sons, 1873), pp. 333-6 (Coles Canadiana Collection).

THE GREAT MIGRATION: THE ENGLISH

1 W. Catermole, *Emigration: The Advantages of Emigration to Canada* (London: Simpkin and Marshall, May 1831), pp. 203-4 (Coles Canadiana Collection).

2 *Ibid.,* pp. 206-8.

3 *Ibid.,* p. 44.

4 J. Howison, *Sketches of Upper Canada* (Edinburgh: Oliver & Boyd, 1821), pp. 237-46 (Coles Canadiana Collection).

THE GREAT MIGRATION: THE IRISH

1 Quoted in Cecil Woodham-Smith, *The Great Hunger* (New York: Harper & Row Co., 1962), p. 237.

2 *Ibid.,* pp. 32, 34, 412.

3 *Ibid.,* p. 47.

4 *Ibid.,* p. 159.

5 *Ibid.,* p. 205.

6 *Ibid.,* p. 226.

7 *Ibid.,* p. 222.

8 Nicholas Davin, *The Irishmen in Canada* (Shannon, Ireland: The Irish University Press, 1968), p. 245.

THE GREAT MIGRATION: THE FUGITIVES

1 Benjamin Drew, *The Refugee; or the Narratives of Fugitive Slaves in Canada* (Boston: John P. Jewell and Company, 1856), p. 3. Facsimile edition published by Coles Publishing Company, Toronto, *c.* 1972.

2 *Ibid.,* p. 49.

3 *Ibid.,* pp. 86-87.

4 *Ibid.,* p. 134.

5 *Ibid.,* p. 151.

6 *Ibid.,* p. 370.

7 *Ibid.,* p. 374.

8 *Ibid.,* p. 3.

9 *Ibid.,* p. 152.

10 *Ibid.,* p. 153.

11 *Ibid.,* p. 147.

12 *Ibid.,* p. 159.

13 *Ibid.,* p. 190.

14 *Ibid.,* pp. 279-80.

15 *Ibid.,* p. 371.

16 *Ibid.,* p. 151.

17 *Ibid.,* p. 342.

THE GREAT MIGRATION: OPENING THE WEST

1 John T. Saywell and John C. Ricker, *Nation-Building. Original Documents on the Founding of the Canadian Nation and the Settlement of the West, 1867-85* (Burns & MacEachern, 1967), p. 161.

2 James J. Talman, *Basic Documents in Canadian History* (Toronto: Van Nostrand, 1959), pp. 20-23.

3 Sealey and Kirkness, *op. cit.,* p. 117.

4 *Ibid.,* p. 23.

5 D. Bruce Sealey, *Cuthbert Grant and the Métis. We Built Canada* (Toronto: Book Society of Canada, 1976), pp. 37-38.

6 Saywell and Ricker, *op. cit.,* p. 161.

7 Toronto *Globe.* J.T. Copp and Marcel Hamelin, *Confederation: 1867.* Problems in Canadian History (Toronto: Copp Clark, 1966), p. 6.

8 The Nor'Wester. P.B. Waite. *Confederation, 1854-1867.* Canadian History Through the Press Series. Gen. eds. David P. Gagnan, Anthony W. Rasporich (Toronto: Holt, Rinehart and Winston, 1972), p. 65.

9 *Quebec Daily Mercury, ibid.,* p. 122.

10 Edward Watkin. Copp and Hamelin, *op. cit.,* p. 9.

11 *The Globe,* July 12, 1866.

12 Historical and Scientific Society of Manitoba, *Papers,* Series III, No. 26. 1969-70.

13 Saywell and Ricker, *op. cit.,* pp. 161-2.

14 Sealey and Kirkness, *op. cit.,* p. 51.

15 Saywell and Ricker, *op. cit.,* p. 15.

16 *Ibid.* p. 164.

17 *Ibid.,*

18 Urquhart, *op. cit.,* pp. 27-28.

THE GREAT MIGRATION: THE MEN IN SHEEPSKIN COATS

1 Cited in Vladimir J. Kaye, *Early Ukrainian Settlements in Canada 1895-1900* (Toronto: University of Toronto Press, 1964), pp. 3-4.

2 *Ibid.,* pp. 15-16.

3 *Ibid.,* p. 17.

4 Cited in J.G. MacGregor, *Vilni Zemli (Free Lands). The Ukrainian Settlement of Alberta* (Toronto: McClelland & Stewart, 1969), pp. 75-76, 105-6.

5 Kaye, *op. cit.,* pp. 192-3.

6 MacGregor, *op. cit.,* p. 93.

7 *Ibid.*

8 *Ibid.,* pp. 109-10.

9 Kaye, *op. cit.,* p. 350.

10 *Ibid.,* p. 356.

11 Joan Forman, *Westward to Canaan* (Holt, Rinehart and Winston, 1972).

12 Kaye, *op. cit.,* p. 350.

13 *Ibid.,* p. 372.

14 *Ibid.,* p. 364.

15 J.S. Woodsworth, *Strangers Within Our Gates. (Toronto: University of Toronto Press, 1972), pp. 110-12.*

16 *Census of Canada,* 1971.

THE GREAT MIGRATION: THE CHINESE

1 Woodsworth, *op. cit.,* pp. 144-152.

2 Hwuy-ung, *A Chinaman's Opinion of Us and of His Own Country,* trans. J.A. Makepeace (London: Chatto & Windus, 1927), quoted in David L. Weitzman, *East Meets West* (Berkeley Heights, New Jersey: Field Educational Publications, Incorporated, Asian Studies Inquiry Program, *c.* 1969), pp. 48-50.

3 J.S. Woodsworth, *op. cit.,* p. 142.

IMMIGRATION AFTER WORLD WAR I: IMMIGRATION POLICIES

1 R.B. Bennett, House of Commons *Debates,* June 7, 1928, pp. 3925-6.

[2] *Manitoba Free Press,* June 4, 1919, quoted in Howard Palmer, *Immigration and the Rise of Multiculturalism* (Toronto: Copp Clark Publishing, 1975), p. 198.

[3] John Marlin, *Under the Ribs of Death* (Toronto: McClelland and Stewart Ltd., 1964), pp. 23-24.

IMMIGRATION AFTER WORLD WAR I: THE HUTTERITES

[1] J.A. Hostetler and G.E. Huntington, *The Hutterites in North America* (New York: Holt, Rinehart and Winston, 1967), p. 5.

[2] *Ibid.,* p. 95.

IMMIGRATION AFTER WORLD WAR I: JAPANESE CANADIANS

[1] Bruce Cushing, Japanese Canadians. Did Canada Treat Them Fairly During World War II? *Canada and the World,* Vol. 39, February 1974, pp. 26-27.

IMMIGRATION AFTER WORLD WAR II

[1] Cited in Freda Hawkins, *Canada and Immigration: Public Policy and Public Concern.* (Montreal: McGill-Queen's University Press, 1972), pp. 58-59.

[2] *Canada Year Book 1976-77.*

IMMIGRATION AFTER WORLD WAR II: THE AMERICANS

[1] Joan Rattner Heilman, "We Moved to Toronto," Changing Life-Styles: No. 8, *Family Circle,* February 1974, pp. 46-50.

IMMIGRATION AFTER WORLD WAR II: THE GERMANS

[1] Wolfgang Friedman, *German Immigration into Canada,* Contemporary Affairs series No. 23 Canadian Institute of International Affairs (Toronto: Ryerson, 1952).

[2] *Toronto Star,* June 3, 1972.

IMMIGRATION AFTER WORLD WAR II: THE ITALIANS

[1] *Census of Canada,* 1961.

[2] C. Jansen, "The Italian Community in Toronto" in J.L. Elliot, *Minority Canadians* (Toronto: Prentice-Hall of Canada Ltd., 1971), p. 208.

[3] Robert Reguly, *Toronto Star,* May 23, 1972.

[4] *Ibid.*

[5] *Ibid.*

[6] *Census of Canada,* 1961.

[7] A. Spada, *The Italians in Canada* (Montreal: Canada Ethnic Press Federation, Riviera Printers and Publishers, 1969), p. 266.

[8] The Dominion Bureau of Statistics, quoted in Spada, *op. cit.,* p. 139.

WHO CAN IMMIGRATE TO CANADA?

[1] *New Directions. A Look at Canada's Immigration Act and Regulations,* Minister of Supply and Services, Canada, 1978.

[2] Richard Needham, *Globe and Mail,* February, 1974.

[3] *Canada and the World,* Vol. No. 38, January 1973, pp. 3,4

[4] Norman Hartley, *Globe and Mail,* December 29, 1973.

[5] An immigration official, quoted by Norman Hartley, *Globe and Mail,* December 29, 1973.

[6] Richard Tait, quoted by Norman Hartley, *Globe and Mail,* January 24, 1974.

CANADA: A MOSAIC OF PEOPLES?

[1] *Toronto Star,* April 6, 1972.

[2] Sam Fox, of the Amalgamated Clothing Workers Union, reported to the *Toronto Star,* April 6, 1972.

[3] *Toronto Star,* September 11, 1972.

[4] Julian Fantino, a constable with the Metro Toronto Police Force, quoted in the *Toronto Star,* September 23, 1972.

[5] Marlene Tomlinson, founder of a Caribbean Club.

[6] Walter Pitman, *Now Is Not Too Late* (Toronto: Metropolitan Task Force on Human Relations, 1977), p. 32.

[7] *Ibid.,* p. 81.

[8] *Ibid.,* p. 279.

9 R.T. Samuel, "The East Indian Presence in Canada" in G.W. Bancroft, ed., *Outreach for Understanding* (Toronto: The Ministry of Culture and Recreation, 1977), pp. 71-73.

10 G.W. Bancroft, ed., *Outreach for Understanding: a report of the intercultural seminar program conducted in Toronto between 1973 and 1975* (Toronto: The Ministry of Culture and Recreation, 1977), p. 5.

11 *Ibid.,* p. 10.

RESOURCES FOR TEACHERS

LOOKING AT CANADIANS

Baker, Eunice Ruiter. *Searching for Your Ancestors in Canada.* Ottawa: Heritage House Publishers Ltd., 1974.

Baxter, Angus. *In Search of Your Roots: A Guide for Canadians Seeking Their Ancestors.* Toronto: Macmillan of Canada, 1978.

The Canadian Family Tree. Ottawa: Department of the Secretary of State, 1967.

THE FIRST PEOPLE

American Heritage. *The American Heritage Book of Indians.* William Brandon, Editor in Charge. American Heritage Publishing Co., 1961.

Angus, T. and White, S. *Canadians All: Portraits of Our People.* Toronto: Methuen Publications, 1976.

Asp, George. "Land for Living." *Canada and the World.* Volume 41, Number 1, September 1975.

Berger, Thomas R. *Northern Frontier, Northern Homeland. The Report of the Mackenzie Valley Pipeline Inquiry: Volume One.* Ottawa: Minister of Supply and Services, 1977.

Briggs, Lyman J. and Weaver, Kenneth P. "How Old Is It?" *The National Geographic Magazine.* Vol. CXIV. July-December 1958. Washington: The National Geographic Society.

Canadian Association in Support of the Native Peoples. *And What About Canada's Native Peoples?* Ottawa: CASNP, 1976.

Canadian Association in Support of the Native Peoples. *Bulletin.* Ottawa: CASNP.

Cardinal, Harold. *The Rebirth of Canada's Indians.* Edmonton: Hurtig Publishers, 1977.

———. *The Unjust Society.* Edmonton: M.G. Hurtig Ltd., 1969.

Claiborne, Robert and the Editors of Time-Life Books. *The First Americans.* The Emergence of Man. New York: Time-Life Books, 1973.

Clark, Ella Elizabeth. *Indian Legends of Canada. Toronto: McClelland & Stewart, 1960.*

Cowan, Susan, ed. *We Don't Live in Snow Houses Now.* Edmonton: Hurtig Publishers, 1976.

Dewdney, Selwyn. *They Shared to Survive: The Native Peoples of Canada.* Toronto: Macmillan of Canada, 1975.

Eber, Dorothy, ed. *People from Our Side: A Life Story with Photographs by Peter Pitseolak.* Edmonton: Hurtig Publishers, 1975.

Eisenberg, J. and Troper, H. *Native Survival.* Canadian Critical Issues Series. Toronto: O.I.S.E., 1973.

Elliott, Jean Leonard. *Minority Canadians I. Native Peoples.* Toronto: Prentice-Hall, 1971.

Hall, E., comp. *Early Canada: A collection of historical photographs by officers of the Geological Survey of Canada.* Ottawa: Queen's Printer, 1964.

Heindenreich, Conrad E. and Ray, Arthur J. *The Early Fur Trades: A Study in Cultural Interaction.* Toronto: McClelland & Stewart, 1976.

Howell, F. Clark. *Early Man.* Life Nature Library. New York: Time-Life Books, 1965.

LaForme, Harry. "Wards of the State." *Canada and the World,* Volume 41, Number 1, September 1975.

LaRoque, Emma. *Defeathering the Indian.* Toronto: Book Society of Canada, 1975.

Mandamin, Tony. "The Forgotten Poor." *Canada and the World,* Volume 41, Number 8, April 1976.

Patterson, E. Palmer. *The Canadian Indian: A History Since 1500.* Toronto: Collier-Macmillan, 1972.

People of Native Ancestry. A Resource Guide for the Intermediate Division. Toronto: Ontario Ministry of Education, 1977. This contains an excellent list of audio-visual resources.

Rogers, E.S. *Algonkians of the Eastern Woodlands.* Toronto: Royal Ontario Museum, 1970.

———. *The Indians of Canada: A Survey.* Toronto: ROM, 1970.

———. *Indians of the North Pacific Coast.* Toronto: ROM, 1970.

———. *Indians of the Plains.* Toronto: ROM, 1970.

———. *Indians of the Subarctic.* Toronto: ROM, 1970.

———. *Iroquoians of the Eastern Woodlands.* Toronto: ROM, 1970.

Rowley, G.W. "What are Eskimos?" *Canada and the World,* Volume 39, Number 6, February 1974.

Sealey, D. Bruce and Kirkness, Verna J., eds. *Indians Without Tipis. A Resource Book by Indians and Métis.* Toronto: Book Society of Canada, 1974.

Surtees, R.J. *The Original People.* Toronto: Holt, Rinehart and Winston, 1971.

Taylor, J.G. *The Canadian Eskimos.* Toronto: Royal Ontario Museum, 1971.

Turner, C. Frank. "The First Inhabitants." *Canada and the World,* Volume 41, Number 1, September 1975.

Walsh, Gerald. *Indians in Transition: An Inquiry Approach.* Curriculum Resource Books Series. Toronto: McClelland & Stewart, 1971.

White, Charles A. "The Only Good Indian. . . ." *Canada and the World,* Volume 41, Number 1, September 1975. (The Beothuks of Newfoundland.)

DID THE VIKINGS SETTLE IN NORTH AMERICA?

Anderson, John. *Vineland Voyage.* New York: Funk and Wagnalls, 1967.

Brondsted, Johannes. *The Vikings.* Harmondsworth, Middlesex, England: Penguin, 1976.

Mowat, Farley. *West Viking.* Toronto: McClelland & Stewart, 1965.

Washburn, W.E. *Proceedings of the Vinland Map Conference.* Chicago: University of Chicago Press, 1971.

THE FRENCH IN CANADA

Beaudry, Yvonne. "Quebec Roots." *Weekend Magazine.* August 27, 1977.

Casanova, Jacques-Donat with the collaboration of Landrey, Armour. *America's French Heritage.* A joint publication of La Documentation Française and the Quebec Official Publisher, 1976.

Coulson, Gary F. *Seventeenth-Century Canada Source Studies.* Toronto: Macmillan, 1970.

Cybulski, Lynn. "Living in Peace." *Canada and the World,* Volume 44, Number 7, March 1979 (Acadians).

Eccles, W.J. *France in America.* Toronto: Fitzhenry & Whiteside, 1972.

———. *The Government of New France.* The Canadian Historical Association Booklets. No. 18. Ottawa: Public Archives, 1965.

———. *The Ordeal of New France.* Part I of a Four-Part History of Canada. Toronto: The Canadian Broadcasting Corporation, 1967.

Griffiths, N.E.S. *The Acadian Deportation: Deliberate Perfidy or Cruel Necessity?* Issues in Canadian History. Toronto: Copp Clark, 1969.

———. *The Acadians: Creation of a People.* The Frontenac Library. Toronto: McGraw-Hill Ryerson, 1973.

Harris, R.C. *The Seigneurial System in Early Canada.* Madison: University of Wisconsin Press, 1966.

Marshall, Joyce. *Word from New France. The Selected Letters of Marie de L'Incarnation.* Toronto: Oxford, 1967.

Moir, John S. and Saunders, Robert E. *Northern Destiny: A History of Canada.* Toronto: Dent, 1970.

Neatby, Hilda. *Quebec, the Revolutionary Age, 1760 1791.* Canadian Centenary Series. Toronto: McClelland & Stewart, 1966.

Nish, Cameron, ed. & trans., *The French Régime.* Vol. I. Canadian Historical Documents Series. Scarborough: Prentice-Hall, 1965.

Sully, Robert Guy. "To be French in North America." *Canadian Forum.* October 1975.

Trudel, Marcel. *The Seigneurial Regime.* The Canadian Historical Association Booklets. No. 6. Ottawa: Public Archives, 1967.

Trussler, Lloyd G. *Canadian Settlement Patterns.* Canadian Geography Resources. Dent, 1972.

Zoltvany, Yves F., ed. *The French Tradition in America.* New York: Harper & Row, 1969.

CANADA AND GREAT BRITAIN: A UNIQUE ASSOCIATION

Ashley, Maurice. *England in the Seventeenth Century.* Toronto: Penguin Books (Canada) Ltd., 1952.

Bindoff, S.T. *Tudor England.* Harmondsworth, Middlesex, England: Penguin Books Ltd., 1950.

MacKenzie, Kenneth. *The English Parliament.* Harmondsworth, Middlesex, Engand: Penguin Books Ltd., 1950.

Medlicott, W.N., general editor. *A History of England* (in ten volumes). London: Longmans, Green and Co. Ltd.

Plumb, J.H. *England in the Eighteenth Century.* Harmondsworth, Middlesex, England: Penguin Books Ltd., 1950.

Trevelyan, G.M. *England Under the Stuarts.* Harmondsworth, Middlesex, England: Penguin Books Ltd., 1960.

Audio-Visual

Cole. G.D.H. *Agriculture and the Land.* Common Ground filmstrip CGB44, distributed in Canada by Carman Educational Associates, Pine Grove, Ontario.

Cole, G.D.H. *Coal, Metal and Steam.* Common Ground filmstrip CGB47, distributed in Canada by Carman Educational Associates, Pine Grove, Ontario.

THE SCOTS IN CANADA

Campbell, D. and MacLean, R.A. *Beyond the Atlantic Roar: A Study of the Nova Scotia Scots.* The Carleton Library No. 78. Toronto: McClelland & Stewart, 1974.

Dunn, Charles W. *Highland Settler, A Portrait of the Scottish Gael in Nova Scotia.* Toronto: University of Toronto Press, 1953.

Galbraith, John Kenneth. *The Scotch.* Boston: Houghton Mifflin, 1964.

Gray, John Morgan. *Lord Selkirk of Red River.* Toronto: Macmillan, 1964.

Hill, Douglas. *The Scots to Canada.* Vol. I. Great Emigrations. London: Gentry Books, 1972.

Pottle, Frederick A. and Bennett, Charles H., eds. *Boswell's Journal of a Tour to the Hebrides with Samuel Johnson, LL.D. 1773.* London: Heinemann, 1963.

Prebble, John. *The Highland Clearances.* Penguin Books, 1963.

Reid, W. Stanford, ed. *The Scottish Tradition in Canada.* Generations. A History of Canada's Peoples. Toronto: McClelland & Stewart, 1976.

Roy, James A. *The Scot and Canada.* Toronto: McClelland & Stewart, 1947.

Traill, Catharine Parr. *The Backwoods of Canada.* Toronto: McClelland & Stewart, 1966.

Audio-Visual
Culloden. BBC. 16 mm b/w.

THE UNITED EMPIRE LOYALISTS

Lapp, Eula C. *To Their Heirs Forever.* Belleville, Ont.: Mika Publishing Co., 1977.

Lower, A.R.M. "Loyalist Cities: Saint John, New Brunswick, and Kingston, Ontario." *Queen's Quarterly,* Vol. LXXII, Winter, 1966, pp. 657-664.

Shelton, W.G. "The United Empire Loyalists: A Reconsideration." *Dalhousie Review,* Vol. XLV, No. 1, 1965, pp. 5-16.

Upton, L.F.S., ed. *The United Empire Loyalists: Men and Myths.* Toronto: Copp Clark Publishing Co., 1967.

Wrong, G.M. *Canada and the American Revolution.* New York: Cooper Square, 1968.

For information from the United Empire Loyalist Association write to National Headquarters, 23 Prince Arthur Ave., Toronto, Ontario M5R 1B2.

THE GREAT MIGRATION: *Why They Left Home*

Ashton, T.S. *The Industrial Revolution 1760-1830.* London: Oxford University Press, 1948.

Erickson, Charlotte. *Emigration from Europe 1815-1914.* London: Adam & Charles Black Co. Ltd., 1976.

Thomson, David. *Europe Since Napoleon.* New York: Alfred A. Knopp, Inc., revised, 1962.

THE GREAT MIGRATION: *The Atlantic Crossing Under Sail*

Cowan, Helen. *British Emigration to British North America: The First Hundred Years.* Toronto: The University of Toronto Press, 1961.

Guillet, Edwin C. *The Great Migration: The Atlantic Crossing by Sailing Ships Since 1770.* Toronto: University of Toronto Press, 1937.

Woodham-Smith, Cecil. *The Great Hunger.* New York: Harper & Row Publishers, 1962.

THE GREAT MIGRATION: *The English*

Atwood, Margaret. *The Journals of Susanna Moodie.* Toronto: Oxford Univeristy Press, 1970.

Catermole, W. *Emigration. The Advantages of Emigration to Canada.* London: Simpkin and Marshall, 1831 (Coles Canadiana Collection).

Cowan, Helen. *British Emigration to British North America: The First Hundred Years.* Toronto: University of Toronto Press, 1961.

Howison, J. *Sketches of Upper Canada.* Edinburgh: Oliver & Boyd, 1821

THE GREAT MIGRATION: *The Irish Immigration (1846-1849)*

Cowan, Helen. *British Emigration to British North America: The First Hundred Years.* Toronto: The University of Toronto Press, 1961.

Halévy, Elie. *Victorian Years (1841-1895).* London: Ernest Benn Ltd., 1961.

Woodham-Smith, Cecil. *The Great Hunger.* New York: Harper & Row, Publishers, 1962.

THE GREAT MIGRATION: The Fugitives

"Blacks in Canada: A Forgotten History." *Toronto Star,* February 17, 1979.

Drew, Benjamin. *The Refugee; or the Narratives of Fugitive Slaves in Canada.* Boston: John P. Jewett and Company, 1856. Facsimile edition published by Coles Publishing Company, Toronto, *c.*1972.

Fraser, Douglas. "The Forgotten Canadians." *Canada and the World,* Volume 43, Number 4, December 1977.

Tait, Terence. *Black and White in North America.* Curriculum Resource Books Series. Toronto: McClelland & Stewart, 1970.

Tulloch, Headley. *Black Canadians: A Long Line of Fighters.* Toronto: NC Press Limited, 1975.

Winks, Robin William. *The Blacks in Canada; A History.* Montreal: McGill-Queen's University Press, 1971.

THE GREAT MIGRATION: Opening the West

Ganzevoort, Herman. *A Dutch Homesteader on the Prairies: The Letters of Willem de Gelder 1910-13.* The Social History of Canada. Toronto: University of Toronto Press, 1973.

Hall, E., comp. *Early Canada; A collection of historical photographs by officers of the Geological Survey of Canada.* Ottawa: Queen's Printer, 1964.

Harney, Robert and Troper, Harold. *Immigrants. A Portrait of the Urban Experience, 1890-1930.* Toronto: Van Nostrand Reinhold, 1975.

Hill, Douglas. *The Opening of the Canadian West.* Toronto: Longmans, 1967.

Macdonald, Norman. *Canada: Immigration and Colonization: 1841-1903.* Aberdeen University Press, 1966.

Saywell, John T. and Ricker, John C. *Nation-Building. Original Documents on the Founding of the Canadian Nation and the Settlement of the West, 1867-85.* Burns & MacEachern, 1967.

Troper, Harold. *Only Farmers Need Apply.* Toronto: Griffin House, 1972.

Warkentin, Abe. *Reflections on Our Heritage: A History of Steinbach and the R.M. of Hanover from 1874.* Steinbach: Derksen Publishers, 1971.

Woodsworth, J.S. *Strangers Within Our Gates.* Toronto: University of Toronto Press, 1972.

Audio-Visual

The Fourth Wave. Sound filmstrip. NC Multimedia Corporation.

THE GREAT MIGRATION: The Men in Sheepskin Coats

Canadian Centre for Folk Culture Studies of the National Museum of Man. *Continuity and Change: The Ukrainian Folk Heritage in Canada.* Ottawa: National Museum of Canada, 1972.

Forman, Joan. *Westward to Canaan.* Toronto: Holt, Rinehart and Winston, 1962.

Kaye, Vladimir J. *Early Ukrainian Settlements in Canada 1895-1900.* Toronto: University of Toronto Press, 1964.

MacGregor, J.G. *Vilni Zemli (Free Lands). The Ukrainian Settlement of Alberta.* Toronto: McClelland & Stewart, 1969.

Woycenko, Ol'ha. *The Ukrainians in Canada.* 2nd rev. ed. Canada Ethnica IV. Winnipeg: Trident Press, 1968.

Audio-Visual

I've Never Walked the Steppes. 16 mm film. 28 min. col. NFBC, 1975.

Kurelek. 16 mm film. 10 min. col. NFBC, 1966.

Pysanka: The Ukrainian Easter Egg. 16 mm film. 14 min. col. FLMART, 1975.

THE GREAT MIGRATION: The Chinese

Davis, Morris and Krauter, J.F. *The Other Canadians: Profiles of Six Minorities.* Toronto: Methuen, 1971.

Glynn-Ward, Hilda. *The Writing on the Wall: Chinese and Japanese Immigration to British Columbia.* Toronto: University of Toronto Press, 1974.

Hardwick, Francis C., ed. *East Meets West.* Vancouver: Tantalus Research, 1975.

Wetzel, A. *Chinese Immigrants and China.* Toronto: Board of Education, 1969.

Audio-Visual

"The Chinese in Canada," *The Canadian Mosaic.* Toronto: Moreland-Latchford, 1976 (8 filmstrips. 8 sound cassettes).

Quo Vadis, Mrs. Lumb? National Film Board, 1965, B/W 28 min.

IMMIGRATION AFTER WORLD WAR I

Adachi, Ken. *The Enemy That Never Was: A History of the Japanese Canadians.* Toronto: McClelland & Stewart, 1976.

Broadfoot, Barry, *Years of Sorrow, Years of Shame: The Story of the Japanese Canadians in World War II.* Toronto: Doubleday, 1977.

Canada. Department of Manpower and Immigration. *Immigration Policy Perspectives.* Ottawa: Information Canada, 1975.

Davis, M. and Krauter, J.F. *The Other Canadians: Profiles of Six Minorities.* Toronto: Methuen, 1971.

Harney, Robert and Troper, Harold. *Immigrants: A Portrait of the Urban Experience, 1890-1930.* Toronto: Van Nostrand Reinhold, 1975.

Hostetler, J.A. *Hutterite Society.* Baltimore: John Hopkins University Press, 1974.

Palmer, Howard. *Immigration and the Rise of Multiculturalism.* Toronto: Copp Clark, 1975.

_____. *Land of the Second Chance.* Lethbridge, Alberta: Lethbridge Herald, 1972.

Troper, Harold and Palmer, Lee. *Issues in Cultural Diversity.* Toronto: The Ontario Institute for Studies in Education, 1976.

Audio-Visual

The Hutterites. National Film Board, 1963, B/W. 28 min.

IMMIGRATION AFTER WORLD WAR II

Boissevain, Jeremy. *The Italians of Montreal.* Ottawa: Queen's Printer, 1970.

The Canadian Family Tree. Ottawa: Department of the Secretary of State, 1967.

Fretz, J. Winfield. *The Mennonites in Ontario.* Waterloo: The Mennonite Historical Society of Ontario, 1974.

Freidman, Wolfgang. *German Immigration into Canada.* Contemporary Affairs series No. 23. Canadian Institute of International Affairs. Toronto: Ryerson, 1952.

Jansen, C. "The Italian Community in Toronto" in J.L. Elliot, *Minority Canadians.* Toronto: Prentice-Hall, 1971.

Montero, Gloria. *The Immigrants.* Toronto: James Lorimer & Company, 1977.

Reaman, George Elmore. *The Trail of the Black Walnut,* rev. ed. Toronto: McClelland & Stewart, 1965.

Spada, A. *The Italians in Canada.* Montreal: Canada Ethnic Press Federation, Riviera Printers and Publishers, 1969.

Staebler, Edna. *Sauerkraut and Enterprise.* Toronto: McClelland & Stewart, 1974.

White, Charles A. "Oktoberfest and More." *Canada and the World.* Volume 42, Number 1, October 1976.

Audio-Visual

Plain People. 16 mm film. colour. 28 min. CBC, 1972.

WHO CAN IMMIGRATE TO CANADA?

Canada. *New Directions. A Look at Canada's Immigration Act and Regulations.* Ottawa: Ministry of Supply and Services, 1978.

Canada. Department of Manpower and Immigration. *Immigration Policy Perspectives.* Ottawa: Information Canada, 1975.

Gayn, Mark. "The Plight of the World's Refugees." *Toronto Star.* January 13, 1979.

Hawkins, Freda. *Canada and Immigration: Public Policy and Public Concern.* Montreal: McGill-Queen's University Press, 1972.

Linton, Marilyn. "A 'Second Heaven' in Canada." Toronto: *The Sunday Sun.* October 15, 1978.

Vyhnak, Carol. "Refugees' Recipe Is Hard Work." *Toronto Star.* January 16, 1979.

Audio-Visual

This Business of Immigration. Toronto: Ontario Educational Communications Authority. Colour. 60 mins.

CANADA: A MOSAIC OF PEOPLES?

Ashworth, Mary. *Immigrant Children and Canadian Schools.* Toronto: McClelland & Stewart, 1975.

Bailey, Leuba, ed. *The Immigrant Experience.* Toronto: Macmillan, 1975.

Berry, J.W. *et al. Multiculturalism and Ethnic Attitudes in Canada.* Ottawa: Minister of Supply and Services, Canada, 1977.

Brown, Ina Corinne. *Understanding Other Cultures.* Toronto: Prentice-Hall, 1963.

Canada. Department of the Secretary of State. *Let's Take a Look at Prejudice and Discrimination: A Study Guide.* Ottawa: Queen's Printer, 1970.

Canada. Royal Commission on Bilingualism and Biculturalism. *The Cultural Contribution of the Other Ethnic Groups.* Ottawa: Queen's Printer, 1970.

Canadian Consultative Council on Multiculturalism. *First Annual Report of the Canadian Consultative Council on Multiculturalism.* Ottawa, 1975.

Clairmont, D.H. and Magill, D.W. *Africville: The Life and Death of a Canadian Black Community.* Toronto: McClelland and Stewart, 1974.

Danziger, K. *The Socialization of Immigrant Children.* Toronto: Institute for Behavioural Research, York University.

Doughty, Howard A. *Culture and Country.* Toronto: Wiley, 1976.

Ferguson, T. *A White Man's Country: An Exercise in Canadian Prejudice.* Toronto: Doubleday (Canada), 1975.

Gwyn, Sandra. "Multiculturalism: A Threat and a Promise." *Saturday Night,* Vol. 89, February 1974, pp. 15-18.

Harney, R.F. "The New Canadians and Their Life in Toronto." *Canadian Geographical Journal,* April/May 1978, pp. 20-27.

Head, Wilson. *The Black Presence in the Canadian Mosaic: A Study of the Perception and Practice of Discrimination Against Blacks in Metropolitan Toronto.* Toronto: Ontario Human Rights Commission, 1975.

Hughes, David R. and Koller, Evelyn. *The Anatomy of Racism: Canadian Dimensions.* Montreal: Harvest House, 1974.

Johnson, Valerie. "Our Isolated Immigrants." *Saturday Night,* Vol. 86, February 1971, pp. 16-20.

Migus, P.M., ed. *Sounds Canadian: Languages and Cultures in Multi-Ethnic Society.* Toronto: Peter Marlin Associates, 1975.

Mingi, Julian. *Peoples of the Living Land: Geography of Cultural Diversity in British Columbia.* Vancouver: Tantalus Research Ltd., 1972.

Munro, Iain R. *Immigration.* Toronto: Wiley, 1978.

Norris, John, ed. *Strangers Entertained: A History of the Ethnic Groups of British Columbia.* Vancouver: British Columbia Centennial '71 Committee, 1971.

Palmer, Howard. *Immigration and the Rise of Multiculturalism.* Toronto: Copp Clark, 1975.

_____. *Land of the Second Chance: A History of Ethnic Groups in Southern Alberta.* Lethbridge: Lethbridge Herald, 1972.

Porter, John A. *The Vertical Mosaic: An Analysis of Social Class and Power in Canada.* Toronto: University of Toronto Press, 1965.

Troper, H. and Palmer, Lee. *Issues in Cultural Diversity.* Toronto: The Ontario Institute for Studies in Education, 1976.

Wolfgang, A., ed. *Education of Immigrant Children.* Toronto: The Ontario Institute for Studies in Education, 1975.

Wood, Dean. *Multicultural Canada. A Teachers' Guide to Ethnic Studies.* Toronto: The Ontario Institute for Studies in Education, 1979.

Audio-Visual

Bill Cosby on Prejudice. International Telefilm Enterprises. 16 mm film, 1976, 20 mins.

Canada: Melting Pot or Mosaic? C.B.C. audio tape. Cat. No. 656, 30 mins.

Everybody's Prejudiced. N.F.B. 16 mm film. B/W. 21 mins.

Immigrants to Power. C.B.C. audio tape. Cat. No. 797, 1 hour.

Manitoba: Festival Country. Manitoba Government Film Library. 16 mm.

McFadden, Fred *et al. The Canadian Mosaic.* Multi media kit #40. Toronto: Moreland, Latchford Co. Ltd., *c.*1977.

Neidhardt, W.S. *The Peoples of Canada: Our Multicultural Heritage.* cassettes and filmstrips. Toronto: See! Hear! Now! *c.*1976.

This Business of Immigration. OECA 16 mm film. Colour. 60 mins.

The Threshold. N.F.B. 16 mm. film. B/W. 23 mins.